D1525271

The Markets for Force

The Markets for Force

Privatization of Security Across World Regions

Edited by

Molly Dunigan

and

Ulrich Petersohn

PENN

UNIVERSITY OF PENNSYLVANIA PRESS

PHILADELPHIA

Published by
University of Pennsylvania Press
Philadelphia, Pennsylvania 19104-4112

Printed in the United States of America on acid-free paper
1 3 5 7 9 10 8 6 4 2

Library of Congress Cataloging-in-Publication Data

The markets for force : privatization of security across world regions /
edited by Molly Dunigan and Ulrich Petersohn. — 1st ed.
    p. cm.
    Includes bibliographical references and index.
    ISBN 978-0-8122-4686-5 (hardcover : alk. paper)
    1. Private security services.   2. Private security companies.   3. National
security.   4. Security sector.   I. Dunigan, Molly.   II. Petersohn, Ulrich.
HV8290.M375 2015
355.3'5—dc23

2014028287

CONTENTS

ABBREVIATIONS

ANA	Afghan National Army
ANP	Afghan National Police
ANSF	Afghan National Security Forces
APPF	Afghan Public Protection Force
ASD	alternative service delivery
ASG	armed support group
BAPSC	British Association of Private Security Companies
CANSOFCOM	Canadian Special Operations Forces Command
CAT	counter-assault team
CF	Canadian Forces
CFB	Canadian Forces Base
CICIG	Commission Against Impunity in Guatemala
CIDA	Canadian International Development Agency
CNPC	China National Petroleum Corporation
CONOC	contractor operation cell
CORREPI	Coordinadora Contra la Represion Policial e Institucional (Coordinate Against Police and Institutional Repression)
CPA	Coalition Provisional Authority
CSPIA	China Security and Protection Industry Association
CSOR	Canadian Special Operations Regiment
DFAIT	(Canadian) Department of Foreign Affairs and International Trade
DIAG	Disbandment of Illegal Armed Groups program
DND	(Canadian) Department of National Defence
DoD	(U.S.) Department of Defense
DoS	(U.S.) Department of State
EIC	(British) East India Company
EU	European Union
FCO	Foreign and Commonwealth Office

FDD	Focused District Development Program
GNI	Gross National Income
ICoC	International Code of Conduct
IGO	international governmental organization
ILETA	International Law Enforcement Training Agency
ISAF	International Security Assistance Force
JTF2	Joint Task Force 2
KBR	Kellogg, Brown, and Root
LOGCAP	Logistics Civil Augmentation Program
MoD	Ministry of Defense
MoI	Ministry of the Interior
NATO	North Atlantic Treaty Organization
NGO	nongovernmental organization
NPM	New Public Management
PA	Public Affairs party
PASA	Pan-African Security Association
PLA	People's Liberation Army
PMC	private military company
PMSC	private military and security company
PPP	public-private partnership
PRC	People's Republic of China
PRT	Provincial Reconstruction Team
PSB	public security bureau
PSC	private security company
PSI	private security industry
PSP	private security provider
RDR	recursos directamente recaudados (resources directly collected)
SAS	Special Air Service
SEZ	special economic zone
SOF	Special Operations Forces
SOFA	Status of Forces Agreement
TCO	transnational criminal organization
TGP	Transportadora de Gas del Peru
UKMFTS	United Kingdom Military Flying Training System
UN	United Nations
USAID	U.S. Agency for International Development
USPI	U.S. Protection and Investigations

USSR   Union of Soviet Socialist Republics
VRAE   Valley of the Apurimac and Ene Rivers
WPPS   Worldwide Personal Protection Service
WTO   World Trade Organization

FOREWORD

As armed men took over two airports in Crimea after the ouster of embattled Ukrainian President Viktor Yanukovich in February 2014, some reports suggested they were forces employed by Vnevedomstvenaya Okhrana, a private security contracting bureau inside the Russian interior ministry that hires forces to protect Russian Navy installations and assets in Crimea ("Russian 'Blackwater'" 2014). If this is indeed the case, what can we expect of Russian security firms? Are they shoring up the Russian state's monopoly on force or undermining it? Will their use lead to greater public security or less? This volume endeavors to address just these kinds of questions.

A significant literature has amassed focusing on the global growth of a market for force and particular manifestations of it in individual cases. Fewer, however, have systematically examined the variations within this market. Molly Dunigan and Ulrich Petersohn set out to do just that. They pose a typology of different kinds of markets: a neoliberal market, a hybrid market, and a racketeering market. They and their colleagues then analyze how these different market forms should impact the state's monopoly on force and the provision of security as a public good and investigate how the markets have affected individual cases. Though some may take issue with their formulations and predictions, Dunigan, Petersohn, and their colleagues take a step toward better describing and understanding the various forms that marketized security takes and the consequences of these different forms.

Beyond the general formulations, this volume also offers new empirical detail on cases from Latin America to Europe to North America to Asia. Much of the analysis in the literature on the private military and security industry has focused on the United States and Europe or on various countries in Africa. This volume includes cases from less studied regions. The inclusion of a broader array of cases and regional overviews is a welcome addition, even though reliable data on many of these cases is hard to obtain.

Particularly intriguing are the different relationships between governments and militaries and the various private actors—from state-owned and -managed security companies in China, to militaries working for private sector extractive industries in Ecuador and Peru, to the overlap between warlord forces and private security companies in Afghanistan.

Though this volume presents convincing evidence of variation in market dynamics across regions and cases, it also tells of increasing interaction between these more local markets and global forces and firms. Following these interactions will be important for understanding how both the global market and associated markets unfold. Regardless, the analyses in this volume make a compelling argument that marketization in the security sector is vast and varied. I hope it generates much research in this important area.

Deborah Avant
Sié Chéou-Kang Chair for International Security and Diplomacy
Josef Korbel School of International Studies, University of Denver

Reference

"Russian 'Blackwater' Takes over Ukraine Airport." 2014. *The Daily Beast* (February 28).

CHAPTER 1

Introduction

Ulrich Petersohn and Molly Dunigan

In the early 1900s, Max Weber developed his definition of the modern state as a sovereign entity holding a *monopoly on the legitimate use of force* within a territory. Ever since, many have taken Weber's definition to depict the actual characteristics of a state. However, Weber's use of the term *modern state* and his reference to historical development underscore his awareness that this form of organizing violence has been volatile over time (Weber 1999: 815–22). In keeping with this, Janice Thomson (1994: 3) points out that there is nothing natural or timeless in the state-centric organization of violence. Exploring European history dating back to the fourteenth century, she highlights the prevalence of various forms of mercenarism, privateering, and mercantile companies capable of raising their own armed forces (ibid.: 27–42). Other historians, meanwhile, note the presence of mercenaries in the Middle East and North Africa as far back as 1479 B.C. (Lanning 2005: 3–4).

Though Weber's idea of the state having a monopoly on the legitimate use of force has been the predominant conception of the control of force over the past 200 years, a vibrant market for force has become a major player in international politics and military operations again over the course of the last two decades (Abrahamsen and Williams 2011; Avant 2005; Singer 2003). Many authors have already considered the driving forces behind the emergence of this new market, attributing it to an increase in violent conflict, the failure of governments in the Third World, and/or the massive demobilization of state-run armed forces and a decrease in the willingness to intervene abroad since the end of the Cold War (Kinsey 2006: 95–96; Shearer 1998; Singer 2003: 49–70). Another reason often cited is the "privatization revolution," which was based on the belief in the efficiency and effectiveness of the marketplace as well as a reduction in military operations' political risk through the deployment of private contractors in place of regular military personnel (Mandel 2002: 57–60; Schreier and Caparini 2005: 3–6). Deborah Avant (2005: 38), by contrast, claims that states have chosen privatization because they are unable to deal with global security threats alone and multilateral institutions have been unable to adequately cope with these challenges. The marketplace, according to Avant, therefore offers a more workable solution.

Yet, all of these approaches to understanding the underlying drivers of the market for force are incomplete to the extent that they treat the market as single, homogenous, and neoliberal, that is, as a market organized around privately owned business entities where property rights prevail and clients and providers enter into legal contracts for the voluntary exchange of goods and services. Such assumptions regarding the nature of the market for force currently operating globally overlook the fact that this market appears to be a very diverse system, varying along a number of dimensions in different areas of the globe. For instance, in some areas, the market for force is characterized by the involvement of only domestic firms; in others, the market is marked by the presence of a large number of international actors. Moreover, some firms only provide security domestically (i.e., "internally focused" firms), while others appear to be primarily "externally focused," exporting their services abroad. Still others reportedly provide a mixture of internally and externally focused services. Even the kind of providers trading security services fluctuates, with private firms, local militias, organized crime rings, and/or warlords entering the market in various areas to provide security.

In short, our analysis in this volume takes as its starting point that the market for force is actually a conglomeration of different types of markets, rather than a singular neoliberal entity. Because little scholarly attention has been devoted thus far to any sort of empirical, comparative investigation of the various causes and effects of different forms of markets for force operating across the globe, we seek to perform such a comparison here through an analysis of the markets for force in twelve states: Argentina, Guatemala, Peru, Ecuador, United Kingdom, the Czech Republic, Ukraine,

Russia, Afghanistan, China, Canada, and the United States. In performing this comparison, we hypothesize that the different market types and their different characteristics have different causes and effects. The more specific questions we are interested in, therefore, are the following:

1. What are the particular characteristics of the respective markets?
2. What has caused the markets to evolve into their current forms, and to what extent do these causes vary across different markets?
3. What are the consequences of the different types of markets for the state's monopoly on force and the provision of security as a public good, and to what extent do these consequences vary across the different markets?

The significance of the answers to these questions stretches beyond mere academic interest, particularly in the context of the rapid expansion of security privatization and force marketization that the world has seen since September 11, 2001 and the beginning of Operation Iraqi Freedom (OIF) in 2003. Because states across the globe are increasingly turning to nonstate actors to perform security functions—either intentionally or unintentionally—it is important for the persistence of state power to develop a more complete understanding of the implications of such outsourcing of security functions. Moreover, if, as postulated here, this marketization of force takes different forms in different areas of the globe, it is important for policymakers and scholars alike to better understand how each form of marketized force interacts with the local politics and geostrategic context of the particular area in which it occurs—in addition to its effects on state power in that region—so that policies may be adapted accordingly.

The remainder of this chapter proceeds first by defining how we conceive of and utilize the term *market* throughout the volume. We then provide a brief overview of the debate in the scholarly literature regarding the *causes* of the market for force. Next, we identify the specific areas on which the volume focuses its analysis of the *consequences* of the markets for force, elaborating upon the concepts of the state's monopoly on force and the provision of security as a public good. We then define more specifically the existing literature's explanations of the variation within the neoliberal market model, situating this volume's argument in relation to these explanations. Finally, we outline our analytic framework, provide further details regarding the case selection process, and acknowledge several caveats regarding the scope and design of this study.

Conceptualizing a Market

The term *market* is rarely defined in the literature on security privatization. This is partly due to much of the existing literature's focus on things other than the market itself, and partly due to the fact that the literature has taken the neoliberal approach as given. Neoliberals subscribe to the notion that the market is merely a virtual arena for actors to engage in voluntary economic exchange, and it does not exert any influence on the interaction or the conditions of exchange (Jackson 2007: 235). The outcome of a neoliberal market is, therefore, only determined by the interaction of rational actors and not by characteristics of the market itself. Although this is not wrong, the neoliberal approach is only one way of conceptualizing a market, and it is very specific regarding the factors shaping the market and the mode of exchange. This approach thereby excludes other potential organizational forms of markets, such as casual trade markets, collusive trade markets, open security markets, or oligopolistic security markets (for other forms, see Jackson 2007; Branovic and Chojnacki 2011).

In order to grasp the full range of variation between different types of markets for force, we utilize a broad definition of a market as *a locally specified "set of formal and informal rules" under which actors engage in exchange* (Fligstein and Dauter 2007: 113). However, not all forms of exchange qualify as market exchange. Barter, for instance, does not depend on money but on the direct exchange of goods. In contrast to this, *markets are arenas where commodities are sold and bought and property rights are transferred upon monetary payment* (Jackson 2007: 236). Second, *market exchange is always a two-way street, wherein one party provides a commodity for future payment*. This distinguishes market exchange from one-way transfers such as gifts (ibid.). Third, *market exchange takes place regularly, and commodities are characterized by a certain degree of similarity*. Markets require a regular exchange, in contrast to a single unique event. To achieve regular exchange, commodities need to be similar to some extent, as otherwise prices necessary for monetary exchange could not form and there would simply be a multitude of unconnected exchanges (Rosenbaum 2000: 470).

Although market exchange has to fulfill all of these criteria, we acknowledge that the specific exchange conditions and the mode of exchange may differ. This is in contrast to neoliberal theory, which suggests that the mode of market exchange is always the same: based on mutual voluntary agreement between the two parties (Rosenbaum 2000: 466–68). Furthermore, mutual agreement is not necessary to allocate commodities on markets. For instance, Donohue and Levitt argue that on illegal markets, the use of force is the prime mechanism to allocate resources (Donohue and Levitt 1998: 463; Reuter 2009).

We also acknowledge that markets can vary in their degree of openness and competitiveness. "Openness" means that new actors can enter the market freely, and "competitiveness" means that multiple suppliers and sellers compete (Jackson 2007: 236–37). This is considered an important mechanism of market efficiency because under the condition of competition, suppliers constantly attempt to surpass competitors by offering better contractual conditions, which ensures low prices and high-quality services (Rosenbaum 2000: 472). However, perfect competition and openness are not necessary requirements for market exchange. Both may be impaired by legal requirements, government policies, personal relationships, or market power (Drutschmann 2007: 450; Burt 1993). Thus, competition and openness vary from market to market.

The Underlying Causes of the Markets for Force

There is no agreement among scholars regarding the cause(s) of the market for force. Prominent explanations include an increase in violent conflict, the failure of governments in the Third World, and/or the massive demobilization of state-run armed forces and a decrease in the willingness of states to intervene abroad since the end of the Cold War (Singer 2003: 49–70; Shearer 1998; Kinsey 2006: 95–96). Abrahamsen and Williams (2011: 26, 89) move beyond this post–Cold War explanation to argue that the emergence of private security is part of the wider process of globalization that disassembles the state and restructures power relations. As discussed above, many scholars also cite the "privatization revolution" as a cause of the market (Schreier and Caparini 2005: 3–6; Mandel 2002: 57–60), and Avant (2005: 38) argues that privatization is the result of both states and multilateral institutions being unable to deal with global security threats alone.

Others have analyzed variation in the market's causes. Elke Krahmann (2010), for instance, argues that there is variation in the extent to which states embrace privatization. Some have acknowledged that the demand for market services may have different roots in weak and strong states (Petersohn 2010). However, because all of these approaches implicitly understand the market to be a neoliberal market, the discussion of the causes is, thus far, unable to account for the variation in the types of markets for force that exist. The volume at hand seeks to remedy this shortfall by inductively exploring the emergence of the various market types, looking for patterns of conditions yielding particular types of markets.

The Consequences of the Markets for Force: The Monopoly on Force and Provision of Security as a Public Good

Ever since the reappearance of marketized forms of force in recent years, scholars have engaged in a spirited debate about their consequences. Some authors have investigated repercussions for the democratic control of force (Verkuil 2007), while others have been more concerned with the market's impact on the armed forces (Kidwell 2005) or the market's reconfiguration of state power (Abrahamsen and Williams 2011). However, some of the most fundamental questions that scholars have raised with regard to the effects of marketized force relate to their impact on the state. As many analysts have pointed out, the state's monopoly on violence (Coker 1999) and its provision of security as a public good (Mandel 2002: chap. 2; Krahmann 2008) are potentially affected by marketized forms of force. We elaborate upon these two concepts below.

The State Monopoly on Force

Although the literature on the privatization of force extensively addresses the impact of marketized force on the state's monopoly on the use of force (Singer 2003: chap. 10), a universal understanding of what comprises that monopoly on force is lacking. Some straightforwardly define it as the "monopoly over the possession and use of the instruments of violence" (Edmonds 1999: 118). Deborah Avant (2005: 5–6), in contrast, relaxes the monopoly aspect and rather focuses on the level of functional control (i.e., the ability of the troops to exercise their mission), social control (i.e., to what extent the conduct of the violent actors reflects current norms), and the political dimension (i.e., who makes decisions regarding the use of force). In other words, there is a distinction between a state's *authority* to use force and a state's *capability* to use force. Elke Krahmann argues that it is this political or authority dimension, the question of who makes decisions regarding the use of force, that is of central importance: "The norm of the state monopoly on violence rests on the assumption that a general expectation of peaceful cooperation and conflict resolution can only develop among all citizens if private individuals are prohibited from using armed force to further their own interests" (Krahmann 2009: 2–3).

For the purposes of this study, we focus solely on the political/authority dimension of the monopoly on force. Considered in this way, if the state monopoly on force is fully implemented, the state has the exclusive ability to effectively regulate the use of force and to decide autonomously its use (Thomson 1994: 8).

Security as a Public Good

This volume also investigates how the provision of security services through markets affects the extent to which security is provided as a public good. Security is understood here in a narrow manner. First, we are not interested in nonhuman threats, such as environmental disasters or accidents. The investigation deals only with human-based threats, such as crime or violence. Second, the achievement of security does not necessitate the complete removal or suspension of any threat. For the purposes of our analysis, it suffices to achieve security if protection against a threat is provided.

In general, it is assumed that one of the state's primary functions is to provide security as a public—as opposed to private—good. A public good is characterized by being *nonexcludable*; that is, everyone can consume it. A private good, in contrast, is by definition *excludable* and cannot be enjoyed by everyone. Furthermore, public goods are characterized by nonrivalry; that is, the consumption of the service by one person does not diminish its utility for others, while private goods are reduced by consumption (Krahmann 2008: 383–84). The provision of security as a public good, therefore, means that the entire population has access to protection against human-based threats, and the level of protection does not decrease when protection is consumed.

Explaining the Variation in the Markets' Consequences

Although the literature predominantly treats the market as a neoliberal market, few authors would deny that conditions in markets differ. Charles Lindblom (2001: 4), for instance, points out that this ideal single coherent space where actors buy and sell a commodity does not exist in reality. Still, the different conditions are rarely the center of attention, and very often these differences are not even made explicit. When looking closely, however, the following differences in market conditions can be identified in the current literature on the privatization of force: (1) differences in the goods and services that are being traded; (2) differences in the regulatory environment; (3) differences in the quality of the state; and (4) differences in whether the services are exported or imported. We examine these differences in greater detail below.

Differences in the Goods and Services Traded

The commodities traded on the market for force are often considered to make a difference in the consequences of the market (Avant 2005: 16–22; Singer 2003: 92–100). It is noteworthy that the scope of the market for force is a matter of debate in the literature. We focus here on situations in which the direct use of force, either lethal or nonlethal, for combat or security services is actually traded as a commodity. We conceive of force to vary along a force continuum (see Figure 1.1). On the lower end of the spectrum, watchmen who provide guard services operate in a generally low-risk environment, for instance, shopping malls or other similar venues in which the most dangerous threat is random criminality. Force is used to incapacitate or arrest a suspect, and lethal force is a rare exception. Therefore, the ability to employ nonlethal force is much greater than the ability to exert lethal force. In contrast, security guards work in high-risk environments or even conflict zones and are meant to protect a compound, person, or convoy from a coordinated attack. Their ability to employ nonlethal force is very limited, and they have various options to apply lethal force. Security guards carry military weapons—assault rifles and sometimes even grenades—and

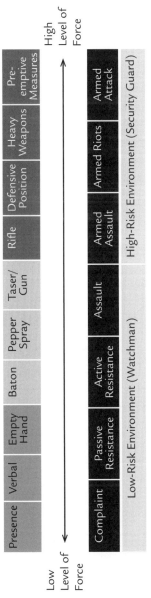

Figure 1.1. Force continuum.

use military tactics to prepare fighting positions and to break (or break free from) an attack by superior firepower. Sometimes, they even go beyond purely defensive measures and resort to preventive or preemptive uses of force. The following chapters focus primarily on the lethal services markets. In two cases, China and the Czech Republic, the internal market only allows for nonlethal services.

The different kinds of force, nonlethal and lethal, are argued to have different effects on the monopoly of force and security as a public good. Although "fighting forces should retain their status as a monopoly," nonlethal and support capabilities are not considered to be exclusively a public domain (Verkuil 2007: 189, 27). Moreover, lethal services have the potential to undermine public security, and nonlethal services are considered to pose a lesser risk. Although the markets for armed security lead to an increase in aggressive actions where the services are delivered (Carmola 2010: 140–41), nonlethal services are usually deemed to be less controversial and harmful (House of Commons 2002).

Differences in the Regulatory Environment

In different markets, different regulatory frameworks may apply. Such frameworks are like intangible borders between markets; accordingly, exchange takes place under particular sets of legal regulations that differ across local markets (Fligstein and Dauter 2007: 113). The absence of tight regulation is considered to be a permissible condition for private security companies (PSCs) to wield force unrestrained, without any accountability, leading to escalation and increased turmoil (Mandel 2002: 82). In such cases, the authority dimension of the state's monopoly of force may be affected as an unchecked market allows companies to provide potentially any services to anyone and to therefore undermine a state's foreign policy (Percy 2006: 7–8). The presence of regulation, in contrast, may mitigate any negative market repercussions on the monopoly of force and public security, while at the same time harnessing the positive effects of private security actors.

Likewise, it is assumed that the absence of regulation has a negative effect on public security. Without any regulation, accountability cannot be assured, which opens up the possibility that market actors will misbehave or, at the very least, fail to prioritize the interests of the public. Many scholars consider the presence of effective regulation and the involvement of criminal courts to be necessary to prevent negative externalities associated with a market for force (Cockayne et al. 2008: 11–12). Some arguments conclude that regulation allows the state or other clients to effectively harness the market's potentially positive effects (Avant 2009).[1]

Differences in the Quality of the State

Deborah Avant has argued that the market for force affects states differently, depending on the quality of the state in question. According to Avant (2005: 7), strong states are "coherent, capable, and legitimate" and are therefore able to handle the risks and harness the benefits of privatization. In contrast, those countries with an ineffective and weak government are expected to have more problems managing private actors. However, the market's effects are not clear-cut. Strong states, for instance, are expected to gain from private security actors through an increase in their capabilities. Simultaneously, however, because they have a relatively tight grip on authority over the use of force—at least as compared to weaker states—strong states are at risk of losing authority over the use of force when private security providers enter the equation. On the other hand, weak states' relative lack of a monopoly on force to begin with means that the option to hire private security providers may enable the leaders of such states to increase their authority over the use of force by hiring a capable agent. With regard to the provision of security as a public good, it has been posited that market capabilities may offer weak states the possibility to increase and broaden the provision of security (Kinsey 2007). In contrast, some authors expect negative consequences for the provision of public security if strong states turn to the market, as private sources of protection may exacerbate the tension between those able to afford private security and those who cannot (Mandel 2002: 120).

Differences in Where Services Are Produced and Employed (Foreign Versus Domestic Consumption)

Although the literature rarely explicitly discusses the issue of *where* a particular marketized form of force is employed (either abroad or domestically), many authors deem this distinction to be crucial to the consequences of the force in question. Deborah Avant (2005: 143), for instance, argues that exporting security services may undermine the public security of the exporting state by building up future enemies or implicating the government in a conflict. Other authors take an alternative view, considering the export of security to often be a means through which the exporting country can increase its security. Additional capabilities purchased on the market for force allow states to fill capability gaps and extend the capabilities of their existing missions, while also offering flexibility and the ability to project power abroad. However, PSCs are not integrated into either the military chain of command or a government agency, which may result in the state's loss of authority over the use of force (Petersohn 2008).

Domestic employment of private force is argued to have different ramifications for the state's monopoly on force and for security as a public good. Robert Mandel (2002: 85) highlights the possibility of tensions arising between public and private security forces. The public forces may consider PSCs to be interfering with their duty to provide public security, while PSCs assume that their employment proves the ineptitude of public forces. Additionally, the emergence of gated communities with private security may lead to crime displacement and an increase in social fragmentation, as some can afford security while others cannot (Boemcken 2012: 20). However, due to the fact that domestically employed PSCs operate on the territory of the state supplying them, the state is better able in such cases to control and restrain these actors than it is when exporting their services abroad. As the government can implement laws regulating the security industry and rules regarding its use of force when such force is to be used domestically, we would not expect the state to lose as much authority as it might through the export of these services abroad.

In sum, we would expect the export of security services abroad to lead to an increase in the provision of domestic public security and a decrease in the state's authority over the use of force. We expect that domestic markets for force, on the other hand, should decrease the provision of public security domestically and have a relatively less negative (though still not positive) impact on the state's authority over the use of force.

Methodology and Analytic Framework

We employ Alexander George and Andrew Bennett's method of "structured focused comparison," a method "structured" around standardized general questions that are developed to reflect the research goal, and which guide each case investigation. This assures standardized data collection and permits for systematic comparison. The term *focused* reflects the desire to not provide a holistic explanation of each case, but to deal with particular aspects only (George and Bennett 2005: 67). The method is well suited for collaborative exploratory studies for two main reasons: First, bringing together a number of distinguished scholars involves a great deal of coordination, and a framework assures that the analysis of each author is guided by the same questions and makes certain that the volume as a whole has a common focus. Second, the general structure also guides the collection and selection of data and guarantees the comparability of the findings.

As mentioned above, the aim of the study is threefold: to identify different types of markets for force, briefly explore the causes underlying the formation of each type of market, and explore the consequences of different types of markets. Building upon the analysis of these three issues in each of the case study chapters, our goal for the volume as a whole is to discover and categorize different *types* of markets for force, determining how these types develop and what their consequences are for the state's monopoly on force and the provision of security as a public good. In doing so, we also seek to determine whether the causes and consequences of each market type are consistent across types or whether significant differences exist. We expect significant differences in the causes and consequences across the various types of markets explored in the following chapters. Even if causes and consequences are found to be consistent across market types, the analysis will be valuable in demonstrating that no single market type is responsible and that there are different types generating similar outcomes.

Given the limited number of cases we include in this volume, we do not claim to comprehensively catalogue all types of markets for force (George and Bennett 2005: 242). However, in order to strengthen our argument and to identify as many types as possible, we aimed to include cases displaying a broad variety of scope conditions. Assuming that market transactions are underpinned by cultural, political, and economic factors, we selected our cases for variation in terms of region, regime type, and level of economic development. We first included cases from different world regions and different countries from each region in order to include a broad variety of cultural factors that might affect market relations.[2] Second, we included different regime types because different regime types appear to have varying effects on a state's economy (Przeworski and Limongi 1993). In order to measure the

Table 1.1. Summary of Case Characteristics

Case	World Region	GNI per Capita*	Freedom Index[†]
United States	North America	Very High	Free
Canada	North America	Very High	Free
Argentina	South America	High	Free
Guatemala	South America	Low	Partly Free
Ecuador	South America	Low	Partly Free
Peru	South America	Medium	Partly Free
United Kingdom	Europe	Very High	Free
Ukraine	Europe	Low	Free
Russia	Europe	High	Not Free
Czech Republic	Europe	Very High	Free
China	Asia	Low	Not Free
Afghanistan	Asia	Very Low	Not Free

* Source: United Nations, *Human Development Report, 2010* (http://hdr.undp.org/en/data/map/). This report measures, among other factors, the gross national income per capita in USD. It differentiates between five different income levels: > 20,000 (Very High); 14,000–20,000 (High); 8,000–14,000 (Moderate); 2,000–8,000 (Low); < 2000 (Very Low).
[†] The Freedom House *Freedom Index* measures different democractic freedoms, such as democratic governance and free elections (Freedom House 2010).

regime type, we employ Freedom House's Freedom Index (Freedom House 2010).[3] According to the index, the more "free" a country is, the more democratic it is. Third, we included countries in different stages of economic development, indicated by the gross national income (GNI) per capita of those countries (see Table 1.1).

Admittedly, other cases fulfilling these or similar criteria do exist, and we could have chosen them for this study. However, due to the broad variety in the included cases' characteristics, and due to the fact that the number of included cases (twelve) still exceeds all previous studies on the market for force, we feel confident that the results will have broad applicability. Additionally, the number of included cases allows us to present in-depth investigations of each. The individual chapters are, therefore, able to explore the relationship between the consequences of each market and the various possible explanations for the variation in those consequences across the markets and to then assess the relative power of the various explanations. This should further increase confidence in the findings.

Based on these cases, in Chapter 11 we identify three different types of markets operating globally: a neoliberal market, a hybrid market, and a racketeer market. We then analyze the relevance of each of the four alternative explanations in the literature that seek to account for variation in the consequences of a market for force—type of commodity (lethal or nonlethal), level of regulation, state quality, and export versus domestic markets—and compare them to the relevance of our market types argument. To do so, we draw upon Charles Ragin's qualitative comparative analysis (QCA) method to evaluate whether the conditions dictated by each of the four alternative explanations are sufficient and/or necessary for the outcome in each of the case studies examined in the volume (Ragin 2000: chap. 4). Finally, we seek to elaborate upon various causes that could potentially be responsible for the various types of markets and explain how and why each market type creates particular consequences for the state's monopoly on force and the provision of security as a public good.

We acknowledge that there are also limitations to this construct. Due to the limited number of cases, the study may not illuminate the entire range of possible types of markets for force. However, the aim of the study was to include a broad variety of cases in order to cover as much ground as possible and to provide a solid basis for the conclusion. Furthermore, we can make no inferences as to the frequency with which particular types of markets arise in the entire universe of cases. Nonetheless, the cases and empirical evidence presented in the following chapters are sufficiently varied and compelling to enable us to derive useful conclusions regarding the markets for force.

Plan of the Book

The remainder of the volume is organized as follows. We begin in Chapter 2 with Latin America, as Kristina Mani explores the domestically oriented private security market in Argentina and the criminal force market in Guatemala. In Chapter 3, Maiah Jaskoski explores military protection markets operating in Latin America in her counterpart to Mani's work, which focuses on the tendency of local army units in both Peru and Ecuador to sell the state's military services to private interests. The volume then focuses on both Western and Eastern European cases, with chapters examining the United Kingdom, Czech Republic, Russia, and Ukraine, authored by Carlos Ortiz, Oldrich Bures, and Olivia Allison, respectively. In Chapter 7 we move our analysis to Asia, with Jake Sherman exploring the activities of both corporate and criminal actors in the market in Afghanistan, and Jennifer

Catallo examining the largely state-controlled, "quasi-managed" or "hybrid" market for force in China. Last, we turn to North America, with Christopher Spearin reporting on the growing Canadian market for force in Chapter 9 and Scott Fitzsimmons examining the United States' market for lethal combat services in Chapter 10. The volume concludes in Chapter 11 with the development of a typology of the markets for force derived from the preceding case studies and an assessment of the variation in the causes and consequences of each type of market for the state's monopoly on force and the provision of security as a public good.

Notes

1. Many have argued in recent years that regulation of the security industry is absent or incomplete at best (Singer 2003; Carmola 2010: 99). Different types of regulation have been developed at the national level. Some aim at outlawing the private military and security company (PMSC) industry; others seek to accommodate the industry by setting up soft regulations, such as licensing regimes, or relying entirely on self-regulation. A third alternative tries to integrate the industry into existing legal frameworks by extending their scope. The most promising options for regulation of the private security industry are found in interrelated international initiatives that have been established through multi-stakeholder processes since 2008: the International Code of Conduct (ICoC; building upon the 2008 *Montreux Document*) and the American National Standards Institute/ASIS International *Management System for Quality of Private Security Company Operations: Requirements With Guidance* (the so-called PSC.1 Standard) developed in 2012 (Geneva Centre for the Democratic Control of Armed Forces (DCAF), n.d.; American National Standards Institute 2012). As an initiative aimed at effectively implementing the ideas embedded in the ICoC, the PSC.1 Standard appears to hold substantial promise: Compliance with this standard is now mandated in the U.S. Department of State's Worldwide Personal Protective Services (WPPS II) contract for diplomatic security and in U.S. Department of Defense (DoD) and U.K. Foreign & Commonwealth Office contracts for security services. However, the PSC.1 Standard is limited solely to regulation of the private *security* industry, omitting any regulation of the broader private military industry (i.e., those involved in base maintenance operations, logistical support, or other military-related nonsecurity functions) or of other types of force bought and sold on various markets around the globe. Moreover, the extent to which auditing of private security companies and contractors for compliance with the PSC.1 will be effectively carried out remains to be seen.

2. Related to this, it is important to point to the fact that—mainly due to the limited space available in this volume—no African cases were included in the study. This was a pragmatic choice guided by the fact that Africa has already been covered extensively in numerous other books (Abrahamsen and Williams 2011; Cilliers and Mason 1999; Musah and Fayemi 2000; Mills and Stremlau 1999). We do not expect the ab-

sence of an African case to have a negative effect on our ability to draw conclusions. We selected a broad variety of cases across different regions, regime types, state quality, and gross national income. If one of the conditions suggested in the literature or our market structure argument accounts for the variation across these different regions, there is little ground to assume that an African case would show different effects than, for instance, a case in Asia, provided they share similar characteristics in terms of types of commodity traded, state quality, the domestic versus export focus of the market, and level of regulation.

3. Because most of the case studies in this volume refer specifically to events taking place from 2009 to 2011, we use the 2010 Freedom Index as our baseline measurement of regime type.

References

Abrahamsen, Rita, and Michael C. Williams. 2011. *Security Beyond the State: Private Security in International Politics*. Cambridge, UK and New York: Cambridge University Press.

American National Standards Institute/ASIS International. 2012. *Management System for Quality of Private Security Company Operations: Requirements with Guidance*. New York.

Avant, Deborah. 2005. *The Market for Force: The Consequences of Privatizing Security*. Cambridge, UK and New York: Cambridge University Press.

Avant, Deborah. 2009. "Making Peacemakers Out of Spoilers." In *The Dilemmas of Statebuilding*, ed. Roland Paris and Timothy Sisk, 104–26. London and New York: Routledge.

Boemcken, Marc von. 2012. "Commerical Security Markets." In *Commercial Security and Development*, ed. Marc von Boemcken, 9–15. Bonn: Bonn International Center for Conversion.

Branovic, Zeljko, and Sven Chojnacki. 2011. "The Logic of Security Markets: Security Governance in Failed States." *Security Dialogue* 42(6): 553–69.

Burt, Roland. 1993. "The Social Structure of Competition." In *Explorations in Economic Sociology*, ed. Richard Swedberg, 65–103. New York: Russell Sage Foundation.

Carmola, Kateri. 2010. *Private Security Contractors and New Wars: Risk, Law, and Ethics*. London: Routledge.

Cilliers, Jakkie, and Peggy Mason. 1999. *Peace, Profit or Plunder*. Pretoria: Institute for Security Studies.

Cockayne, James, Emily Speers Mears, Iveta Cherneva, Alison Gurin, Sheila Oviedo, and Dylan Yaeger. 2008. *Beyond Market Force*. New York: International Peace Institute.

Coker, Christopher. 1999. "Outsourcing War." *Cambridge Review of International Affairs* 13(1): 95–113.

Donohue, John J., and Steven D. Levitt. 1998. "Guns, Violence, and the Efficiency of Illegal Markets." *American Economic Review* 88(2): 463–67.

Drutschmann, Sebastian. 2007. "Informal Regulation: An Economic Perspective on the Private Security Industry." In *Private Military and Security Companies*, ed. Thomas Jäger and Gerhard Kümmel, 443–55. Wiesbaden: VS Verlag für Sozialwissenschaften.

Edmonds, Martin. 1999. "Defence Privatisation: From State Enterprise to Commercialism." *Cambridge Review of International Affairs* 13(1): 114–29.

Fligstein, Neil, and Luke Dauter. 2007. "The Sociology of Markets." *Annual Review of Sociology* 33: 105–28.

Freedom House. 2010. *Freedom in the World 2010.* Accessed October 10, 2013. http://www.freedomhouse.org/report/freedom-world/freedom-world-2010.

Geneva Centre for the Democratic Control of Armed Forces (DCAF). n.d. "International Code of Conduct for Private Security Providers." Accessed July 7, 2012. http://www.dcaf.ch/Project/International-Code-of-Conduct-for-Private-Security-Service-Providers.

George, Alexander L., and Andrew Bennett. 2005. *Case Studies and Theory Development in the Social Sciences.* BCSIA Studies in International Security. Cambridge, Mass.: MIT Press.

House of Commons. 2002. *Private Military Companies, Ninth Report of Session 2000–2001.* London: Stationery Office Limited.

Jackson, William. 2007. "On the Social Structure of Markets." *Cambridge Journal of Economics* 31(2): 235–53.

Kidwell, Deborah. 2005. *Public War, Private Fight? The United States and Private Military Companies.* Global War on Terrorism Occasional Paper 12. Fort Leavenworth, Kans.: Combat Studies Institute.

Kinsey, Christopher. 2006. *Corporate Soldiers and International Security: The Rise of Private Military Companies.* Contemporary Security Studies. New York: Routledge.

Kinsey, Christopher. 2007. "Problematising the Role of Private Security Companies in Small Wars." *Small Wars and Insurgencies* 18(4): 584–614.

Krahmann, Elke. 2008. "Security: Collective Good or Commodity?" *European Journal of International Relations* 14(3): 379–404.

Krahmann, Elke. 2009. *Private Security Companies and the State Monopoly on Violence: A Case of Norm Change?* Prif-Reports. Frankfurt: Peace Research Institute.

Krahmann, Elke. 2010. *States, Citizens, and the Privatisation of Security.* Cambridge, UK and New York: Cambridge University Press.

Lanning, Michael Lee. 2005. *Mercenaries: Soldiers of Fortune, from Ancient Greece to Today's Private Military Companies.* New York: Ballantine Books.

Lindblom, Charles Edward. 2001. *The Market System: What It Is, How It Works, and What to Make of It.* Yale ISPS Series. New Haven, Conn.: Yale University Press.

Mandel, Robert. 2002. *Armies Without States: The Privatization of Security.* Boulder, Colo.: Lynne Rienner.

Mills, Greg, and John Stremlau. 1999. *The Privatization of Security in Africa.* Johannesburg: South African Institute of International Affairs.

Musah, Abdel-Fatau, and J. Kayode Fayemi. 2000. *Mercenaries: An African Security Dillemma*. London: Pluto Press.

Percy, Sarah. 2006. *Regulating the Private Security Industry*. Adelphi Paper 46(384). London: International Institute for Strategic Studies.

Petersohn, Ulrich. 2008. *Outsourcing the Big Stick: The Consequences of Using Private Military Companies*. Cambridge, Mass.: Weatherhead Center Working Paper.

Petersohn, Ulrich. 2010. "Sovereignty and Privatizing the Military: An Institutional Explanation." *Contemporary Security Policy* 31(3): 531–52.

Przeworski, Adam, and Fernando Limongi. 1993. "Political Regimes and Economic Growth." *Journal of Economic Perspectives* 7(3): 51–69.

Ragin, Charles. 2000. *Fuzzy-Set Social Science*. Chicago: The University of Chicago Press.

Reuter, Peter. 2009. "Systemic Violence in Drug Markets." *Crime, Law and Social Change* 52(3): 275–84.

Rosenbaum, Eckehard. 2000. "What Is a Market? On the Methodology of a Contested Concept." *Review of Social Economy* 58(4): 455–82.

Schreier, Fred, and Marina Caparini. 2005. *Privatising Security: Law, Practice and Governance of Private Military and Security Companies*. Occasional Paper. Geneva: Geneva Centre for the Democratic Control of Armed Forces.

Shearer, David. 1998. *Private Armies and Military Intervention*. Adelphi Paper. Oxford and New York: Oxford University Press for the International Institute for Strategic Studies.

Singer, Peter W. 2003. *Corporate Warriors: The Rise of the Privatized Military Industry*. Cornell Studies in Security Affairs. Ithaca, N.Y.: Cornell University Press.

Swiss Federal Department of Foreign Affairs. 2008. *The Montreux Document on Private Military and Security Companies*. Accessed July 7, 2012. http://www.eda.admin.ch/etc/medialib/downloads/edazen/topics/intla/humlaw.Par.0057.File.tmp/Montreux%20Document%20(e).pdf.

Thomson, Janice. 1994. *Mercenaries, Pirates, & Sovereigns*. Princeton: Princeton University Press.

United Nations Development Programme. 2010. *Human Development Report 2010*. Accessed October 10, 2013. http://hdr.undp.org/en/data/map/.

Verkuil, Paul R. 2007. *Outsourcing Sovereignty: Why Privatization of Government Functions Threatens Democracy and What We Can Do About It*. New York: Cambridge University Press.

Weber, Max. 1999. *Wirtschaft und Gesellschaft: Grundriss der verstehenden Soziologie*. Tübingen: J.C.B. Mohr (P. Siebeck).

CHAPTER 2

Diverse Markets
for Force in Latin America:
From Argentina to Guatemala

Kristina Mani

Contemporary Latin America appears to be plagued with the problem of insecurity. Across the region, citizen insecurity regularly tops public opinion surveys of problems that governments must better address, making recourse to gated communities and security guards the new norm. Mexico and the countries of Central America face the additional challenge of drug and gang wars that appear unrelenting. Meanwhile, the military remains indispensable for protecting oil pipelines and mining enterprises, particularly in the Andean countries. Yet while the range of security problems appears bewildering, in fact it reflects a disturbingly rich array of markets for force that engage both public and private actors in legal and illegal security enterprises.

In this chapter, I identify three distinct markets for force that operate in Latin America today: the private security market, the criminal force market, and the military protection market. I sketch out the features of each of these markets and look at two of them in the context of a particular case: the private security market in Argentina, and the criminal force market in Guatemala. The third market for force, the military protection market, is captured in Maiah Jaskoski's chapter, which details army provision of security to private actors in Ecuador and Peru. Given its complex range of force markets and actors, Latin America demonstrates not only that there are multiple markets for force, but that they can operate within a single region and also within a single country.

Three Types of Markets for Force in Latin America

Cases of all three types of markets for force conceptualized in this volume—neoliberal, racketeer, and hybrid—occupy a place in Latin America, making it particularly dynamic and complex as an object of study. Therefore, a useful way to conceptualize the security environment in contemporary Latin America is as one of multitiered markets for force, with a base layer in common and potentially more specialized market configurations that characterize individual countries.

The region's most pervasive base layer market is the commercially oriented private security market. Most private security services are consumed within the global North, with Europe the most densely privatized at 30 percent of the world market (with 11 percent of the world's population). Within the global South, it is Latin America and the Caribbean that hold a similar distinction, with 14 percent of the global market (and 8 percent of the world's population) and growth rates projected to be among the highest in the world at 8 to 10 percent annually (Securitas 2013). In consequence, private security markets exist in every country in the region. They provide an estimated 4 million agents employed to protect individuals, neighborhood communities, and corporate and government facilities, and to do surveillance and monitoring work, including for the transport of money and people. Because privately owned firms are the main actors in Latin America's private security sector, this market type is neoliberal. However, state regulation has struggled to keep up with the growing industry, particularly since the administrative capacity of the state throughout the region was rolled back following the debt crisis of the 1980s and turned to structural economic reforms that favored an unfettered private sector and lightweight state. Overall, state regulation of the security sector is extremely weak, and analysts estimate that more than half of the 4 million engaged in the sector are not legally registered (OAS 2008: 3).

Beyond the private security market, countries in the region frequently have additional markets for force. In criminal force markets, actors hire armed agents to use force illegally in ways that enable other criminal activity.

Drug cartels frequently rely on criminal gangs to protect and extend their trafficking routes. The infamous Zetas cartel got its start this way, as a group of Mexican former special forces hired by the Gulf cartel to provide protection and enforcement. Yet the agents in this market are not necessarily nonstate actors. There are cases of local army units in Colombia aiding drug traffickers, and weapons of the Guatemalan and Honduran armies have "mysteriously" turned up in the hands of drug traffickers (Forero 2007; Ramsey 2011). Although these markets exist, to some extent, in other parts of Latin America, they are particularly dynamic in Central America and the major countries flanking it, Colombia and Mexico. Criminal force markets are clearly of the racketeer type, as illegal groups systematically wield force for illicit gain, without legitimation through the state and legal system; indeed, state and legal actors may be co-opted into the criminal force market to provide cover for illegal acts. This market is likely to reflect features that generally characterize criminal trafficking organizations: operating transnationally, organizing through flexible networks, and relying in part on state-based corruption to exist (Williams 2002).

Finally, in military protection markets, militaries are contracted to provide security that is legal but serves interests narrower than those of the nation as a whole. The most common form of military protection is for economic activities that can be considered vital to national development and, by extension, state security. The protection of the oil, gas, and mining sectors by military units, as Jaskoski describes in Chapter 3, is typical. Military protection markets in Latin America are most common in the Andean region, where the mining and hydrocarbon sectors are substantial *and* where there is resistance from societal and armed groups to successful exploitation of these resources. Both states and private corporations contract militaries for protection. In 2002, the U.S. government added oil pipeline protection to the agenda of its military aid programs for Colombia, which had previously focused on counter-drug assistance. It provided the Colombian military with $98 million dedicated to the dual task of securing the Caño-Limón oil pipeline and combating the insurgency in Arauca; additionally, the corporations that jointly operate the pipeline paid more than USD 17 million annually to the Colombian military for their security work (U.S. GAO 2005). In Ecuador, state-owned Petroecuador contracted with the military for USD 10 million to provide security over a four-year period ("Las refinerías" 2007). Although military forces are hired for protection work both formally and informally, and deals are made both at the national/ministerial level and local/unit level, military forces essentially operate as agents of the state. Thus military protection markets constitute a hybrid type, in which the state's coercive apparatus serves as the go-to provider for private commissions. Crucial in military protection markets is the fact that, as a formal agent of the state (and often the only significant state presence in the areas where natural resource extraction takes place), the military provides a unique authority with its protection work.

Causes Underlying the Markets for Force in Latin America

The development of private security, criminal force, and military protection markets in Latin America is rooted in the problem of diminished state capacity. Paradoxically, the problem persists in a period of remarkable achievement in the region: Latin America today has more democratic regimes with market-based economies than ever before. A wave of political and economic transitions in the 1980s and 1990s ended the repression of military rule that had spread throughout South America and the devastating civil wars that rent societies in Central America.

The historical moment of these liberalizing transitions, coinciding in many cases with the region's debt crisis in the no-growth "lost decade" of the 1980s, required rolling back the state to accommodate the market-based features of neoliberalism: privatization, trade openness, and deregulation. The neoliberal turn of the 1990s stabilized the region's economies, but it did not stem the rapidly increasing social and economic inequality that resulted. Even among advocates of economic liberalization there is agreement that building more effective state institutions and promoting greater social equity through social provisioning were sorely neglected (Birdsall, de la Torre, and Valencia Caidedo 2010). Although traditional social safety nets diminished, many state security forces maintained old practices and protections, from military training programs to military justice systems, without civilian oversight. "Democratic security" reforms, which require transparency, public accountability, and the goal of securing citizens rather than the state, have remained pending in most countries in the region (Diamint 2008).

The security consequences of this diminished state capacity have been dire. In many countries, the lack of education and job opportunities for youth has spawned the growth of common and organized crime as the region's new sources of insecurity. The most common response to the rise of crime has been to develop private force solutions—private security for those who can afford it, as in Argentina (and forced resignation, or occasionally vigilantism, for those who cannot). Yet rolling back state resources has also had the effect of leaving traditional security and defense institutions scrambling for resources and individuals scrambling to make their own ends meet; the result is military protection services for private actors, in lucrative tasks, as in Ecuador and Peru. In situations of extreme economic and social insecurity, criminal organizations take advantage of the perfect storm of social, institutional, and geographic conditions: a ready base of marginalized youth; weak and corrupt law enforcement and justice institutions; and an established, lucrative market for drug production driven by demand in the United States. That the region's primary security threats to its citizens manifest themselves at the local community level belies the transnational factors that underlie them, as in Guatemala.

Consequences of the Markets for the State Monopoly on Force and Public Security

As a result of the erosion of state capacity and the rise of various types of markets for force, security in Latin America has increasingly become a private, excludable commodity available to those who can buy or self-provide it— whether as private security, military protection, or criminal force. However, it is worth recalling that Latin American states historically struggled with the challenge of exercising a monopoly on force and that security has rarely been a "true" public good in the region. Frequently in the twentieth century (and certainly in earlier periods as well), authoritarian regimes policed their societies, providing "public" security that was, in fact, highly partial to political and social groups supporting the regime (Huggins 1998). In areas where the state's power was absent, private elites managed their own security. In Colombia, the long-surviving leftist FARC insurgents and their right-wing paramilitary foes may be the most famed, but many more have existed, including rural landowner paramilitaries in Guatemala and Brazil and peasant-based *rondas* (patrols) organized to counter insurgents in Peru. Yet what is critically important and distinctive in today's climate is the high level of insecurity persisting in urban as well as rural areas *under democratic regimes.*

The problem of insecurity and the state's inability to provide security reliably as a public good gains added urgency in the contemporary Latin

American context where, in many cases, the consolidation of democracy is at stake. The economic costs of insecurity in countries debilitated by criminal violence are one significant aspect of the challenge. For instance, the drug- and gang-fuelled violence that has swept Central America is estimated to cost afflicted countries an average of nearly 10 percent of GDP annually due to expenditure on law enforcement, private security, and health care (World Bank 2011: 7). Similarly costly are violent attacks against the infrastructure of extractive sectors, which are usually located in areas remote from state control. In Colombia, the Caño-Limon pipeline runs 450 miles through territories long neglected by state authorities. Insurgent groups have demanded protection "fees" and threatened to bomb the pipeline, which has occurred hundreds of times, with a loss of revenues of nearly USD 500 million in the year before the United States began funding its protection (U.S. GAO 2005: 7). Overall, in states where social expenditure and public welfare nets have already been reduced due to neoliberal restructuring of state priorities, the cost of insecurity poses an additional burden the contemporary democratic state appears to have passed on to its citizens.

As a result, there are also costs in terms of continued citizen support for democratic institutions. Although actual crime rates vary significantly (per capita homicide rates remain relatively low south of the equator but have skyrocketed in some cities of Colombia, in Venezuela, and in the northern half of Central America), in public opinion surveys across the region "public insecurity" has become an essential citizen concern, displacing concern for economic well-being. On average, 58 percent of Latin Americans believe that life in their country *daily* grows more unsafe (Latinobarómetro 2010: 93). In response, governments have turned to *mano dura* (iron fist) policies that dramatically toughened punishments for common crimes, limited due process of law, and actually expanded gang networks by exposing youths to hardened gang members in the adult prison system (Sibaja et al. 2006: 13).

Overwhelmingly, the scaling up of the state's repressive capacity through such *mano dura* policies has failed to stem crime and is a disappointment to most citizens. Public approval of governments exceeds approval of state security policies by an average of nearly 20 percent (Latinobarómetro 2010: 79). Yet particularly disturbing are surveys finding that crime and the perception of insecurity are significant determinants of support for military coups (Pérez 2009), although a majority of people in the region (61 percent) continue to prefer democracy above all other forms of government (Latinobarómetro 2010: 25). Therefore, much is at stake if public security in the region continues to worsen unabated. Democracy itself, so hard-won over the course of the twentieth century, may be at risk.

The Private Security Market in Argentina

Argentina is one of the region's wealthiest countries. Despite numerous economic cycles of boom and bust, it remains a middle-income country and is one of the region's three G-20 members. Geographically sprawling and sparsely populated, in the late nineteenth century Argentina employed U.S.-style frontier policies and encouraged European immigration, transforming the country into one of Latin America's most ethnically homogeneous ("white") countries, with a sizable working and middle class and an activist political culture. The astonishing human rights violations and economic mismanagement of the last military regime (1976–83) thoroughly discredited the military as a political arbiter; today, Argentina's military is the least funded, farthest fallen in terms of prestige, and most strongly civilian controlled of the armed forces in the region.

The market for force most prominent in the country today is the private security market. Though steadily growing, this market remains modest compared with others in the region. For instance, Argentina has about the same number of private security agents as Guatemala, but it has nearly three times Guatemala's population (Arias 2009: 27). In short, Argentina should be a promising environment for the effective control of private security, as it is one of the region's most economically advanced societies and most demanding of accountability. Yet even in Argentina, important issues of transparency and accountability persist in this sector.

Most private security firms in Argentina are recently established, born in the 1990s under the embrace of the neoliberal reforms implemented during the presidency of Carlos Menem. As is typical in the region, Argentina's private security market is national in scale and populated primarily by local, small, and medium-sized firms (fewer than 150 employees), though subsidiaries of transnational giants like Securitas and G4S predominate in high-value protection markets such as armored transport of money and high-profile personal security. According to the Argentine labor ministry, by 2010 there were more than 1,400 private security firms registered nationwide, employing about 111,000 individuals; in addition, an estimated 100,000 work illegally (Fleitas Ortiz 2011; OAS 2008: 5).

Argentina has a federal system providing its provinces with significant autonomy, so federal government oversight of the private security sector is minimal. The most important national legislation regulating the sector is the National Decree 1002, enacted in 1999. Under this law, the federal government serves mainly to define criteria for legal registration of private security firms and to oversee the national registry of firms and of the arms and armored material they use. Practical oversight resides at the provincial level with each of the twenty-three provinces, plus the capital, Buenos Aires, defining its own regulatory framework for licensing, auditing, and sanctioning the firms and individuals operating in the industry in its jurisdiction. Firms that intend to operate in more than one provincial jurisdiction must seek licensing in each. However, most private security agents (80 percent) operate in the city of Buenos Aires and the surrounding province of Buenos Aires that together are home to one-third of the country's population.

Private security practices in Argentina and elsewhere in Latin America suggest that regulatory frameworks for the industry need to be evaluated with an understanding of the political cultural context in which they are embedded. For instance, in Argentina the private security market is defined by informal, collaborative structures maintained between state security actors and their private security peers. As in other countries in the region, a significant sector of owners and agents of private security firms are former military and police officers—about 25 percent in formally registered firms (OAS 2008: 7). Yet the appeal of a growing small business sector run by experienced professionals belies important dysfunctions perpetuated through the public security–private security link.

In particular, systemic impunity in the public security sector has not only persisted within the police but has been "recycled" into the private security sector. As a lawyer at CORREPI (Coordinate Against Police and Institutional Repression, the country's leading human rights organization against police impunity) noted, the most useful place to begin their searches for fugitive police who have committed *gatillo fácil* (trigger happy) killings, torture, or arbitrary detention is inside private security firms where they have taken second career jobs (Lacunza 2009). As CORREPI and other nongovernmental advocacy groups have documented, a number of prominent firms have employed and even been run by men with criminal antecedents.

Moreover, ties persist between corrupt police institutions and the private security agents they generate. Both private security guards and the infamous Bonaerense (police of Buenos Aires province) were clearly implicated

in the infamous killing in 1997 of investigative photographer José Luis Cabezas, who had both investigated corruption in the Bonaerense and auda-
ciously photographed the reclusive and corrupt "businessman" Alfredo
Yabrán (Sagasti 2003; "Condenados por el asesino" 2011). The Cabezas murder became a watershed event in social mobilization in post-authoritarian
Argentina. It ignited public outrage at the chain of impunities and cover-ups
of the murder that was orchestrated by Yabrán's personal security detail and
the Buenos Aires police, most likely on his orders. The case marked initial
efforts to make the private and public security sectors more transparent and
led to the creation of the federal law (1002/99) noted earlier. Yet more than a
decade later, the problem of collaborative impunity by police and private
security agents persists. Following several shocking *gatillo fácil* incidents in
2012, the Minister of Security, Nilda Garré, established a special commission to investigate the cases and warned against "all forms of corporatism"
that might sacrifice individual officers in the interest of saving the security
institutions' reputation (Britos 2012).

The Argentine case suggests that even in Latin American societies that
Yet legal structures and strong political stances do not necessarily eliminate impunity. Rather, the persistent mobilization of Argentine civil society
groups, conducting their own investigations of security agents' records and
histories, has played an essential role in pressuring political leaders to institute tougher regulatory reforms of the private security sector. Now private
security firms operating in the city of Buenos Aires (though not in Buenos
Aires province or other jurisdictions) must make public via the Internet the
names and work histories of their owners and employees, in order to enable
greater public oversight (Lacunza 2009). The norm, therefore, affects about
20 percent of the country's registered firms and an important segment of the
national market.

The Argentine case suggests that even in Latin American societies that
have come quite far from their authoritarian pasts, the most effective guard
of the guardians (public or private) is likely to be civil society, rather than
state officials. The fact that Argentina's private security market is a neoliberal type, which operates through contract-based privately owned firms, in
theory offers civil society the important ability to insure that transparency
and accountability are the norm in this industry. Yet in practice such ability
is only as powerful as the will that sustains it. In Argentina, it was only recently, in 2010, that government initiatives began to substantially demilitarize the structures of the federal police forces and to train for community-based
policing (Kollmann 2011). That year, the government initiated a major re-

form of the security sector by creating a new Ministry of Security, which the aforementioned Garré was the first to head. In her previous post as Minister of Defense, Garré had presided over promotional shake-ups and dismissals in the military high command in an effort to further civilian control of the military. Among her first tasks at Security was a purge of corrupt federal police forces and temporary use of Argentina's respectable Gendarmería (Gendarmerie, the national frontier guard) in the capital to address a wave of crime and public insecurity.

Thus, the government focus of the last several years has been to enhance public security provision, rather than address issues of concern regarding the private security sector. Yet given the close association between state security and private security actors, reform on the state side of the equation is an essential component of reform in the private security sector. Importantly, the government of Cristina Fernández de Kirchner prides itself on advancing human rights protections, so civil society groups advocating for greater transparency and checks on security sector impunity have finally found committed allies at the national government level. Yet the process of security sector reform, requiring the transformation of long-existing institutional structures and practices, is unlikely to be swift. Sustained societal pressure will be crucial to its success.

Overall, the Argentine experience suggests that the development of private security industries in post-authoritarian countries must be carefully regulated from their inception, as reliance on the market alone is no guarantee that "good" practices will trump the persistence of traditional impunities that can carry over into the new private security sector.

The Criminal Force Market in Guatemala

In almost every respect, Guatemala resides on the opposite end of the spectrum from Argentina. Poor, small, and densely populated, Guatemala has one of the region's largest rural and indigenous populations, with nearly 50 percent of Guatemalans identifying as ethnic Maya. Long the domain of oligarchic rule, Guatemala was the last of the region's current democracies to make the transition away from authoritarian rule. In 1996, the brutal three-decade civil war ended with the military's defeat of the leftist insurgency and a United Nations–brokered peace and reconstruction process that remains incomplete. The civil war was, in fact, an ethnic genocide perpetrated under the argument that rural Guatemalans were aiding the leftist insurgency. In this genocide, state-based security forces and private militias systematically decimated indigenous populations in the countryside, taking the lives of more than 200,000. Despite the end of the civil war and despite significant international attention for democracy building, Guatemala's military and security forces are arguably the region's most staunchly unreformed. The armed forces remain largely autonomous from civilian oversight, and impunity has persisted for human rights crimes of the past, with no charges for human rights crimes brought against anyone in the military until 2009.

Yet most disturbing is the finding, described in a landmark report by the advocacy group Washington Office on Latin America (2003), that illegal armed groups operate strategically at the behest of clandestine "hidden powers" embedded within the state and linked to and protected by powerful political parties and officials; thus, hidden powers operate racketeering operations, embezzle state funds, and engage in widespread corruption with political and legal immunity. The extraordinary impunity of Guatemala's hidden powers led to the unprecedented creation of the special United Nations–sponsored International Commission Against Impunity in Guatemala (CICIG), at the request of the Guatemalan government. CICIG is mandated to assist judicial institutions in investigating and prosecuting illegal and clandestine security groups. Since its creation in 2006, CICIG has aided the Guatemalan state in numerous proceedings, yet it has also met frequent resistance to its efforts, as cases carefully brought to court have often been thrown out on legal technicalities and prosecutions have been stonewalled (International Crisis Group 2011).

Thus Guatemala's security environment remains rife with impunity, and this context sets the stage for the operation of Guatemala's most prominent market for force: the criminal force market.[1] This market connects the country's two most acute security challenges: *mara* criminal gangs and transnational criminal organizations (TCOs). Together, they commit enormous violence—the *maras* mainly in Guatemalan cities, while TCOs operate mainly in coastal areas and rural communities, most notably in the province of Petén bordering Mexico. *Maras* control entire sectors of cities, while TCOs have come to control about 40 percent of national territory. Although there are important ways that these two collective actors cooperate within the market, they are distinct from each other and play different roles in the criminal force market in which they operate.

The *maras* are street gangs born of the refugees who fled to Los Angeles and other U.S. cities and brought the gang cultures they adopted there back to their home countries at the war's end. Numbering 70,000 across Central America and about 14,000 within Guatemala, the *maras* are known for their brutal violence, including the killing of innocent victims as part of induction into the gang (Boraz and Bruneau 2006). Although their primary impact on public security is through common (street) crime such as robbery, extortion, and drug selling, some *maras* are employed by major TCOs, primarily from Mexico, that have outsourced specialized services provided by the gangs. Although their roles are generally limited to conducting street-level drug distribution and killings on behalf of Mexican cartels (UNODC 2010: 239–40), it is worth emphasizing that *maras* are unique among the region's gangs in their transnational reach and organization. For instance, according to Boraz and Bruneau, MS-13, one of the two key *mara* confederations, has about 20,000 members in the United States and several thousand in Canada and Mexico. They describe *mara* organizational structures as "elaborate, flexible, and redundant": leadership cadres often have backup cadres, and internal functions are specialized into recruitment, logistics, attacks, intelligence gathering, and murder, trafficking, and extortion (Boraz and Bruneau 2006: 37).

Within this context, the key rationales laid out by Guerrero-Gutiérrez (2010: 21) for gangs and TCOs to "contract" with each other are particularly compelling. I summarize them here.

Cartels hire gangs for the following reasons:

1. *Risk reduction.* The semi-autonomous cells supplied through gang-level association diminish the likelihood of infiltration by government agents and other criminal groups. When gang members are arrested or defect to cartel rivals, they are unable to provide information about the cartel's workings because they are not integrated into its structures.
2. *Logistical advantage.* Gangs are networked but still locally based, so they aid cartels by providing information about conditions within their turf and facilitating information flows from various locations about which the cartel itself may know little.
3. *Credible violence.* Their violence skills and the fear they generate, both core assets for any organized crime group, define gangs.

4. *Economization.* By outsourcing tasks to gangs, cartels require less organizational infrastructure of their own.
5. *Market expansion.* Gang members themselves consume drugs and
   use arms, adding a reliable client base to cartel business.

Gangs work for cartels for the following reasons:

1. *Financial gain.* Cartels readily provide resources, rewards, and incentives for continued cooperation, as well as "concessions" to sell their
   illicit products.
2. *Reliable supplies.* Drugs and arms become more readily available,
   often at a discount.
3. *Protection.* Association with powerful cartels aids in insulating gangs
   from police interference, as poorly resourced police will likely be de-
   terred from taking on cartel-backed gangs.
4. *Recognition.* Alliances with cartels enhance gang reputation.

However, TCOs rely on more than the force of gangs for their operations
to succeed. Like legal corporations, TCOs require reliable market conditions
in which to operate and expand; corruption allows this. Therefore high-level
protection—the *withholding* of the use of force—by state-based actors (the
aforementioned hidden powers) is another crucial, paid-for service TCOs
commonly provide. Guatemalan law enforcement and justice institutions
stand out in the region for their pervasive corruption, particularly at the highest levels, despite various purges of the public security sector. Numerous police chiefs, drug enforcement officials, and legislators at all levels of government
have been implicated in drug and arms trafficking (UNODC 2010: 240–41).
    Although many TCOs rely on their own ability to use force, there are
also less typical examples of cartels hiring specialized armed forces away
from the state to support them. The outstanding case in Guatemala is the
Zetas, initially several dozen junior officers who defected from the Mexican
military's Air Mobile Special Forces Group to work for Mexico's Gulf cartel
in the late 1990s. The Zetas' specialized military training allowed them to
plan sophisticated operations and use advanced weaponry, enabling its pa-
tron to become one of the most powerful TCOs in the region. Zetas also
trained the enforcers of an allied group, the Familia Michoacana, which became one of the most ruthless and feared cartels in the region. By the mid

2000s, Zetas were using former Kaibiles, Guatemala's special forces, both to train their own new recruits (now from police and civilian cohorts) and likely to aid in the Zetas' expansion into Guatemalan territory (CRS Report for Congress 2007: 7–8).

The Kaibiles were infamous for their horrific killings and scorched earth operations during the civil war in Guatemala. At the war's end in 1996, the Kaibiles continued to exist, but about 4,000 were discharged. It is not surprising that former military forces like these have found ready employment in the "private" sector—both criminal and private security. As studies by scholars and human rights organizations have documented, former military officers were informally reincorporated into society through work for private security firms and organized crime (Argueta 2013: 80–82; Washington Office on Latin America 2003). This aspect suggests that the criminal force (and certainly also private security) markets have networked elements (e.g., on the gang front), but in the main they are fundamentally collaborative in structure. From their new private sector placement, they can continue to maintain perverse links within state structures, as the remarkably dense web of state-complicit corruption demonstrates.

The criminal force market in Guatemala demonstrates that such markets are not simply about violence-for-hire farmed out to the highest bidder. They involve, at times, complex relationships and structures, in which "payments" involve a dizzying array of far more than money—protection, prestige, operational advantage, and not least survival and reinvention are among the resources exchanged—though always it is the ability to use violent force of the most extreme kind that makes these hired enforcers so useful. Beyond this, however, the *mara* component is, to some extent, surprising within the Latin American context, where most private forces-for-hire have been trained as agents of the state through the military or police. The terrible irony of the *maras* is that they got their start-up training on the streets of the most powerful and stable democracy in the hemisphere. Demonstrating the significance of *transnational* force markets, the *maras* show that a migrant nonstate actor, in terms of origins and training, can become an important participant in Latin America's criminal force markets.

The Guatemalan case suggests that, of all the markets for force in the region, criminal force markets are the most absolutely debilitating to state institutions and society. Their enormous profit motive and their de facto autonomy from all legal regulation make them the region's force market that is surely hardest of all to restrain, and that warrants the most serious attention from the international community, as no state can tackle the challenge alone.

Conclusion

The cases studied in this chapter demonstrate the range of markets for force operating in contemporary Latin America. Regardless of market type—whether the neoliberal private security market, the racketeer criminal force market, or the hybrid military protection market—the causal factors bringing about specific markets for force in Latin America were heavily driven by the dynamics of rolling back state regulatory capacity and moving toward market-driven economic models. The resulting social and economic dislocation of the Washington Consensus era of the 1990s generated new forms of citizen insecurity that public sector forces were ill equipped to meet. Recourse to private markets for force became common, though the consequences have varied across types and depending on national characteristics. Still, we can determine some basic consequences of the force markets in Argentina and Guatemala.

In Argentina, it is fair to assume that the reliance on private security undermines public security institutions, effectively filling in for them in places where they are weak or absent, so that there is a diminishing incentive to rectify faulty public forces. Yet the reality in Argentina is more complex. Although certainly many in the elite can (and likely always have) relied on privately contracted force to protect their interests, many vocal and progressive citizens have considered defects in the security forces—both public and private—grounds for institutional reform. Enhanced vetting of private forces due to citizen-led initiatives was the outcome of reforms promoted in the national capital, and the federal police forces became the object of formal investigation and review. Although Argentina's federal system inherently limits the ability of national reforms to take hold, citizen-led reform initiatives in the capital set the powerful normative standard that ties of impunity and collaboration should not exist between public and private security forces.

Perhaps most important in observing the Argentine case is the caution with which we should consider the "positive" effects of the neoliberal force market. Although in Argentina it is certainly true that the neoliberal concept of the market, defined in terms of contracts among private actors and privately owned enterprises, predominates, it is the organizational capacity of civil society groups that empowers change. Anchored in a historical culture of progressive political activism, civil society mobilization gives momentum to all security reform efforts pursued by political leaders. In particular, the state's repressive capacity as exercised during the 1976–83 dictatorship, which mobilized both private and public agents to perform more than 30,000 extrajudicial killings and disappearances, remains under constant scrutiny from human rights groups. This political culture of mobilization and resistance to repression drives positive outcomes in the provision of security as a public good, likely trumping purely market-based contributions. In short, although the structure of the private security market as neoliberal may be a necessary condition for the market to have a positive effect on the provision of security as a public good, in the Argentine case it is clearly not a sufficient condition.

In Guatemala, the consequences following from the criminal market for force are wide ranging and disturbing. The criminal market has enhanced the position of existing spoilers, and perhaps created new ones, as transnationally based criminal groups fight over turf in the "ungoverned spaces" of Guatemala. The illicit provision of force for hire has also allowed corrupt individuals from the public security and military forces to reinvent themselves in second careers, while gang members who work for the trafficking cartels gain new connections, prestige, and survival opportunities.

The criminal market clearly undermines state institutions. One reason for this is the daunting challenge that criminal groups pose to regular security forces, as they are often better armed and equipped with communications technologies than their counterparts. Another reason is that they are often successful in demanding protection for powerful state-based actors, creating perverse linkages between state and criminal actors that must be severed in order to construct any semblance of state capacity for good governance. Finally, in pressuring the state to up the ante and draw the armed forces into the counter-drug fight, criminal groups open the door to a remilitarization of security functions in Guatemala, at a time when efforts had been underway to demilitarize, especially in rural areas that had been focal zones for military action during the civil war.

Finally, there is no question that the criminal market deepens citizen insecurity. Whether in terms of the economic costs required for investment in both public and private security, or the social cost of vigilantism and cycles of violence, or the political-institutional cost of militarizing anti-crime and anti-drug efforts, the rise of criminal force markets is utterly debilitating. Although it is encouraging that international organizations and states from outside the region have pledged substantial aid to target citizen insecurity in

Guatemala and throughout Central America, the effort must center on established but elusive criminal ties that are extremely difficult to reveal and break. As the experience of CICIG shows, gross corruption and criminality *can* be successfully prosecuted, but it requires both practical reforms (e.g., witness protection programs) in the short term and a deeper cultural shift among elites away from normative acceptance of impunity.

Markets for force have a long history in Latin America, but they operate in a new era, at a time when civil society in every country of the region has gained unprecedented networking ability and mobilizational capacity. The trend of recent years, toward mass protest based on widespread dissatisfaction with political leadership and state provision of services, may well be an indicator of future challenges that citizens will direct toward markets for force. Civil society resilience and the responsiveness of political leaders may well determine the outcome.

Note

1. The focus here on the criminal force market does not negate the importance of a private security market, as much a base layer phenomenon in Guatemala as elsewhere in Latin America. On the private security market's dynamics, see Argueta 2013.

References

Argueta, Otto. 2013. *Private Security in Guatemala: Pathway to Its Proliferation.* Baden-Baden: Nomos Verlagsgesellschaft.

Arias, Patricia. 2009. *Seguridad Privada en América Latina.* Santiago, Chile: FLACSO.

Birdsall, Nancy, Augusto de la Torre, and Felipe Valencia Caidedo. 2010. *The Washington Consensus: Assessing a Damaged Brand.* Working Paper 211 (May). Washington, D.C.: Center for Global Development.

Boraz, Steven C. and Thomas C. Bruneau. 2006. "Are the *Maras* Overwhelming Governments in Central America?" *Military Review* (November-December): 36–40.

Britos, Juan Diego. 2012. "Garré recibió a familiares de víctimas." *Tiempo Argentino* (Buenos Aires), February 2.

"Condenados por el asesino de Cabezas trabajan como seguridad en Pinamar." 2011. *La Razón* (Buenos Aires), January 9.

Congressional Research Service (CRS). 2007. *Report for Congress: Mexico's Drug Cartels.* Washington, D.C.: Author. http://www.fas.org/sgp/crs/row/RL34215.pdf.

Diamint, Rut. 2008. "Defensa, Seguridad y Estado de Derecho." In *Reforma de las Fuerzas Armadas en América Latina y el impacto de las amenazas irregulares*, ed. José Raúl Perales, 105–17. Washington, D.C.: Woodrow Wilson International Center for Scholars.

Fleitas Ortiz de Rozas, Diego M. 2011. *La Seguridad Privada en Argentina.* Buenos Aires: Asociación para Políticas Públicas.

Forero, Juan. 2007. "Traffickers Infiltrate Military in Colombia." *Washington Post,* September 8.

Guerrero-Gutiérrez, Eduardo. 2010. "Security, Drugs, and Violence in Mexico." Paper prepared for the Sixth North American Forum, San Miguel de Allende, Mexico, September 30–October 2. http://insyde.org.mx/images/naf_rev_2010.pdf

Huggins, Martha K. 1998. *Political Policing: The United States and Latin America.* Durham, N.C.: Duke University Press.

International Crisis Group. 2011. "Learning to Walk Without a Crutch: An Assessment of the International Commission Against Impunity in Guatemala." *Latin America Report* 36(May): 31.

Kollmann, Raul. 2011. "Es preciso dejar atrás el molde militar." *Página 12* (Buenos Aires), March 5.

Lacunza, Sebastián. 2009. "Argentina: Dubious Past? No Problem for Private Security Firms." *Inter Press Service,* October 2.

"Las refinerías, bajo el cuidado de las FFAA." 2007. *El Comercio* (Quito), December 22. http://www.bittium-energy.com/cms/content/view/1302/

Latinobarómetro. 2010. *Informe 2010.* Santiago, Chile: Corporación Latinobarómetro.

Organization of American States (OAS). 2008. *Seguridad Privada: Respuesta a las necesidades de seguridad pública en conglomerados urbanos.* Washington, D.C.: OAS Secretaría General, Departamento de Seguridad Pública.

Ramsey, Geoffrey. 2011. "Cable: Honduran Military Supplied Weaponry to Cartels." *Insight Crime,* April 25. http://www.insightcrime.org/news-analysis/cable-honduran -military-supplied-weaponry-to-cartels.

Sagasti, Ramiro. 2003. "Investigan a 40 Policías Bonaerenses." *La Nación* (Buenos Aires), July 23.

Securitas. 2013. *Annual Report 2012.* Stockholm.

Servicios Privados de Seguridad y Custodia. Decreto 1002 (Argentina, 1999).

Sibaja, Harold, Enrique Roig, Christina del Castillo, Patty Galdamez, and Marlon Carranza. 2006. *Central America and Mexico Gang Assessment, Annex 1: El Salvador Profile.* Washington, D.C.: U.S. Agency for International Development.

United Nations Office on Drugs and Crime (UNODC). 2010. *World Drug Report, 2010.* Vienna.

United States Government Accountability Office (U.S. GAO). 2005. *Security Assistance: Efforts to Secure Colombia's Caño-Limón-Coveñas Oil Pipeline Have Reduced Attacks, but Challenges Remain.* GAO-05-971. Washington, D.C.

Washington Office on Latin America. 2003. *Hidden Powers in Post-Conflict Guatemala: Illegal Armed Groups and the Forces Behind Them.* Washington, D.C.

Williams, Phil. 2002. "Transnational Organized Crime and the State." In *The Emergence of Private Authority in Global Governance*, ed. Rodney Bruce Hall and Thomas J. Biersteker, 161–82. Cambridge, UK: Cambridge University Press.

World Bank. 2011. *Crime and Violence in Central America: A Development Challenge.* Washington, D.C.

CHAPTER 3

The Military Protection Markets in Peru and Ecuador: A Detailed Analysis

Maiah Jaskoski

Introduction

Latin America's markets for lethal force bring together public and private actors from the international and domestic arenas. The markets are particularly complex in the Andean region, given that natural resource extraction, insurgency, and/or cocaine production and trafficking often take place in the same space. The work of private security companies is extensive. The U.S. Department of State has hired the U.S. firm DynCorp to support the eradication of coca (the raw material used to process cocaine) in Bolivia, Colombia, and Peru (Richani 2005: 135). International as well as domestic private security companies also work to protect private investments in extractive industries in remote areas of this region, where oil and mining company workers face the prospect of kidnappings, guerrilla attacks, and popular mobilizations that can halt production. In Colombia, Occidental Oil has maintained contracts with the U.S. company AirScan (ibid.), foreign oil companies operating in Ecuador have employed companies such as British Defense Systems Limited, and Peruvian mining companies have relied on firms that include the domestic companies Forza and Orus.

Private firms are not the only actors hired to provide security in the Andes. As recounted during interviews by private security officials and private mining and oil company representatives with extensive experience working in Latin America, companies often find that paying local army units can be the most effective means of security provision. This is particularly so when companies deem that the situation requires a rapid mobilization of large forces that can legally traverse territory while carrying weapons.[1] The U.S. government is another renowned "client" of Andean militaries and police forces, as U.S. assistance has drawn both institutions into antinarcotics (Youngers and Rosin 2005). It is this dimension of the Andes' hybrid market for force—the hiring of national militaries by actors other than the central government—that serves as the focus of the present analysis.

This chapter analyzes two cases of "military protection markets" discussed in Kristina Mani's chapter on Latin American markets for force. Specifically, the study examines financing of the Ecuadorian and Peruvian armies by third parties. The research finds that clients, especially private mining and hydrocarbon companies, have paid the armies for their security services. To a significant degree, deals occur at the local level. The study can be situated next to prior work on Latin American militaries in the local sphere, and in particular Ferreyra and Segura's (2000) comparative analysis of Mexico and Colombia. With regard to the Mexican case, the authors pose the following three questions: "Who are the 'clients' of the armed forces in the different regions? What are the local dynamics that shape their policies and activities at the local level? Are these activities consistent with the national discourse?" (ibid.: 29). These three questions frame this chapter's finding that private actors have financed army security work through local deals to a great extent; examination of the causes of this local, third-party influence; and examination of the direct consequences of private clients' hiring the armies.

Research for this chapter was conducted in both Peru and Ecuador during 2005–6 and 2009 and involved interviews and review of newspaper and government archives, army doctrinal materials, and secondary sources. Interviews were conducted with more than 150 army officers of all ranks who had recently served in different capacities and in different locations in the countries. In Ecuador, officers were interviewed in the capital city of Quito and on seven bases throughout the country. I interviewed Peruvian officers in the capital of Lima and on an important base in an insurgency zone. Subjects included instructors and students from the army war college and from the different service schools. I also interviewed more than 170 journalists; academics; nongovernmental organization (NGO) representatives; private-sector actors; navy, air force, and police officers; elected and appointed local and regional political officials; and officials from the U.S. defense and state departments.

The Market: Local Third-Party Financing

Ecuador's northern region faces two types of security challenges. First, on an ongoing basis, residents, including indigenous groups, mobilize against the practices of oil companies and government oil policy (see Gerlach 2003; Sawyer 2004). Second, Colombian guerrillas have used the north to rest, supply, and train for combat back home, bringing to Ecuador's northern border provinces of Sucumbíos, Carchi, and Esmeraldas challenges ranging from drug and weapons trafficking to kidnappings to extortion. When in 2000 the joint initiative between Colombia and the United States entailing a major military offensive against insurgents, the so-called "Plan Colombia," was implemented, it exacerbated northern insecurity.[2] The Ecuadorian military—especially the army—responded with a force buildup in the north.[3]

In this context, army commanders have received significant financing from third-party actors. After 2000, the U.S. military supplemented its relations with the army in Quito with direct contact with Ecuadorian army units in the north in order to encourage army border defense and counter-drug efforts. In 2005 and 2006, these local army commanders used U.S. logistical support—including communications equipment, patrol supplies, and vehicles—for antinarcotics. Army units also have conducted patrols to protect wealthy landowners from crop and livestock theft, extortion, and kidnapping. In return, landowners have given army personnel food, fuel, lodging, and tires for their vehicles. Mayors and prefects have used (public) local and provincial resources, respectively, to furnish army units throughout the north with base improvements and fuel in return for security in cities.

Finally, northern army units have provided considerable security for the oil industry against popular protest. Local army commanders and private oil company representatives have negotiated directly the amount and location of army services—including security for oil wells, refineries, and pipelines—and company payments for army security, in the forms of base improvements, communications equipment, food, fuel, lodging, and vehicles. More than 2,000 men in the Fourth Division, responsible for security in the northeast, were assigned to perform ongoing oil security ("Las FF.AA. ofrecen" 2007).[4] Within that division, the Nineteenth Brigade has devoted significant resources to oil security. All battalions in the brigade have worked in oil security, and one of the brigade's five combat units that operate directly from the brigade base has focused only on oil security, supplemented on occasion with help from the other combat units. Regularly, personnel from the Special Forces brigade have rushed north from their permanent location in the highland city of Latacunga, south of Quito, to assist in protest control.

Some of the army's oil work has been triggered by national actions, for example, when by emergency decree the executive has ordered the army to control a major protest. Additionally, until 2007 the military and oil companies engaged in national-level contracts (see below). However, such contracts only established broad terms, leaving local company and army officials to negotiate the details of payments and services.

In Peru, third-party financing has occurred amid an ongoing insurgent threat posed by the Maoist Shining Path (Sendero Luminoso). Although by the mid-1990s much of the armed threat had been eliminated, the group has continued training to a limited extent, ambushing military and police patrols, and kidnapping residents of remote towns in the Valley of the Apurímac and Ene Rivers (VRAE)—where the army most actively conducts operations—and in the southern highlands and the Upper Huallaga Valley zone in Peru's central highlands. Representatives from private hydrocarbon and mining companies have reimbursed army units that patrol company infrastructure and personnel against guerrilla attacks in the VRAE. In accordance with such agreements, all of the country's main mines enjoyed security from army units in the 1980s and 1990s. Though most army/company deals in Peru have occurred at the subnational level, Peru's military joint command and head of the army have been involved when major army equipment is needed, such as during the renting out of army helicopters.

As an example of ongoing third-party financing of the Peruvian army at the local level, there is the case of the private natural gas conglomerate Camisea, which owns and operates a major pipeline that passes through the VRAE. As of 2005, the army had a small unit near each of Camisea's fourteen installations along the pipeline. At the time, all counterinsurgency bases (more than ten) in the Ayacucho brigade—which has been responsible for a considerable amount of army security services in the VRAE—protected the pipeline, as did bases in the neighboring department of Cusco. These army commitments were significant: At the time, the army had only between twenty-seven and thirty-five active counterinsurgency bases in the VRAE in total.[5] Camisea security was performed consistent with agreements between company officials and army commanders. As an example of the terms of financing, in accordance with arrangements made between the brigade commander and Transportadora de Gas del Perú (TGP)—the Camisea consortium that operates the pipeline—TGP constructed and stocked the pipeline bases used by the Ayacucho brigade's personnel.

In both Peru and Ecuador, one characteristic of the local market for army services is ongoing and even increasing pressure by army leadership on local commanders for the latter to fund their bases through entrepreneurship. Such pressure suggests that local, third-party financing of the armies may be on the rise. Due to resource shortages, local commanders have pursued many entrepreneurial activities, in addition to the security deals described above.[6] For instance, not including salaries and food, the army only paid for approximately 20 percent of the operating expenses of the Special Forces brigade in Latacunga. Almost 20 percent of the remaining operating expenses were covered by the brigade's sale of its farm products. An officer familiar with the brigade's finances said in an interview that the colonel in charge of the unit was in a difficult position, in that he had to ensure that the brigade carried out the work assigned by army leaders in Quito.

The Ecuadorian army unit reputed to be most active in terms of conducting security operations was the Nueva Loja battalion in the province of Sucumbíos, which is known for a significant Colombian guerrilla presence. Annually, the army provided that battalion a mere USD 200 to maintain its thirty vehicles. The battalion sold fish and chicken from its farms to raise USD 6,000–7,000 each year to put toward fuel. An officer who had managed finances for the battalion characterized the position as stressful because he had been perpetually late in paying the unit's bills. Local resource scarcity extended to units beyond the north. For instance, the army provided the brigade in the southern coastal city of Machala roughly one-tenth of the diesel and one-sixth of the gasoline that the unit used.

In Peru, too, army leaders have pressured commanders to support base functions with outside resources. One army officer said, "The army has its priorities, which include rations for the troops, ammunition, and fuel. But what is not prioritized by the army is electricity, water . . . paper for the office . . . so the units have to come up with this, to make up the difference." In addition to security deals with mining and hydrocarbon companies in Shining Path zones, local army commanders have engaged in other types of entrepreneurship, such as the leasing of their base infrastructure to third parties. As in Ecuador, Peruvian army units have sold products from their farms to the community. These sales have occurred, for example, in the southern departments of Puno and Tacna, the northern department of Tumbes, and the eastern city of Iquitos. Engineering battalions have supported themselves by selling their construction services. Through these different efforts, units covered a substantial proportion of their operating costs—for instance, approximately 15–20 percent in Tumbes, 20–30 percent in the department of Arequipa, and 50 percent in Tacna.

Pressure from army leadership on local commanders to finance their units apparently has been on the rise, as reported by an Ecuadorian officer who had experience working in finances on more than ten bases throughout the country. Similarly, a mid-ranking Peruvian officer said, "I tell the general that we raised 80,000 *soles* last year, and I say that to run the [unit] I need 300,000 *soles* for . . . this year. He gives me 200,000 and tells me to work harder this year to come up with the extra 100,000 *soles*." A retired officer from the army corps of engineers described how the corps operated in this environment: "We need resources to fix the equipment, for maintenance . . . So the units might work for twelve hours, rent the equipment and men out for that period of time, but then report to [the army in] Lima that they worked for only three hours."

Causes of the Market

This section turns from describing the characteristics of the local market for army services in Ecuador and Peru to identifying potential forces that may have advanced local third-party financing of the armies. Two contextual factors—Latin America's shift to a market-led economic model and the conclusion of the Peru-Ecuador border conflict—have led to cuts in national defense spending and privatization of the extractive industries, which, in turn, seem to encourage third-party financing. At the same time, regulatory shifts, especially increased oversight of the armed forces, in combination with the historically weak capacity for Latin American governments to control remote regions of their countries, push army-client relations to the local level.

National defense spending has decreased in importance relative to other sectors in the two countries, possibly motivating the armed forces to look beyond the state to third parties for resources.[7] In Ecuador, the 1995 Peru-Ecuador Cenepa War and the subsequent 1998 peace agreement that resolved the longstanding international border conflict left the military without a salient combat mission. (In contrast, in Peru the military had ongoing counterinsurgency responsibilities following that peace agreement). In this context, Ecuador's defense budget dropped from 10.9 to 7.3 percent of national spending between 1995 and 2006 (Ministerio de Economía y Finanzas, Ecuador n.d.). Peru's military experienced steady budget cuts throughout the 1990s when, amid a deep economic crisis, the government of Alberto Fujimori (1990–2000) implemented one of Latin America's most radical liberal economic reform projects. As a percentage of the national budget, Peruvian defense spending dropped from 14.4 percent in 1989 to 8 percent in 2006 (Palomino Milla 2004; Ministerio de Economía y Finanzas, Perú n.d.).

At the same time that budget cuts may have pushed the armies to seek third-party financing, the opening of the critical extractive industries to private investment may have expanded the armies' potential client base, paralleling dynamics in Colombia (Richani 2005: 127–28). In the aftermath of highly nationalist military regimes in Ecuador and Peru during the 1960s and 1970s, privatization of extractive industries as part of Latin America's broader shift to a liberal economic market has been noteworthy. Private actors gained a major role in Ecuador's oil industry in the 1990s (Sawyer 2004: 95–97). In Peru in 1999, 95 percent of the country's mineral production was carried out by the private sector, as compared to 55 percent in 1990 (Bury 2005: 225). For their part, seeking to protect their investments, private companies subsidize national security forces in a setting in which weak states wish to avoid the difficult task of funding those forces through taxation (Avant 2005: 180–81).

If cuts in national defense spending and the availability of private clients can encourage armies to look for private funding sources, increasingly that financing may be obtained through local negotiations, due to the combination of (a) government oversight of national military financial practices and (b) ongoing military autonomy at the local level. In an effort to increase civilian control of the armed forces, governments in Ecuador and Peru have enhanced their oversight of military financial practices in ways specifically relevant to the question of third-party influence on the armed forces. Within Ecuadorian society, open opposition to military deals with the private sector grew in 2005, when the national press reported on a 2001 contract between the military and sixteen private oil companies ("FFAA acuerdan con empresas petroleras" 2001; Ministerio de Defensa Nacional, Ecuador 2001; "2000 militares vigilarán" 2005; "Siete meses más" 2005). Subsequently, a 2007 defense law prohibited direct resource transfers from the private sector to the military as part of a broader effort on the part of the executive to bolster civilian control of the armed forces. Security experts interviewed in 2009 reported that in response to the 2007 law, Ecuador's military halted national contracts with private oil companies.

In Peru, too, the government has sought to strengthen its control of the military through greater financial oversight. This effort has been a component of broader efforts toward enhanced government transparency and accountability since the conclusion of the highly corrupt, repressive, and militarized Fujimori government.[8] Particularly relevant to the present discussion has been the regulation of army contracting services. Legally, the army can provide services and rent out its infrastructure to state and private third parties in return for *recursos directamente recaudados* (resources directly collected, or RDR). RDR are then incorporated into the official defense budget.[9] According to army officers, due to oversight of military finances since Fujimori left office, the armed forces have increased their reporting of RDR.

In contrast to this supervision of national military (and army) financial practices, research for this study revealed no civilian oversight of individual army units' finances. The proposition that the governments have little ability to monitor local commanders is consistent with Ferreyra and Segura (2000), who find that Latin American military units can become deeply entrenched in local political and economic realities. Their findings indicate that this dynamic is especially true in countries that face major security threats in remote areas known for a lack of nonmilitary state presence. It seems, in fact, that the government's added control of the military in the capital city has merely pushed third-party financing of the armies to the local level, where such control does not exist. The above analysis suggests that these local exchanges have continued and even expanded. In spite of the 2007 legislation outlawing army/private sector contracting in Ecuador, local deals between army units and private oil companies continued as of early 2009, according to a journalist with extensive experience reporting on the army and its operations in the north. In Peru, brigades and battalions often contract out services and infrastructure for income that goes unreported, thereby remaining outside of the RDR system.

Consequences of the Market

Private financing of the two armies has constituted a particular kind of state capture by the private sector, with two main consequences relevant to this volume. First, the capture has undermined the military as an institution by diverting the armies from their national security functions, a clear challenge to the state's monopoly of force. Second, it has diminished security for the general public.

As mining and hydrocarbon companies prove central in this analysis of state capture, a preliminary note is in order about the distinction between the (public) national security interest, on the one hand, and demands from private mining and hydrocarbons, on the other. Hydrocarbons and, in Peru, mining, in fact are considered critical for national security. Furthermore, security for the sectors has been one component of the armies' assigned security work. Ecuador's 1979 National Security Law, still in effect when research for this analysis was being carried out, assigns the armed forces to protect "strategic" areas, including oil. Peruvian military and civilian security experts justified military work to protect hydrocarbon interests by pointing to successive national constitutions that have mandated that the armed forces "participate in the country's social and economic development."

Yet although the armies have a legal obligation to provide security for these sectors, they are not supposed to put that work ahead of other key missions in the complicated zones of northern Ecuador and Peru's VRAE. A 2001 directive from the commander of the Ecuadorian army's Fourth Division commits the unit to security for oil companies, but "without neglecting [the division's] fundamental missions and assignments" (Jarrín Román 2001: Section D). During interviews, officers also ranked oil security lower than other work. Forty-six Ecuadorian army officers were asked to identify the army's most important missions. In their first three responses, thirty-three of them mentioned border defense and/or reducing Colombian insurgent activities in Ecuador, and only four mentioned oil security. Similar to the Ecuadorian case, neither law nor security experts interviewed in Peru identified hydrocarbons or mining security as being the army's primary reason for working in Shining Path zones. Instead, the army was to focus on most effectively eliminating the guerrilla threat. Of the fifty Peruvian army officers asked to name the army's most important missions, twenty-two mentioned counterinsurgency as one of their first three responses, and no officer mentioned security for natural resources or resource extraction.

In spite of the obligation to put border defense and counterinsurgency first in Ecuador and Peru, respectively, in fact local battalions in northern Ecuador and Peru's Shining Path zones have prioritized security for paying, private companies in the extractive industries, indicating state capture.[10] As we have seen, army leaders placed significant pressure on local commanders to finance their own units, and clients generally have reimbursed army units with in-kind payments, thereby ensuring that the army has used the resources for the financed functions. In this context, commanders have decided when and where to provide security in response to resource transfers from clients. In Ecuador, wealthy oil companies have exercised a high level of influence on army behavior relative to other clients. U.S. military representatives have competed openly with oil companies for army services and have lost.[11] In Carchi, a province that does not have oil or oil infrastructure, the army unit has focused intensively on security for wealthy landowners in return for resources. In contrast, officers who described army security services for the wealthy landowners in the province of Esmeraldas—where many African palm plantations are located—spoke little of that work, which was relatively limited compared to the unit's security services for the private oil pipeline of OCP Ecuador S.A.

Further evidence that third-party financing has transformed army security services into excludable, private goods is that contracting mainly has occurred between army units and private, not state, companies. When research was conducted for this study in zones where the Ecuadorian state oil company (Petroecuador) operated, local army commanders there dealt with private companies. Furthermore, in the 1980s, before Ecuador's government actively encouraged major private participation in oil, the army still served the private sector in exchange for compensation. A retired army helicopter pilot described in an interview that starting in the mid-1980s, either the army aviation commander or the head of the army signed with oil companies, according to contracts. In such cases, the army helped to conduct seismic evaluations and transported exploration materials to company encampments, among other tasks. Similarly, Peru's army performed work for the small private mining sector in return for company resources in the 1980s, prior to the large-scale privatization of resource extraction. In fact, the U.S.

Southern Peru Copper Corporation, the sole private mining company that had avoided being nationalized under military rule (1968–80), was the only company that Peruvian officers named when describing the army's work for mining companies in the 1980s, despite the fact that guerrillas targeted both foreign private companies and the large national companies at the time (Bury 2005: 223).[12]

Through capture, the very institution of the military, which is expected to protect national security interests, has been undermined. That negotiations between the army and third parties seem to take place increasingly at the local level is particularly disconcerting for those concerned about the state's monopoly on force: The local dynamic suggests not only that the military as an institution has been threatened through capture, but also that the very unity and cohesion of the armed forces has been challenged, as local commanders focus on raising funds rather than on effectively performing security missions designed in the capital city by military leadership.

These militaries that are distracted by private-sector security demands and financing have left the general public facing heightened insecurity. The Ecuadorian army forces that patrol for wealthy landowners in Carchi have not provided security for the impoverished people who also live within the same zones, according to an army officer. Even in Sucumbíos, which experiences the ongoing presence of Colombian guerrillas, one of the four battalions in the province (in Shushufindi) has been devoted entirely to oil security. The other three battalions in the province also have provided services to private oil companies, according to ongoing relations between company officials and battalion commanders. In Peru, when research was being conducted for this study, the TGP agreement with the Ayacucho brigade that committed the latter's counterinsurgency bases to Camisea pipeline security meant that the brigade's counterinsurgency services were unlikely to lead to direct combat between the army and Shining Path guerrillas: Pipeline patrols were carried out during the daytime only, immediately along the pipeline, which did not pass directly through Shining Path's main training and operation zones. Thus, by causing army patrol routes to concentrate on private company infrastructure, local army/company contracts have interfered with the Peruvian army's mission to protect the public from insurgents.

Notes

I thank Deborah Avant, Molly Dunigan, Candelaria Garay, Elke Krahmann, Anna Leander, Stephanie McNulty, Ulrich Petersohn, Arturo Sotomayor, and Harold

Trinkunas for feedback on earlier versions of this chapter. Portions of this chapter are adapted from Jaskoski 2013b. The study would not have been possible without the generosity of many individuals in Ecuador and Peru who shared with me their time and views, and for their help I am deeply grateful. Fieldwork was supported by a National Security Education Program David L. Boren Graduate Fellowship and the Naval Postgraduate School Research Initiation Program. The findings presented here are those of the author and do not represent positions of the U.S. Navy, Department of Defense, or government.

1. For a more detailed analysis of the motivations of private companies in extractive industries when turning to public security forces for security in Latin America, see Jaskoski 2013c.

2. For further discussion of insecurity in northern Ecuador since 2000, see Andrade 2002a, 2002b; Montúfar 2003; and International Crisis Group 2004.

3. In 2001, the command center of the army's fourth division moved north to the city of Francisco de Orellana, in the province of Orellana just south of Sucumbíos, and the army had added 7,000 personnel to the north as of September 2003 ("Entrevista Grab" 2003).

4. In the army, which according to a journalist with expertise on the Ecuadorian military is made up of approximately 34,000 personnel, the 2,000 number is large.

5. This estimate is based on interviews with army officers, private-sector officials, and research conducted by Peruvian security expert Ricardo Soberón Garrido (2006).

6. The following discussion of army entrepreneurship is based on information provided by local army commanders and other officers with direct knowledge of the units' finances, gained through working on those bases.

7. The apparent effect of budget cuts in the two countries, and particularly the Peruvian case of extreme neoliberal economic reforms, is in line with Cruz and Diamint's (1998: see especially 117–18) observation that defense spending reductions that have accompanied Latin America's broader shift to a liberal economic model have encouraged military entrepreneurship.

8. On the Fujimori government's authoritarian tendencies, see Carrión 2006.

9. In 2003 and 2004, RDR contributed roughly 11 percent of the national defense budget (Robles Montoya 2005: 159–60). Approximately one-half of RDR was earned through the provision of services such as air and sea transportation and medical assistance (Palomino Milla 2004: 144–45).

10. For analysis of the limits of private client influence on the two armies, see Jaskoski 2013a: 181–83. Importantly, the limits are not defined by national security interests but, rather, the interest of the armies as organizations in maintaining predictability for their work.

11. For example, in late 2007 there were popular protests in Dayuma, in the northeastern province of Orellana, and the army was involved in establishing order there. U.S. military representatives wanted the army forces instead to focus on antinarcotics and border defense farther north. In an effort to calm the protesters and thereby free

up the army, U.S. officials gave supplies to a local school. Details of this case were provided by a U.S. official in Ecuador.

12. On the history of Southern's investment in Peru, see Kuramoto 1999.

References

Andrade, Pablo. 2002a. "Diagnóstico de la frontera Ecuador-Colombia." *Comentario internacional* 4 (Semester II): 189–240.

———. 2002b. "La seguridad en las relaciones Ecuador-Colombia." *Comentario internacional* 4 (Semester II): 77–88.

Avant, Deborah D. 2005. *The Market for Force: The Consequences of Privatizing Security*. New York: Cambridge University Press.

Bury, Jeffrey. 2005. "Mining Mountains: Neoliberalism, Land Tenure, Livelihoods, and the New Peruvian Mining Industry in Cajamarca." *Environment and Planning* 37(2): 221–39.

Carrión, Julio F. 2006. *The Fujimori Legacy: The Rise of Electoral Authoritarianism in Peru*. University Park: Pennsylvania State University Press.

Cruz, Consuelo, and Rut Diamint. 1998. "The New Military Autonomy in Latin America." *Journal of Democracy* 9(4): 115–27.

"Entrevista Grab. Luis Aguas: 5000 armados están frente a Ecuador." 2003. *El Comercio* (Quito), September 21.

Ferreyra, Aleida, and Renata Segura. 2000. "Examining the Military in the Local Sphere: Colombia and Mexico." *Latin American Perspectives* 27(2): 18–35.

"FFAA acuerdan con empresas petroleras." 2001. *Hoy* (Quito), August 1.

Gerlach, Allen. 2003. *Indians, Oil, and Politics: A Recent History of Ecuador*. Wilmington, Del.: Scholarly Resources.

International Crisis Group. 2004. *Colombia's Borders: The Weak Link in Uribe's Security Policy*. ICG Latin America Report 9. Quito and Brussels.

Jarrín Román, Oswaldo R. 2001. *Directiva No. 2001-13 para el cumplimiento del Convenio de cooperación de seguridad militar entre el Ministerio de Defensa Nacional y las empresas petroleras que operan en la región amazónica*. Quito.

Jaskoski, Maiah. 2013a. *Military Politics and Democracy in the Andes*. Baltimore, Md.: Johns Hopkins University Press.

———. 2013b. "Private Financing of the Military: A Local Political Economy Approach." *Studies in Comparative International Development* 48(2): 172–95.

———. 2013c. "Security for Latin America's Extractive Industries: Private Financiers and Public Security Forces." Paper presented at the International Congress of the Latin American Studies Association, Washington, D.C., May 29–June 1.

Kuramoto, Juana R. 1999. *Las aglomeraciones productivas alrededor de la minería: El caso de minera Yanacocha S.A.* Documento de Trabajo 27. Lima: Grupo de Análisis para el Desarrollo (GRADE).

"Las FF.AA. ofrecen tres tipos de seguridad a las petroleras." 2007. *El Comercio* (Quito), December 28.

Ministerio de Defensa Nacional, Ecuador. 2001. *Convenio de cooperación de seguridad militar entre el Ministerio de Defensa Nacional y las empresas petroleras que operan en el Ecuador.* Quito: Ministerio de Defensa Nacional.

Ministerio de Economía y Finanzas, Ecuador. n.d. *Budget statistics.* Accessed 2007. http://mef.gob.ec/40.

Ministerio de Economía y Finanzas, Perú. n.d. *Budget statistics.* Accessed 2006. http://ofi.mef.gob.pe/transparencia/default.aspx.

Montúfar, César. 2003. "El Ecuador entre el Plan Colombia y la Iniciativa Andina: Del enfoque de los 'efectos' a una perspectiva de regionalización." In *Turbulencia en los Andes y Plan Colombia*, ed. César Montúfar and Teresa Whitfield, 205–34. Quito: Centro Andino de Estudios Internacionales, Universidad Andina Simón Bolívar Ecuador.

Palomino Milla, Fernando. 2004. *Economía de la defensa nacional: Una aproximación al caso peruano.* Serie: Democracia 10. Lima: Comisión Andina de Juristas.

Richani, Nazih. 2005. "Multinational Corporations, Rentier Capitalism, and the War System in Colombia." *Latin American Politics and Society* 47(3): 113–44.

Robles Montoya, José. 2005. "Transparencia y control en la asignación de recursos para la defensa: Discurso y realidad." In *Los nudos de la defensa: Enredos y desenredos para una política pública en democracia*, ed. Lourdes Hurtado, José Miguel Florez, César San Martín, Rossy Luz Salazar, José Robles, Gustavo Sibilla, Rut Diamint, and Ana María Tamayo, 123–52. Serie Democracia y Fuerza Armada. Lima: Instituto de Defensa Legal.

Sawyer, Suzana. 2004. *Crude Chronicles: Indigenous Politics, Multinational Oil, and Neoliberalism in Ecuador.* Durham, N.C.: Duke University Press.

"Siete meses más para el convenio del 2001." 2005. *El Comercio* (Quito), December 19.

Soberón Garrido, Ricardo. 2006. *Listado de bases antisubversivas en el Perú.* Inventory. Lima.

"2000 militares vigilarán el sistema petrolero." 2005. *El Comercio* (Quito), December 19.

Youngers, Coletta A., and Eileen Rosin. 2005. *Drugs and Democracy in Latin America: The Impact of U.S. Policy.* Boulder, Colo.: Lynne Rienner.

CHAPTER 4

The Market for Force in the United
Kingdom: The Recasting of the Monopoly
of Violence and the Management of Force
as a Public-Private Enterprise

Carlos Ortiz

On February 12, 2002, the U.K. Foreign and Commonwealth Office released the green paper *Private Military Companies: Options for Regulation.* Although at the time this chapter was being written the regulation of British PMCs remained in its infancy, the green paper is a testament to the role this type of firm plays in British politics and the world stage. PMCs (or private security companies—PSCs—if the reader prefers this alternative term) are the main entities populating the U.K. market for force, which has been historically a neoliberal and export-oriented market. The United Kingdom, together with the United States, leads the supply of PMCs and high-caliber private military and security personnel.

Besides the market lead that makes the United Kingdom a noteworthy case study, the British experience presents us with a rich trajectory in which it is possible to trace the modern genesis of private military enterprising. Against this backdrop, the U.K. market for force has had a rapid evolution since the Cold War, when regimes of collaboration between British PMCs and government started to galvanize. The latest link on this trajectory builds on reform inspired by New Public Management (NPM) policies, whereby defense contractors and PMCs have become essential state partners for the handling of military and security-related tasks. This chapter explores this transition and dissects certain historical causal trends leading to the characteristics that distinguish the U.K. market for force.

The main service areas covered by PMCs are combat, training, support, security, intelligence, and reconstruction (Ortiz 2010b: 48). The potential to exercise lethal force primarily materializes when combat-related and protective security services are rendered in, hence exported to, dangerous environments. In the third part of the causes section of the chapter, however, the analysis departs from the lethal realm and covers nonlethal service areas such as logistics support and training. This wider approach is necessary to understand trends toward the privatization of security broadly, as well as the reorganization of the U.K. monopoly of violence in the twenty-first century.

The first part of the chapter provides an analysis of the two overarching models that appear to characterize the current U.K. market for force: contingency and proxy partnerships. The second part examines the causal development of the market. I explore the early modern history of the U.K. market for force to the bifurcation of the Cold War mercenary trade, which led to the emergence of the first British PMCs and the introduction of NPM-style reform in the late 1980s. The analysis shows how in addition to the legitimation of the private military trade and the consolidation of a private military class, the step-by-step implementation of this reform program has led to the emergence of long-term security partnerships between the public and private sectors for the support and management of force. The last part of the chapter highlights tensions engendered by this fusion of public and private culture and its impact on the constitution of the U.K. monopoly on violence and the provision of security as a public good.

Characteristics of Today's Export Market in the United Kingdom: Contingency and Proxy Partnerships

Two trends currently converge in the provision of private military and security services of a lethal nature in the U.K. market for force. First, the security partnerships model exerts some influence on the provision of security services that involve the possible application of lethal defensive force; for example, the protection of people and infrastructure in medium- to high-risk environments. Security partnerships, a modality of primarily *nonlethal* service provision outlined in greater detail in the next section, entail the establishment of formal and long-lasting patterns of collaboration between government and private firms for the support and management of force. The various official defense reviews published since the early 1990s continue to guide the trend toward the establishment of security partnerships, which commonly last three decades (see, e.g., Ministry of Defence [UK] 1998: paras. 4, 170; Ministry of Defence [UK] 2005: para. A3.6; Ministry of Defence [UK] 2010: 5). Second, the proxy culture that permeated the provision of military assistance during the Cold War remains an intrinsic element in the provision of services incorporating high levels of force, such as combat-related services. I refer to the model of service provision enmeshing the proxy culture and the delivery of highly lethal services in high-risk environments as "proxy partnerships." Proxy partnerships are not formal public-private partnerships, but an analytical construct outlining a modality of service provision typical to the U.K. market for force.

Contingency partnerships are conceptually located somewhere between security partnerships and proxy partnerships. Contingency partnerships, unlike security partnerships, tend to be formalized to fulfill the more immediate requirements of military deployments and diplomatic and reconstruction missions overseas. For example, at the time of writing, the British Embassy Static Guard Force protecting the U.K. diplomatic mission in Afghanistan was handled by G4S, the world's largest security corporation. Thus, contingency partnerships can last for any period of time, from a few months to a few years, as contingencies dictate. While the Aerospace Defence and Security (ADS) group incorporates the broader universe of firms involved in security partnerships, the membership of the British Association of Private Security Companies (BAPSC) comprises a sample of the typical small to medium-sized firms specializing in the provision of protective security services and security advice that often contract with the government to fulfill contingency partnerships.

In addition, some of the support and training needs of the U.K. forces are sometimes delivered away from the homeland and in climates of instability. Hence, sometimes security partnerships for nonlethal support on deployed operations incorporate an armed security cover, whether organized by government as contingency partnerships or directly subcontracted (at arm's length from the state) to smaller players by the two dozen or so trusted corporations in security partnership with the U.K. Ministry of Defence

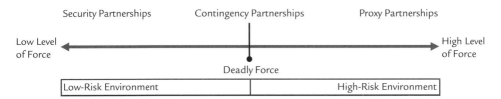

Figure 4.1. The position of security partnerships and proxy partnerships on the force continuum.

(MOD) and other related government departments. Both contingency and security partnerships contain formal patterns of collaboration and efficient contracting between governmental agencies and departments and PMCs, even if the British government prefers not to label smaller and contingent security deals as partnerships or integrate them as yet into long-term strategic reviews. However, there are reasons to suspect that the well-established and tested trajectory of the security partnerships model can offer the basis for the logical evolution of contingency contracts into forms of, or extensions to, security partnerships. Figure 4.1 situates these three models—security, proxy, and contingency partnerships—on the force continuum provided in Chapter 1 and typifies the structure of the U.K. market for force in the twenty-first century.

The different types of partnerships outlined in this chapter might suggest that the firms delivering nonlethal services at home as part of security partnerships are dissimilar from those operating in high-risk environments. That private security in the United Kingdom is essentially an unarmed activity seems to stress the point. Although there are firms that focus on particular types of services, an important proportion of PMCs are equally capable of rendering both nonlethal services in the United Kingdom and armed protection abroad. G4S is a good example of this multifunctional role. Although G4S is capable of protecting British diplomatic missions in high-risk environments, the firm also renders a vast array of nonlethal services to public agencies and commercial clients in the domestic market.

Strong demand for nonlethal security services at home and for those of a more lethal character abroad meets with an abundant supply of former servicemen in the British military and security labor market. In the 1990s, military downsizing as a result of the end of the Cold War provided a boost to this labor market. Another boost is underway as a consequence of the

downsizing of the British forces because of post-recession budget constraints—a planned reduction of 17,000 soldiers by 2015: 5,000 from the
Royal Navy; 7,000 from the Army; and 5,000 from the Royal Air Force
(Ministry of Defence [UK] 2010: para. 2.D.6). Furthermore, U.K.-based
PMCs, like their counterparts throughout the Anglo Saxon world, also tap
international labor markets for highly qualified personnel and recruit locally in the countries to which they deploy. Former servicemen originating
in the former colonial space, for example Gurkhas (soldiers of Nepalese
origin), also figure in many British PMCs. For instance, the private force
protecting the U.K. diplomatic mission in Afghanistan is largely staffed by
Gurkhas.

There will be borderline cases and instances in which British PMCs deliver services in an altogether different fashion than the partnership models
outlined in this chapter or even escape the carefully constructed methodology of this book. For instance, British PMCs focusing on counter-piracy are
broadening their areas of operation in tandem with the expansion of piracy
attacks across the Arabian Sea and the Indian Ocean. These oceanic areas
comprise largely international waters over which no single nation has authority, and the national flags of ships might not be sufficient to disentangle
the jurisdictions of different, and some may say overlapping, markets for
force. The U.K. government fired a salvo in 2011 by arguing for the legal
backing of the inclusion of armed guards onboard U.K.-flagged vessels
(Porter 2011), even though the regulation of the PMCs that could supply
those armed guards, as discussed in the last section of the chapter, is currently a work-in-progress affair. Nevertheless, it is possible to pin down the
activities of most PMCs currently operating in the U.K. market for force to
contingency, proxy, or security partnerships, whether services are rendered
at land or sea.

Underlying Causes: The Development
of Today's Market for Force

The United Kingdom has a long tradition of a market for force. Along this
trajectory, it is possible to identify three important historical stages that
have influenced the development of today's market, in addition to certain
historical characteristics identifiable since at least the seventeenth century. Notably, this evolution shows that British sovereigns have tradition-

ally favored the use of private military actors, particularly those of a corporate type.

From Adventure to Enterprise:
The Early Modern Market for Force

During early modern times (1600–1850), the use of private force for the achievement of political and economic goals, as well as the emergence of a respectable private military class within the fabric of society, metastasized into identity traits of the British state. The key protagonist of the period was the English East India Company (EIC; see, e.g., Chatterton 1933; Keay 1993).

EIC, which at its zenith was the colonial administrator of the Indian subcontinent on behalf of the British Crown, was one of several similar companies chartered in Europe since the late 1590s for overseas exploration and trade. The forces initially recruited by EIC and other British companies to protect their commercial interests abroad comprised ad hoc collections of individuals of diverse backgrounds and ages, with many recruits lacking military or maritime skills. Indeed, the early transoceanic voyages of the chartered companies were voyages of adventure, with uncertain outcomes and high mortality rates. In fact, the term *adventurers* was included in the corporate names of many similar companies and simply meant "merchants engaged in foreign trade" (Braudel 1985: 448).

As trade matured, armies were recruited in Europe and sent overseas. By 1702, the authority of EIC's presidencies in India had been greatly enhanced, giving their presidents the military titles of commanders in chief and granting them full rights for the "organization and disposal of their military forces" (Superintendent Government [India] 1924: 5). By 1805, in Bengal the army had grown to 64,000 men (up substantially from 6,680 men in 1763), in Madras to 64,000 (up from 9,000), and in Bombay to 26,500 (up from 2,550; Callahan 1998: 24, Table 1). Besides the recruitment and training of indigenous forces, the services rendered by the armies and navies of EIC involved various forms of protection (at land and sea), the maintenance of forts, logistics, and the export of weaponry. At sea, EIC Maritime Service, as its navy was known, found itself most active in the same oceanic areas greatly affected by piracy today and in demand of private military seamanship. Indeed, parallels between today's PMCs and the armed forces maintained by the chartered companies can be established (Ortiz 2007).

The expeditionary qualities of the early modern U.K. market for force met with an abundance of personnel available for contracting, by EIC or any other European company. In a study of the records of more than 85,000 recruits from Great Britain serving in EIC's army between 1802 and 1860, about 40 percent of them were English, 47 percent Irish, and 13 percent Scottish (estimations based on Figure 3 in Mokyr and Ó Gráda 1996: 145). Continental Europeans were also targeted, and their regiments in their day were what special forces are to recent generations (Heathcote 1975: 156).

In Asia, EIC also initiated the practice of recruiting Gurkhas. The British Indian Army inherited this practice during colonial times, and the British Army continues it today, along with many PMCs. This labor supply and demand feeding the expansion of the charter system was closely connected to the consolidation of the first modern U.K. market for force.

The U.K. market for force would not have become the most diversified and prolific market of the period in the absence of a climate of permissibility. To begin with, establishment of the chartered companies required governmental consent. Permission to raise private forces to protect monopoly rights was also a public charter privilege and not a unilateral private prerogative. To simplify a discussion that belongs elsewhere, overseas trade generated the wealth needed for governments to be able to fight wars and engage in the building of empires. Yet, the interdependence between the U.K. government and British chartered companies would lose force as the powerful idea of a British Empire and the concomitant need to centralize military power took hold of the public sector imagination. Together with the raising of national armies and the emergence of notions about a state monopoly over (legitimate) violence, the (illegitimate) patterns of military organization with a private element dwindled or were assimilated into the public realm (see, e.g., Ortiz 2010b: 31–33). In the next era, although conventional mercenaries retained their status as an anomaly to the system, the use of PMCs was legitimized.

The Cold War Proxy Partnerships:
The Late Modern Market for Force

During the Cold War, upon the dissolution of the British Empire, a second market for force emerged. Under the veil of proxy politics, the private military class that developed alongside the consolidation of the first modern U.K. market for force became increasingly active.

British mercenaries descended into the many post-colonial conflicts in the Third World, particularly in Africa and the Middle East. There are no exact figures, but an inspection of the literature covering the period suggests a few hundred mercenaries present at any given time in the most protracted theaters of war, for instance, in Angola, Congo, Nigeria, the Arabian Peninsula, and Southeast Asia (see, e.g., Mockler 1985; Tickler 1987). Amid this mercenary resurgence, the bifurcation of the mercenary trade resulted in a robust thread encompassing new types of adventurers: PMCs. A reinvigorated U.K. market for force, still highly expeditionary but lacking private military seamanship, thus resurfaced.

The most-studied case of an early British PMC is Watchguard International. Sir David Stirling, the brain behind the establishment of the elite Special Air Service (SAS), established the firm in 1967. With Watchguard, Stirling went on to pioneer a business concept: the commercial application of the SAS method. He identified a market niche: the need for high-caliber foreign military training and advice tailored for countries in transition (Hoe and Stirling 1994: 367–72).

In addition to PMCs, defense contractors, individual military advisors, and officers seconded by the U.K. government to friendly nations would comprise the bulk of the late modern U.K. market for force (see, e.g., Arnold 1999; Halliday 1977). Among the most prolific consumers of this market was Saudi Arabia, which spent around GBP 1 billion (the equivalent of about USD 11 billion in 2010) between 1965 and 1971 on military hardware and hiring all of these types of private military suppliers (Halliday 1974: 59–62). Airwork Services Ltd., for example, provided about 1,000 aircrew trainers, many of them former members of the Royal Air Force (ibid.: 60), as well as classroom and field translators. However, for every new formally incorporated firm entering this second U.K. market for force, there were many transient mercenary outfits.

The Cold War offered part of the rationale behind the new climate of permissibility that facilitated the development of the late-modern U.K. market for force. As Stirling put it, part of the target market for PMCs was countries to which the U.K. government would like to offer assistance openly "but could not be seen to assist because of political niceties" (Hoe and Stirling 1994: 371). In other words, proxy cooperation between British PMCs and the U.K. government (and between PMCs and foreign governments) crystallized. Confirming this new stance toward the private use of force, the Diplock Committee, launched to investigate the large-scale involvement of British mercenaries in Angola and other newly independent countries, set an important precedent by conveying the view that the "personal freedom" of British citizens to accept service as mercenaries would be justified only if it did not run against the "public interest" of the United Kingdom (Diplock Committee 1976: paras. 10, 15).

It was also during the Cold War that what I will term an "Anglo Saxon model" guiding the use of contractors in areas of defense and security emerged. This model is characterized by a predominant focus on the export of private force, and a large, legal market for doing so organized on the basis of neoliberal economic principles of exchange. The United Kingdom and the United States, as the largest Western defense exporters and spenders, lead this model. However, different norms and identities across countries reflect differences between the U.S. and U.K. markets for force. Historically, for instance, British PMCs originated in the bifurcation of the post-colonial mercenary trade, whereas American PMCs seem to be rooted in the diversification of the "engineering and service sector of the U.S. economy" (Kinsey 2006: 103). Moreover, Fitzsimmons argues in Chapter 10 that the supply of logistical and other support services by these types of corporations has contributed to the legitimation of the combat-related private military business in the United States. At the same time, the British defense corporations supplying military assistance to allied governments during the Cold War were state enterprises rather than private entities. Smaller enterprises, rather than diversified corporations, predominantly populated the private corporate sector of the late-modern U.K. market for force. To some extent, this distinction still permeates the contemporary constitution of the American and British markets.

In the 1980s, when the United Kingdom was well established as a world destination for those tapping international markets for private military services, political attention in the United Kingdom shifted to the war in the Falklands and a reorganization of the British state following a protracted recession. In 1983, when endorsing the privatization program launched by her premiership, Margaret Thatcher (prime minister, May 1979–November 1990) noted her intention "to roll back the frontiers of nationalization," as "it is not public expenditure which leads the way to greater prosperity: it is private enterprise" (Thatcher 1983). This program privatized prime British assets, including the avionics and defense manufacturer British Aerospace (the forerunner of BAE Systems, the largest defense contractor in Europe). British Aerospace was one of the state corporations engaged in Saudi Arabia during the Cold War.

Ronald Reagan was equally positive about the seemingly remedial nature of privatization. However, a distinction to ponder in terms of the development of the Anglo Saxon model is that, while Reagan appeared to emphasize privatization as a blanket solution "for what was wrong with socialist countries" (Poole 2004), Thatcher saw privatization also as a solution to the economic crisis engulfing the United Kingdom. Likewise, Spearin argues in Chapter 9 that financial difficulties partly "catalyzed the Canadian market for force." What followed in the wake of Thatcher's reform agenda, however, evolved into something far more transcendental than privatization as an economic (or ideological) tool. By the late 1980s, the British state started to undergo structural changes that would result in a reorganization of the monopoly of violence based on the establishment of partnerships with the private sector for the support and management of force.

Security Partnerships:
The Emergent Postmodern Market for Force?

As noted in Chapter 1, this volume considers markets to be social structures built up out of numerous relationships between various actors repetitively exchanging goods and services for money (Jackson 2006). Petersohn and Dunigan also note in Chapter 1 that the way in which the exchange is organized in a market, and the specific rules that apply, may vary. At least in the case of the United Kingdom, contingency, proxy, and security partnerships guide exchange transactions in the market. NPM-style reform, in particular, has engendered a climate of national permissibility that has importantly strengthened the broader U.K. security market, covering both lethal and nonlethal services. Within this public managerial universe, public-private partnerships (PPPs) work as a distinctive exchange mechanism primarily, but not exclusively, facilitating the transaction of the domestic supply of nonlethal services.

PPPs work as conceptual compacts in which it is possible to "integrate selected parameters for contractual privatization into a managerial interface linking the public and private sectors in service delivery" (Ortiz 2010a:

39). The application of PPP principles to state defense and security, the modality of service provision I refer to as "security partnerships," incorporates additional features. To begin with, the market exchange of services in these areas touches sovereign ambits, thus involving more specialized tendering methods. The sensitive nature of the services covered by security partnerships and the possible field risk associated with them further require "intelligent" public managers to incorporate into their roles the skills to command and deliver military and security functions (ibid.).

As for the sellers, security partnerships call for the use of specific types of firms, in particular defense contractors and PMCs, as well as the private military class from which these firms draw their labor. The lead the United Kingdom enjoys in the implementation of security partnerships gives rise to a robust demand for private military and security services, which is largely satisfied by firms with strong representation in the U.K. market, if not firms that are fully British owned or staffed. For example, Holdfast Training Services, a consortium that includes Babcock International Group and Carillion, is in charge of the security partnership handling the training of British military engineers. Ascent, a joint venture between VT Group and Lockheed Martin, was designated in May 2008 as the "training system partner" in charge of the United Kingdom Military Flying Training System (UK-MFTS). UKMFTS is a project aimed at creating a tri-service organization delivering flying training to all the sectors of the British forces. In areas of homeland security, the 2009 *Science and Technology Strategy* confirmed the "greater partnership and engagement with industry" established to, for example, improve analytical tools and surveillance, interception, and the collection of data (HM Government [UK] 2009: 13, 26). Effectively, all the support and training needs of the British security forces have security partnerships as their backbone.

NPM-style reform of defense and homeland security can also be considered to be an expression of the evolving Anglo Saxon model. However, variations in norms and identities across countries, again, have an impact on the choice of the particular services selected for incorporation into security partnerships. For example, in the United States, the delivery of lethal security services abroad is sometimes organized as security partnerships. Notably, the U.S. Department of State manages the private provision of personal protective service details under its jurisdiction through the multi-billion dollar Worldwide Personal Protective Services (WPPS) program. In the United Kingdom, in contrast, this type of service is currently outsourced using the contingency partnership model. However, like in the United States, and given the abundant domestic labor supply and the historical affinities that foster reliance on private military actors in the United Kingdom, the provision of lethal defensive services could, in the near future, start migrating from contingency to security partnerships.

Consequences of the U.K. Market for Force for the State's Monopoly on Violence and the Provision of Security as a Public Good

The NPM-style transformation of the British state has been progressive and pervasive, but not flawless. There are many critics of the approach, and security partnerships find themselves increasingly in the spotlight as not offering good value for public money. However, we should not lose sight of the issue that the U.K. market for force is the result of a cumulative historical process that started to take shape during early modernity. In light of fluctuating political and economic circumstances, successive governments have re-engineered the regimes of permissibility facilitating the use of private military actors. This is a key historical trait of the British state implicitly addressed throughout the chapter; security partnerships represent one of its latest expressions. The current structure of the U.K. market for force is thus based on security, contingency, and proxy partnerships, with each type of partnership incorporating the private sector in interrelated but variable fashions. At the same time, as argued, although security partnerships primarily focus on nonlethal services, the model influences the outsourcing of lethal services, broadly. As contingency outsourcing already involves formal patterns of collaboration between government and privately owned business entities, contracts in this area might represent an initial, and perhaps experimental, stage leading to their reorganization as security partnerships. WPPS in the United States sets an important precedent here, as the United States and the United Kingdom are close allies that systematically integrate each other's experience into their military strategies—another characteristic of the Anglo Saxon model. Critically, the ultimate implication of my argument is that the monopoly of force in the United Kingdom has become a fusion of corporate and state involvement because its organization is overlaid by an intricate amalgamation of these partnerships.

In all instances of partnership, the British state continues to enjoy a good degree of decision-making authority on when and where private lethal force can be used or the need for immediate contractor support in order to be able to deploy public force. The specific partnership model used partly denotes this sovereign privilege. The mode of allocation of lethal force can therefore be regarded as authoritative. This applies even when the proxy culture impinges upon market allocation because the British government retains the right to judge the actions of PMCs as not conducive for the public interest of the United Kingdom, if necessary. Nevertheless, there is a certain fortuitousness to the value the British government derives from proxy partnerships: they are not orchestrated by government, they are not regulated, and their benefits are not tangible. This raises the question of whether such deals can achieve any public good.

A guiding aspiration of the fusion of public and private involvement in the U.K. monopoly on force can also be interpreted as an attempt to improve the "efficient quantity" of security as a public good, which would represent the aggregate and equal requirements of people statewide whereby, theoretically, costs are at the lowest possible while the benefits are at the highest attainable level. Hence, it can be argued that when supporting state goals, private security often contributes to the satisfaction of the efficient quantity of security as a public good, as the alternative would be a diminished security for which there is structural demand. Following this line of inquiry, the private military and security services being traded contribute to distinct defense and homeland security goals (as outlined in strategic reviews or policy statements and implemented through security or contingency partnerships), and therefore they can be regarded technically as nonexcludable. In this sense, the U.K. market for force has had overall a positive—or, at the very least, a neutral—effect on the provision of security as a public good. Conceptually, this is clear at the nonlethal end of the force spectrum in Figure 4.1, though the assumption loses meaning the closer we move to the figure's lethal end.

The ambiguities affecting the outsourcing of lethal services could, to some extent, be solved through regulation. However, even though the trade (the commercial activity) has been regulated for a while,[1] the private use of lethal force remains largely unregulated. The regulation of PMCs is an embryonic activity that only started to take shape in 2002, when the green paper on PMCs was published. In addition to mentioning the possible ban of the "direct participation in combat," the green paper outlined two concrete regulation proposals: a licensing system similar to the one used by the United States to sanction the export of lethal and nonlethal articles and services or for PMCs to self-regulate their activities via a trade association, and a "code of conduct for work overseas" (Foreign and Commonwealth Office [UK] 2002: 71–76). A laissez-faire approach continued to be the norm until April 2009, when consultation on an industry-implemented code of conduct applying to the private *security* side of the overall private military industry was opened. The influential *Montreux Document*, endorsed by the British government and incorporating feedback from professional associations such as the BAPSC, is largely behind the new initiatives. The emerging regulatory framework thus draws from a diverse set of ideas originating in organizations and humanitarian law principles endorsed by the British government, including, inter alia:

- **The International Code of Conduct for Private Security Service Providers (ICoC).** Convened by the Swiss government and supporting the *Montreux Document*, the ICoC was created in 2010 and, as of late 2013, had more than 700 private security company signatories. About a third of the signatories are British business entities (Simmonds 2012).
- **ANSI/ASIS PSC.1-2012.** This security standard ensures that companies that adhere to it support the objectives of the *Montreux Document* and comply with the ICoC. The British government has established that this is the applicable standard for the "U.K.-based PSCs working in complex environments on land and overseas" (ibid.). ASIS International is among the oldest and largest security industry associations and was handed the responsibility by the U.S. government to develop the PSC.1 standard. The American National Standards Institute (ANSI) is the preeminent organization behind the creation of internationally recognized business standards.
- **The Security in Complex Environments Group (SCEG).** ADS was designated as the professional association to oversee the development and application of a code of conduct for U.K.-based private military and security companies (PMSCs). SCEG, a branch of ADS, is composed of the private security firms that need to or should adhere to ANSI/ASIS PSC.1-2012.

From theory to practice, it is too early to establish whether the emerging regulation of British PMCs will solve some of the ambiguities that the private use of lethal force engender, or to say that proxy partnerships will eventually become history because they undermine the humanitarian principles underpinning the *Montreux Document*. At this stage, however, it seems relevant to emphasize that the proposed regulation is flexible enough to allow the British government to continue exercising its sovereign privilege to decide who can exercise the private use of lethal force abroad, when, and where.

Conclusion

The historical analysis earlier in this chapter unraveled the roots of the neoliberal and export-oriented character of today's U.K. market for force. The overseas chartered companies were first and foremost business entities, essentially the forerunners of the modern transnational corporation. However, the money they raised in stock markets also paid for the private armed forces they maintained, which protected the companies' monopoly rights from foreign competitors and made distant trade ultimately possible. All these factors were part of an evolving regime of permissibility for the private use of force organized by successive sovereigns and sanctioned by public charter. Names change, however, and the twenty-first-century PMCs are the latest expression of the private corporate enterprises traditionally favored by British governments to engage in the international offering of security services. It is a market overwhelmingly dominated by private firms and market competition, a neoliberal market for force. As argued, the U.K. market for force at the beginning of the twenty-first century is organized primarily around security, contingency, and proxy partnerships. Like a cobweb, these partnerships crisscross the U.K. defense and security apparatus and give rise to a unique fusion of corporate and state resources for the management of force. Clearly, the United Kingdom is not the only country applying PPP principles to defense and homeland security. Nonetheless, the denseness of the public-private interactions lends the U.K. monopoly on violence a very compact architecture, and it is sometimes difficult to disentangle its public from its private components. This uniqueness persuaded me to offer an account of the U.K. market for force in which the types of partnership (lethal or nonlethal) are situated alongside one another, as all partnerships converge on the idea of enhanced efficiency through the systematic integration of private means into public ends.

The complexities inherent in the public-private management of force in the United Kingdom make its market for force a singular edifice. Indeed, the neoliberal environment is conducive for the private military industry to thrive. At the same time, the close connection between government and firms facilitates the U.K. government's ability to control and discriminate between service providers. However, many unsolved problems could affect the future cohesion of the U.K. monopoly on violence and the public good value of collective security. For instance, a key component of the British market for force is its well-established private military class. In April 2009, when announcing the government's chosen route for the regulation of PMCs, the Foreign and Commonwealth Office argued the case for a code of conduct by stating that the high standards of the domestic industry make alternative regulation, namely a licensing mechanism controlled by government, "not proportionate to the scale of the problem in the U.K." (Foreign and Commonwealth Office [UK] 2009: 2). Although the statement reaffirms that the former servicemen commonly employed by the industry are held in high regard within official circles, it also conveys the government's belief that private abuse of force is something that occurs elsewhere. Unlike the U.S. regulatory framework, which now incorporates avenues for the prosecution of contractor abuse, the gestating code of conduct in the United Kingdom effectively enacts market-based regulation—failure to respect the voluntary code is detrimental to the standing of a company but does not necessarily mean prosecution. This regulatory system is "practicable" and "affordable," as the Foreign and Commonwealth Office (2009) qualified it, and certainly cheaper than governmental oversight. Yet, in a world in which the ratio of public to private security personnel will continue shrinking and the security industry will commensurably increase its political influence, can we trust the market as the chief regulator? Diminished governmental control vis-à-vis a broader transfer of security responsibilities to the market can undermine the partnership principles underpinning the U.K. market for force and monopoly on violence because this could harbor a shift from public-private cooperation to dependence on the private sector. Segments of the British electorate disapprove of the idea of a greater use of the private sector in arenas of defense and homeland security. The democratic process so far helps to soften the disjoint between people's expectations about their collective security and what government actually believes is best for its citizens. A few generations down the road, however, will the electorate continue supporting the idea that greater private sector use can only lead to better state security? The flipside of the neoliberal approach to state security is that a market for force could expand to an extent it becomes boundless and difficult to control.

Besides highlighting spoilers, a market model would not be complete without elaborating on its likely evolution. The case for the expansion of security partnerships to cover services involving the use of lethal defensive force has been made, particularly because the use of private security has become a necessary adjunct to diplomatic and reconstruction missions, rather than a sporadic contingency. In addition, it is relevant to note that the private security industry is expanding its footprint in the domestic market and starting to take on policing-related roles. From the running of custody cells to the management of parts of the operation, the cost-cutting strategy so far involves, again, nonlethal roles. In the transition to the post-Cold War world, greater involvement of the private sector in state security has been partly engineered by government to share financial risks because of constrained public finances. We are far away from that scenario, but an outcome of the next financial crisis could therefore be for the U.K. market for force to start making inroads in the homeland.

Note

1. A contract signed between the government of Papua New Guinea (PNG) and the defunct British firm Sandline International on January 31, 1997 offers a relevant precedent of the issue. Sandline was hired to assist the PNG forces to regain control of the Panguna Copper Mine on the Isle of Bougainville, which was shut down when the secessionist Bougainville Revolutionary Army took control of the Island. The operation collapsed soon after it was made public. Nevertheless, the contract stipulated that the agreement was governed by the laws of England, and an arbitration tribunal ruled in favor of Sandline (Somers, Kerr, and Dawson 2000).

References

Arnold, Guy. 1999. *Mercenaries: The Scourge of the Third World*. London: Macmillan Press.

Braudel, Fernand. 1985. *Civilization and Capitalism 15th–18th Century*. Vol. 2, *The Wheels of Commerce*. London: Fontana Press.

Callahan, Raymond. 1998. "The Company's Army, 1757–1758." In *The East India Company: 1600–1858*. Vol. 5, *Warfare, Expansion and Resistance*, ed. Patrick Tuck, 23–24. London: Routledge.

Chatterton, Keble E. 1933. *The Old East Indiamen*. London: Rich & Cowan..

Diplock Committee. 1976. *Report of the Committee of Privy Counsellors Appointed to Inquire into the Recruitment of Mercenaries*. Cmnd. 6569. London: Stationery Office.

Foreign and Commonwealth Office (UK). 2002. *Private Military Companies: Options for Regulation*. London: Stationery Office.

Foreign and Commonwealth Office (UK). 2009. *Consultation on Promoting High Standards of Conduct by Private Military and Security Companies (PMSCs) Internationally*. London: Stationery Office. April.

Halliday, Fred. 1974. *Arabia Without Sultans*. London: Penguin Books.

Halliday, Fred. 1977. *Mercenaries*. Nottingham, UK: Russell Press.

Heathcote, T. A. 1975. *The Indian Army: The Garrison of British Imperial India, 1822–1922*. New York: Hippocrene Books.

HM Government (UK). 2009. *The United Kingdom's Science and Technology Strategy for Countering International Terrorism*. London: Stationery Office.

Hoe, Alan, and David Stirling. 1994. *The Authorised Biography of the Creator of the SAS*. London: Warner Books.

Jackson, William. 2007. "On the Social Structure of Markets." *Cambridge Journal of Economics* 31(2): 235–53.

Keay, John. 1993. *The Honourable Company: A History of the English East India Company*. London: HarperCollins.

Kinsey, Christopher. 2006. *Corporate Soldiers and International Security: The Rise of Private Military Companies*. London: Routledge.

Ministry of Defence (UK). 1998. *Strategic Defence Review*. London: Stationery Office.

Ministry of Defence (UK). 2005. *Defence Industrial Strategy*. Defence White Paper. London: Stationery Office.

Ministry of Defence (UK). 2010. *Securing Britain in an Age of Uncertainty: The Strategic Defence and Security Review*. London: Stationery Office.

Mockler, Anthony. 1985. *The New Mercenaries: The History of the Mercenary from the Congo to the Seychelles*. London: Guild.

Mokyr, Joel, and Cormac Ó Gráda. 1996. "Height and Health in the United Kingdom 1815–1860: Evidence from the East India Company Army." *Explorations in Economic History* 33(2): 141–68.

Ortiz, Carlos. 2010a. "The New Public Management of Security: The Contracting and Managerial State and the Private Military Industry." *Public Money & Management* 30(1): 35–41.

Ortiz, Carlos. 2010b. *Private Armed Forces and Global Security: A Guide to the Issues*. Santa Barbara, Calif.: Praeger.

Ortiz, Carlos. 2007. "Overseas Trade in Early Modernity and the Emergence of Embryonic Private Military Companies." In *Private Military and Security Companies: Chances, Problems, Pitfalls and Prospects*, ed. Thomas Jäger and Gerhard Kümmel, 11–22. Wiesbaden: VS Verlag.

Poole, Robert W., Jr. 2004. *Ronald Reagan and the Privatization Revolution*. Washington, D.C.: Heartland Institute. Available at http://www.heartland.org/.

Porter, Janet. 2011. "UK to Give Legal Backing to Armed Guards on Ships." *Lloyd's List*, May 13.

Simmonds, Mark (UK Under-Secretary of State for Foreign and Commonwealth Affairs). 2012. *Private Security Companies.* HC Deb. 17 December 2012, c. 73WS.

Superintendent Government (India). 1924. *The Army in India and Its Evolution: Including an Account of the Establishment of the Royal Air Force in India.* Calcutta: Superintendent Government Printing.

Thatcher, Margaret. 1983. *Speech to the Institute of Directors.* Albert Hall, London, February 23.

Tickler, Peter. 1987. *The Modern Mercenary: Dog of War, or Soldier of Honour?* Wellingborough: Patrick Stephens.

Somers, Edward Rt. Hon., Rt. Hon. Michael Kerr, and Hon. Daryl Dawson. 2000. "In the Matter of an International Arbitration Under UNCITRAL Rules Between Sandline International Inc. and the Independent State of Papua New Guinea." In *International Law Reports*, ed. Elihu Lauterpacht, C. J. Greenwood, and A. G. Oppenheimer, vol. 117, 552–93. Cambridge: Cambridge University Press.

CHAPTER 5

The Market for Private Force in the Czech Republic

Oldřich Bureš

Introduction

The Czech market for private force has received relatively little attention internationally and, until recently, domestically. This chapter attempts to fill the gap by analyzing the key characteristics, causes, and consequences of this market, which has experienced steady growth since the end of the Cold War. My analysis reveals that the contemporary Czech market exhibits at least three unique characteristics: (1) the historic absence of activity of private military companies (PMCs), domestic or foreign; (2) the fact that the Czech private security companies (PSCs) do not carve out an existing monopoly of force, but engage in the debate on it; (3) the infancy of this debate at both the academic and political levels. Even the Czech media have "discovered" the local market for force only in the aftermath of the June 2010 elections, when a new political party, Věci veřejné (Public Affairs), established by the former owner of the largest Czech PSC, ABL, joined the Czech government.

The structure of this chapter is as follows. The first section maps the key characteristics and causes of the market. Although in the longue durée perspective, its roots can be traced to the Middle Ages, the existing Czech market for private force is only about two decades old. The basic market indicators, nevertheless, point to the activities of several hundred private security companies with a combined annual revenue approaching USD 1 billion. The second section discusses the consequences of the market, focusing in particular on the implications of the persistent lack of clearly defined legal standards for the participants in the Czech market for private force. It also offers an analysis of the recent concerns about undue influence of the largest Czech PSC. The chapter concludes with a plea for greater expert attention to the future developments in the Czech market for private force, which is already exhibiting several unique problems concerning excessive influence of private security actors in public decision-making processes.

Characteristics and Causes of the Czech Market for Force

The first, and in many respects the key, characteristic of the Czech market for force is its nonlethality. The entire post-1989 Czech market for private force encompasses only the lower levels of the force continuum as described by Petersohn and Dunigan in Chapter 1. In the Czech Republic, the term *private security company*, therefore, refers to entities that provide mostly passive security services to counteract "ordinary crimes" such as burglary or mugging. The higher levels of the force continuum are not covered—there are no private military companies providing primarily lethal services in the Czech Republic, domestic or international, though reports have surfaced of individual Czech citizens (mostly retired soldiers) working abroad as private contractors providing lethal services.

Against the backdrop of the history of the Czech market, this is a surprising development. In the longue durée perspective, three different phases can be differentiated. In the late Middle Ages, when the then-Czech Kingdom was an integral part of the Holy Roman Empire, it gained notoriety for supplying numerous soldiers to the so-called "free" and "great" military companies (Ortiz 2010: 14–16) and entire regiments of leased soldiers following the dawn of this era (Percy 2007: 156–57). Moreover, the Thirty Years War (1618–48) not only started in the Czech Kingdom but also led to the rise of the phenomenon of private military entrepreneurs (Redlich 2004: 170). In the absence of regular armies, European kings and emperors were forced to rely on noblemen willing and able to share both the financial and military burden: "A ruler in need of military labor would enter into a formal agreement with a military entrepreneur to supply a number of soldiers for a particular period and at an agreed wage" (Ortiz 2010: 18). A Czech native, Albrecht von Wallenstein, gained international fame as the most successful private military entrepreneur of the Thirty Years War for being able to raise and sustain an army of 20,000 men on behalf of Ferdinand II, the then-Holy Roman Emperor. For his services, von Wallenstein was awarded the title of Duke and subsequently was appointed the commander of the entire Imperial Army (Ortiz 2010: 18; Percy 2007: 87).

The nonlethal quality of today's market is due to two factors. First, despite the considerable benefits of the military services provided by entrepreneurs like von Wallenstein, they were also potential political rivals to the kings and emperors. Hence, the end of the Thirty Years War ushered in an era of state sovereignty, the building of national armies, and gradually limited the power of private military entrepreneurs (Kramer 2007: 23). This development appears to be eminently influential in the case of the Czech Republic, as there is no evidence of a market for private force on the territory of today's Czech Republic during the period between the Thirty Years War and the end of World War II. Second, any potential private security enterprise would have found its end in February 1948, when the Communist Party took over Czechoslovakia and abolished all previously existing private markets. Following the Soviet model, Czechoslovakia implemented a rigid, centrally planned, and state-owned economy. Moreover, all security forces were under the control of the Czechoslovak Communist Party, which was constitutionally granted a monopoly on the use of force.

The second key characteristic of the Czech market for force is its domestic focus. Again, in contrast to its historical predecessor, the current market is dominated by the provision of internal security domestically, exporting only to a small extent. In terms of the services provided, local property and personal protection have clearly dominated the post–Cold War Czech market for private force, with private detective services coming at a distant second place. More recently, there has been a sizeable shift from the provision of direct physical security services (e.g., the deployment of guards) toward greater utilization of electronic monitoring systems (e.g., closed-circuit television systems complemented with distance patrol services; Unie soukromých bezpečnostních sluzeb České republiky 2004: 2). This trend is a result of greater availability, decreasing costs, and increasing sophistication of, as well as trust in, technical security solutions, but it does not challenge either the nonlethal or the domestic fundamentals of the Czech market for force.

The data provided by the Czech Ministry of Trade and Industry and the Czech Statistical Office points to a steadily growing domestic market over the past decade in terms of both the total number of registered PSCs (see Table 5.1) and the employment opportunities created by the industry.

Table 5.1. Number of PSCs and Their Employees in the Czech Republic
(1997–2012)

	1997	1998	1999	2000	2001	2002	2003
PSCs*	3,966	3,482	4,388	4,918	5,460	5,731	5,968
PSCs' employees[†]	?	?	?	?	?	44,174	49,445

Note: ? indicates that the data is not available.
*Source for the 1997–2001 period is Ministry of Industry and Trade; for the 2002–12 period, the Czech Statistical Office.
[†]Source is the Czech Statistical Office.

According to the data, the number grew constantly from 3,966 in 1997 to 7,012 officially registered PSCs with a total of 54,860 employees in 2012. The latter number appears to be valid even as of mid-2013, although—according to the established weekly *Ekonom*—only about 200 of these companies actually offer services (Sýkorová 2011). The private security industry in the Czech Republic is still a significant industrial sector, with the total number of its employees outnumbering national police personnel for several years now (there were about 38,000 police as of 2013). Additionally, the industry generates substantial revenue. According to data from the Association of Private Security Services of the Czech Republic, in 2008 the PSCs' market turnover was nearly CZK 20 billion (USD 1.18 billion; Asociace soukromých bezpečnostních sluzeb České republiky 2010), with at least 30 percent of the orders comings from public sector entities (Unie soukromých bezpečnostních sluzeb České republiky 2010: 5). As with all other sectors of the Czech economy, private security services were negatively affected by the consequences of the global financial crisis, with total revenues declining in 2009 by 5.9 percent (Unie soukromých bezpečnostních sluzeb České republiky 2010: 2). In 2010, according to newspaper sources, the total revenue generated by the officially registered Czech PSCs was CZK 16 billion (USD 941 million), with the "unofficial" shadow market for PSC services[1] adding another CZK 2.5 billion (USD 147 million; Sýkorová 2011). This amounted to almost 0.5 percent of the total Czech GDP in 2011 (CZK 3669 billion/USD 216 billion).[2]

Regarding the almost nonexistent export side, unofficial online sources have alleged "the rumor is that there are private security contractors with Czech equity shares supplying services to various places of conflict" ("Soukromá policie" 2007). Speculation has also emerged about the "training of Czech citizens, who become 'security specialists' for places such as Iraq,"

2004	2005	2006	2007	2008	2009	2010	2011	2012
6,109	6,291	6,385	6,419	6,748	6,748	7,001	7,201	7,094
51,019	53,229	52,963	54,490	56,352	53,403	52,703	56,711	54,860

which is allegedly conducted in various locations of the territory of the Czech Republic, under the guise of private bodyguard training. Moreover, some Czech citizens allegedly "serve as armed contractors, including in places like Iraq" (ibid.). There were also reports in the Czech press that following the U.S.-led invasion of Afghanistan, one Czech PSC had unsuccessfully tried to enter the Afghan security market in cooperation with the Czech–Central Asian Chamber of Commerce (Šmíd 2010).

Nevertheless, the growing interest of various Czech companies in postconflict reconstruction contracts seems to generate occasional demand for personal protection services for officials in Afghanistan. In June 2011, for example, a little-known Czech PSC for the first time actually provided protection to two Czech business managers during their week-long visit to Kabul. The owner of the company, which he already refers to as the "Czech Blackwater," hopes that further contracts will follow (Snidl 2011). If that, indeed, was the case on a larger scale, the Czech market for private force could soon include companies offering their services abroad and, eventually, perhaps even covering the higher spectrum of the force continuum.

This primary focus on the domestic nonlethal market can be explained by a lack of highly qualified personnel to provide their services abroad. Although the Czech Army has undergone substantial force reductions (from more than 100,000 in 1993 to slightly more than 20,000 as of 2011), much of this was achieved by the elimination of mandatory conscription, which provided more than 70 percent of all manpower during the Cold War era. On the demand side, there has been no need for private military services due to the peaceful nature of the transition from communism (the Velvet Revolution) and the smooth break-up of the Czechoslovak Federation in 1993. In contrast, the demand for traditional private security services has been substantial, due to the fact that many Czech employees continue to behave as they were accustomed to under socialism—in other words, following the adage "if you do not steal from the state-owned company, you are stealing from your family." This rather unfortunate legacy continues to trouble many Czech businesses even today. As one PSC representative noted, "You will always keep stumbling on something over which foreign investors shake their heads. A funny example might be a giant slingshot used by workers to shoot poultry from a factory of one well-known company in the nearby fields" (Bartoskova 2007).

The third characteristic of the Czech market for force is the significant presence of major international PSCs. The two biggest players on the Czech market are local subsidiaries of two leading international PSCs. SECURI-TAS CR Ltd., a local subsidiary of the Swedish PSC Securitas AB, is the largest in terms of the annual revenue (CZK 1,435 billion/USD 84 million in 2009) as well as the number of employees (4,500 in 2009). Having been established by 1991, SECURITAS is also one of oldest players in the modern Czech PSC market (Sekuritas CZ 2011). The second-largest firm in the Czech market is the subsidiary of a British PSC, G4S, with an annual revenue of CZK 1.4 billion (USD 82 million) and 2,500 employees (G4S CZ 2011). Only the third-largest player in the market is the aforementioned largest Czech PSC, ABL, with 1,335 employees (ABL 2010). Founded in 1992, its annual revenue in 2010 reached CZK 889 million (USD 52 million; Sýkorová 2011). The leading international PSCs took advantage of their superior know-how, capital base, and better insurance deals and quickly established themselves as the biggest players in the Czech market, where they saw a lot of potential for growth. As discussed in several other chapters in this volume, G4S and Securitas are also trying to establish themselves in a number of other countries, including China (see Chapter 8).

The fourth characteristic of the Czech market for force is a rather extreme diversification in terms of associations. There are at least sixteen professional associations of PSCs working in the Czech Republic. The most important associations include the Chamber of Commercial Security Companies, the Czech Club of Private Security Services, Czech Chamber of Detective Services, Association of Technical Security Alarm Services, the Security Club, and the Association of Private Security Services of the Czech Republic. The last two associations together form the Union of Security Services of the Czech Republic, which is arguably the most active association in terms of providing publicly accessible publications and information about the Czech private security market. The Union is also the only association whose members include both the larger players in the market (members of the Security Club) and the smaller and medium-sized PSCs (members of the Association of Private Security Services of the Czech Republic). Their combined share of the revenues represents about 25 percent of the entire Czech private security market (Unie soukromých bezpečnostních sluzeb České republiky 2004: 2). The large number of PSC associations is largely due to the fact that they have thus far mostly focused on promoting only the specific interests of their own members, in particular when it comes to securing relatively minor, yet potentially lucrative, legislative changes related to the technical standards for the provision of their specific security services (Unie soukromých bezpečnostních sluzeb České republiky 2010: 10). Other informal explanations from PSC representatives for the large number of professional associations in the country include competition between smaller and bigger PSCs, domestic and foreign-owned PSCs, and personal antipathies among some of the top representatives of the leading PSCs.

The final, but in the long run arguably the most problematic, characteristic of the Czech market for private force is the lack of regulation. Emerging after the November 1989 Velvet Revolution that brought down the communist regime, the modern market for private force started with a clean historical slate. Under the leadership of Vaclav Klaus, first as a Czechoslovak minister of finance and later as the Czech prime minister, the Czech Republic embarked on what many economists have subsequently called the "shock-therapy" transition toward a free market economy (Lavigne 1995; Hoehn 1998), which included both the privatization of state assets and the opening of market opportunities for the provision of all kinds of services, including security. This shock-therapy transition is an important explanatory factor for the current shape of the market, which may actually be described as extremely neoliberal in terms of its original ideological foundation. The strong push for speedy privatization was based on the belief that the invisible hand of the market is inherently superior to the public sector in the provision of any service. Moreover, the initial emphasis on establishing the market economy as quickly as possible meant that the necessary legal, regulatory, and bureaucratic changes lagged behind to such an extent that even some of the most basic rules were put in place years after 1989 (Sedlak 2009: 34).

As a consequence, even as of 2013, the Czech Republic remains the only European Union (EU) member state in which the provision of private security services is not regulated by a special statute. Czech PSCs, therefore, operate as any other type of private business under the general 1991 Trade

Licensing Act (455/1991 Coll.), which specifies three types of licensed security services:

1. Services of private detectives
2. Surveillance of persons and property
3. Provision of technical services for the protection of persons and property

The specific content of these licensed trades, however, has only been clarified in the 2000 Government Decree No. 469/2000 Coll., which in Annex 3 offered lists of specific services that fall within the three aforementioned security services. PSCs that are more established have, however, complained that although officially the market is classified as a licensed trade, "in reality there are no such requirements that would make this business any different from any other unregulated trade. Individual trade licensing offices set up the requirements for the conduct of this licensed trade. The monitoring of adherence to these requirements on their part is practically nonexistent" (Unie soukromých bezpečnostních sluzeb České republiky 2004: 4).

The ever-increasing numbers of PSCs and their engagement in more controversial activities, especially in the private detective services area, have prompted a number of public authorities to belated action. In 2007, at the initiative of the Ministry of Trade and Industry (MTI), an amendment to the 1991 Trade Licensing Act brought under one licensed trade private detective services and all PSCs providing security of property and persons, claiming that the two trades share common criteria for their operation. This has generated protest from affected PSCs, which accused the MTI of promoting a "pure 'legal-ideological' approach to the issue of legislative regulation of PSCs' activity, since it is the easiest one" (Unie soukromých bezpečnostních sluzeb České republiky 2010: 16). Another adjustment was made in 2008 with the adoption of Act No. 274/2008 Coll. on the Police of the Czech Republic, which set minimum standards for the provision of private detective services and of property and personal security (a clean criminal record, good health, and minimum professional qualifications for persons performing these activities). Even these adjustments have, however, not been accepted without reservation by some PSCs who held differing views on the qualification and evaluation standards for their employees (ibid.: 17).

The next adjustment was buried in Act No. 353/2003 Coll., which was updated by the Excise Tax Act No. 292/2009 Coll. in July 2009. According to the Union of Private Security Services in the Czech Republic, it again has done more damage than good by creating "confusion concerning the appropriate qualification requirements" (ibid.: 17) by extending the deadlines for completion of the mandatory qualification examinations to July 31, 2012.[3]

The most recent legal changes occurred as a result of the adoption of Act No. 155/2010 Coll., which annulled the remit of the minimum standards definitions published in the aforementioned Act No. 274/2008 Coll. According to the Association of Private Security Services of the Czech Republic, the legislation concerning PSCs has, therefore, returned to the state of the early 1990s, which reportedly serves the interests of "a group of foreign firms, especially from the former USSR, which under the guise of PSC business establish themselves in our country with the worst practices, as well as the corrupt Ministry officials, who got well paid [for these changes]" (Asociace soukromých bezpečnostních sluzeb České republiky 2011).

In 2010, expressing their dissatisfaction with this rather haphazard evolution of the legal framework, seven of the major trade associations of Czech PSCs (out of more than fifteen currently existing) signed a joint memorandum "declaring the need to enshrine into law clear and transparent rules for business in this industry" (Reichl 2010). According to a Ministry of Interior press release, this memorandum became "the first prerequisite for the successful preparation of the Law on Private Security Services because the inconsistency of views from the business environment," along with the "different attitudes of political parties, were the key reasons explaining the past failed attempts to justify such codification" (ibid.). After discussing the need for a specific law on PSCs for two decades, the Czech Ministry of Interior finally produced its first draft in June 2011. Its key features include the following:

1. Requires all PSCs to obtain a license from the Ministry of Interior, which is subject to reevaluation every five years
2. Requires all PSCs to produce an annual activities report for the Ministry of Interior
3. Divides PSCs services into four categories (patrol, detective, technical services, and security consultancy) and sets the conditions for obtaining a license for each of these categories
4. Clarifies the conditions for PSC employee qualification (clean criminal record, appropriate training, standardized qualification exams, and mandatory health checks)

The achievement of all these objectives is, however, dependent upon the hitherto still missing political consensus concerning the rules for, and limits of, privatization of internal security in the Czech Republic. The opposition parties have criticized the draft of the law on various grounds, including the fact that the draft does not push for the creation of a single Chamber of Private Security Companies as a guild authority (Tejc 2011). As of mid-2013, due to the resignation of the national government that drafted the aforementioned law, its adoption appears highly unlikely.

The Market's Effects on the State's Monopoly on Force and the Provision of Security as a Public Good

The absence of effective legal regulation of the market for force in the Czech Republic has serious consequences. There are no legally binding minimum standards for the quality of provision of private security services in the Czech Republic. This has led to cutthroat competition with a downward spiral of quality, especially in personal security services, which account for the biggest share of the market. The public sector apparently even awards contracts to private providers whose price offers cannot even cover the payment of the legally required minimum wage for their employees (Unie soukromých bezpečnostních sluzeb České republiky 2010: 5–6). This practice significantly decreases the quality of the private security services that are provided and encourages the proliferation of PSCs of rather questionable reputation. It is arguably also one of the obstacles to the consolidation of the Czech market for private force, with thousands of registered PSCs located and registered in a country with a population of 10.5 million whose territory is slightly smaller than that of South Carolina. Furthermore, the absence of general legal regulation of PSC services has also led to the proliferation of largely arbitrary certification requirements; excessive labor qualification requirements; and mandatory, yet often meaningless, insurance provisions in the publicly awarded contracts (ibid.: 10). Apart from raising the costs of the contracted services, such requirements can easily be manipulated to fit particular companies in what are officially open bidding tenders. To some extent, this is yet another legacy of the aforementioned neoliberal shock-therapy approach of the Czech economic transition, where the drive for privatization outpaced the necessary changes in the legal and regulatory frameworks. One could argue that such a lack of regulation of the industry necessarily decreases the state's monopoly on force. Indeed, although strong links between PSCs and prominent Czech politicians speak to a certain level of state authority over the industry, because such authority is biased toward a few political actors, it may not be in the interest of the state as a whole.

The absence of a strong legal framework also indicates that the political debate about the limits of privatization of security in the Republic is still in its infancy. The developments on the markets and the actions of PSCs can, therefore, still have significant influence on the debate. Indeed, the Union of Private Security Services of the Czech Republic calls for the improvement of legal standards, but at the same time it openly promotes the outsourcing of state competencies:

> Private providers of property and personal security, as well as private detectives, are able to assume responsibility for many other areas, either independently or in coordination with the Czech Police, with the integrated rescue system, etc., as well as create a major reserve of forces and tools for handling of emergencies—floods, environmental accidents, etc. (Unie soukromých bezpečnostních sluzeb České republiky 2010: 21)

Apparently, Czech PSCs are already taking action to push the boundaries of the debate about the privatization of security in the Czech Republic in their favor. There are indications that at least some Czech PSCs provide services that could fall in the category of so-called "inherently governmental functions"—those "affecting life, liberty, or property of private persons" (Office of Federal Procurement Policy 1992). This particularly concerns the so-called "analytic" services, which include surveillance of persons and obtaining sensitive information about them, often using the latest technologies available (whose utilization even by the public police force requires a court order). Although the current laws do not give the employees of Czech PSCs any more power and/or jurisdiction than that given to other citizens of the Czech Republic, at least some policymakers recognize the behavioral risks inherent in the industry. According to the former deputy minister of interior, "there is a great mass of workers and hundreds of companies for which there are no rules yet. Eventually they might get out of control" (Viktora and Švec 2010).

However, PSCs do not only seek to influence the debate about the public-private balance from outside the political arena. The government of Prime Minister Petr Necas faced criticism for the close linkages between several of its ministers and deputy ministers and the Czech private security firm ABL.

The fact that the founder, and until 2010 the director, of this PSC also became a member of the government as the minister of transport, and that his wife was elected vice-president of the lower (but in terms of legislative powers more important) chamber of the Czech Parliament, raised concerns in the Czech media "that the process of privatization of security will be managed by one man, both as a representative of the state and the founder of one of largest and financially strongest PSCs" (Šmíd 2010). These concerns were further reinforced by a number of widely publicized scandals concerning past ABL contracts,[4] which ultimately almost led to the collapse of the entire Czech government when the other coalition parties demanded an immediate resignation of all Věci veřejné ministers with any connection to ABL. In the end, the former owner of ABL resigned his post of minister of transport after the press printed a transcript of his lecture at a 2008 training session for the top management of ABL, in which he outlined the key points from his strategic plan for ABL for 2009–14 (see Figure 5.1).

Vision:
- Unified building of stable economic and political power

Economic objectives:
- Create the strongest PSC in the Czech Republic with a dominant market position, via the strengthening of fake competition via friendly PSCs
- Development of new categories of customers in the field of public administration (health, education, government agencies, local government, social services)

Economic-political objectives:
- Development of a comprehensive security service for the [Czech] economic elites
- Producing projects leading to government contracts (private prison, luring away the employees in security areas)

Political goals:
- Building a coalition with the Civic Democratic Party [CDP] with the PA in 2010
- City hall control in Prague [districts] 1 and 5 in 2010
- Development of relations with Social Democrats for their government in 2010
- Taking over control of CDP in Prague [districts] 1 and 5 by 2012 (2014)
- In 2014 obtain 30 percent of CDP votes in Prague, or 30 percent of [Prague's] municipal council via PA

Resources:
- ABL, the economic base of power, in the following years to be led to maximum independence and depersonalization
- Public Affairs (PA) party, own political power base

Figure 5.1. Strategic plan for ABL for 2009–14. Source: Kmenta and Dolejší 2011.

This plan clearly indicates intentions to use ABL for political gain and to sway domestic policy. Interestingly, the ultimate dispute among the governing coalition parties concerned the post of the minister of interior (held by the Věci veřejné party leader), whose ministry is formally in charge of writing the long-delayed law on private security services. Subsequently, the minister was also forced to resign. He was replaced by a former head of the special anticorruption police unit, who also founded a small PSC after leaving the public police force in 2008. In April 2011, the founder of ABL and informal leader of Věci veřejné was accused of bribery by several MPs from his own party, for which he was conditionally sentenced to eighteen months of imprisonment a year later. This prompted him to resign from the government, and the Věci veřejné party split right in the middle. The sentence was subsequently suspended by a higher court ruling, according to which the acts of corruption cannot be investigated due to their falling under the broad immunity privileges enjoyed by all Czech MPs. ABL, meanwhile, changed its name to Mark2 Corporation (M2.C), claiming that an English name is more suitable for a planned expansion abroad.

As a consequence, rather than discussing the limits of privatization and its impact on the provision of public security, the Czech political scene has recently been dominated by a controversy about the role of PSCs in shaping the very rules for PSCs' operation. Given the extent of personal connections between political actors and PSCs, there is a risk that can be described, with reference to the experience from other countries, as the risk of "reverse revolving doors": Although in a number of Western countries formerly high-ranking political officials have assumed positions on the boards of national PSCs (Leander 2007: 53), in the Czech Republic the former owner and other top managers of a major PSC have occupied the highest political positions, including the positions in the Ministry of Interior. As such, the Czech variant of the revolving door phenomenon could have an adverse impact on both the political process and the provision of security as a public good. Indeed, the fact that ABL's strategic plan sets as one of its economic-political objectives "Development of a comprehensive security service for the [Czech] economic elites" indicates that the private security industry in the Czech Republic—or at least ABL/M2.C—views security as a private good, to at least some extent.

Conclusion

In terms of the typology developed by Dunigan and Petersohn in Chapter 11, the Czech market for private force can be described as essentially neoliberal. Privately owned security companies are the only market players, although some of them also participate in the "unofficial" shadow market with private security services. It is important to reiterate, however, that both the shadow and the official market participants provide only nonlethal personal security services. There are no private military companies in the Czech market, primarily due to lack of demand for lethal services. In terms of the causes of the market, the domestic demand from private citizens and companies, and the neoliberal shock-therapy approach to privatization, are arguably the key factors explaining the steady growth of the market, both in terms of the number of companies and their employees. The neoliberal approach to security privatization also goes a long way toward explaining the continuing absence of a specific legal regulation for the provision of private security services. In combination with another unique negative market consequence—the phenomenon of reverse revolving doors—the continuing absence of any legal regulation points to a real danger that the Czech market for private force may soon become a textbook example of the excessive influence of private security experts in public decision making and the resulting impact on the provision of security as a public good.[5] The aforementioned ABL Strategic Plan for 2009–14 certainly can be seen as the first step in this direction, both in its spirit and the specifics; however, the market has had a generally neutral impact on the provision of security as a public good up to the present point. Notably, however, the quantity and quality of the personal linkages of this largest Czech PSC to a governmental political party is unique even at the global level. As such, although it has not generally been considered a significant case thus far, the Czech market for private force deserves closer attention of private security experts in the future.

Notes

The author gratefully acknowledges the financial support of the Czech Science Foundation under the standard research grant no. P408/11/0395.

1. The shadow market comprises PSC services that are illegal without a court order and that only the public police force can execute under the current legal framework. This includes, for example, electronic communications interception or phone tapping.

2. All currency conversions in this chapter are based on the May 2011 exchange rate of 17 CZK for 1 USD.

3. The Union of Private Security Services in the Czech Republic estimates that as of 2010, 10–15 percent of employees of Czech PSCs would not meet the minimum qualification requirements (Unie soukromých bezpečnostních sluzeb České republiky 2010: 20).

4. For example, according to a leading Czech daily, *MF Dnes*, in 2006 and 2007 ABL accepted a contract to spy on several local politicians and their family members and to collect sensitive personal data such as driver's license numbers, passport numbers, details of firearm permits, information on the registration plates of cars, and data from police criminal prosecution records (Kmenta and Dolejší 2011). ABL has denied all of these accusations and it has filed a lawsuit against the newspaper.

5. Notwithstanding the numerous differences between the proponents and critics of privatization of security, there is a general consensus on the importance of independent and transparent political decision-making processes that should guarantee that the decisions about security provision are made within a framework that ensures public debate, broad public participation, and access to relevant information (see Barak-Erez 2009; Chesterman and Fisher 2009; Leander 2007; Prado 2009).

References

ABL. 2010. *Výroční zpráva 2009*. Accessed October 5, 2011. http://www.abl.eu/sqlcache /vyrocni-zprava-2009.pdf.

Asociace soukromých bezpečnostních sluzeb České republiky. 2010. *Třetí zpráva o stavu oboru–Příloha c.2*, January 29.

———. 2011. *Celostátní setkání clenských firem a sněm delegátů ASBS ČR o.s.*, September 2.

Barak-Erez, Daphne. 2009. "The Privatization of Violence." In *Private Security, Public Order: The Outsourcing of Public Services and Its Limits*, ed. Simon Chesterman and Angelina Fisher, 71–85. Oxford: Oxford University Press.

Bartoskova, Renata. 2007. "Podezrele levne sluzby." *Profit.Cz.*, June 10.

Chesterman, Simon, and Angelina Fisher. 2009. "Conclusion: Private Security, Public Order." In *Private Security, Public Order: The Outsourcing of Public Services and Its Limits*, ed. Simon Chesterman and Angelina Fisher, 222–26. Oxford: Oxford University Press.

G4S CZ. 2011. *Základní udaje a císla*. Accessed October 5, 2011. http://www.g4s.cz/cs -cz/Info%20centrum/Key%20facts%20and%20figures/.

Hoehn, Herman W. 1998. *The Transformation of Economic Systems in Central Europe*. Cheltenham, U.K.: Edgar Elgar.

Kmenta, Jaroslav, and Václav Dolejší. 2011. *Bárta šel do politiky kvůli zakázkám, vyplývá z jeho tajného plánu*. iDNES.cz, April 8.

Kramer, Daniel. 2007. "Does History Repeat Itself? A Comparative Analysis of Private Military Entities." In *Private Military and Security Companies: Chances, Problems, Pitfalls and Prospects*, ed. Thomas Jäger and Gerhard Kümmel, 23–36. Wiesbaden: VS Verlag für Sozialwissenschaften.

Lavigne, Marie. 1995. *The Economics of Transition*. London: MacMillan Press.

Leander, Anna. 2007. "Regulating the Role of Private Military Companies in Shaping Security and Politics." In *From Mercenaries to Market: The Rise and Regulation of Private Military Companies*, ed. Simon Chesterman and Chia Lehnard, 49–64. Oxford: Oxford University Press.

Office of Federal Procurement Policy. 1992. *Policy Letter 92-1: Inherently Governmental Functions.* Washington, D.C.

Ortiz, Carlos. 2010. *Private Armed Forces and Global Security: A Guide to the Issues.* Santa Barbara, Calif.: Praeger.

Percy, Sarah. 2007. *Mercenaries: The History of a Norm in International Relations.* Oxford: Oxford University Press.

Prado, Mariana Mota. 2009. "Regulatory Choices in the Privatization of Infrastructure." In *Private Security, Public Order: The Outsourcing of Public Services and Its Limits*, ed. Simon Chesterman and Angelina Fisher, 107–32. Oxford: Oxford University Press.

Redlich, Fritz. 2004. *The German Military Enterpriser and His Work Force: A Study in European Economic and Social History.* Vol. 1. Wiesbaden: Franz Steiner Verlag.

Reichl, Jiří. 2010. *Ministr vnitra k zákonu o soukromých bezpečnostních sluzbách.* http://www.mvcr.cz/clanek/ministr-vnitra-k-zakonu-o-soukromych-bezpecno stnich-sluzbach.aspx.

Sedlak, Lubomir. 2009. "Economic Transformation in the Czech Republic: A Relatively Painless Experience." *New Presence: The Prague Journal of Central European Affairs* 116(2): 33–35.

Sekuritas CZ. 2011. *Securitas v České republice.* Accessed October 5, 2011. http://www .securitas.com/cz/cs-cz/O-nas/Securitas-v-eske-republice/.

Šmíd, Tomáš. 2010. "Všechny nitky vedou k ABL." *Lidové Noviny*, September 11.

Snidl, Vladimir. 2011. "V Česku se rozjíždí byznys se soukromými zoldnéry." *Ekonom*, September 9.

"Soukromá policie ve sluzbách státu." 2007. *Policista.cz*, October 1.

Sýkorová, Petra. 2011. "ABL 'vládnutí' prospělo. Loni zvýšila obrat o 30 procent." *Ekonom*, April 20.

Tejc, Jeroným. 2011. "Stanovisko CSSD k zakonu o soukromych bezpecnostnich sluzbach." *CSSD.cz*, May 29.

Unie soukromých bezpečnostních sluzeb České republiky. 2004. *Prvni zprava o stavu oboru.* Accessed October 12, 2010. http://www.securityclub.cz/./PRVNI_ZPRAVA _O_STAVU_OBORU.doc.

———. 2010. *Treti zprava o stavu oboru*, January 29.

Viktora, Antonín, and Petr Švec. 2010. "Jak ohlídat hlídače. Vláda sepíše pravidla pro privátní detektivy." *iDNES.cz*, July 27.

CHAPTER 6

Informal but Diverse: The Market for Exported Force from Russia and Ukraine

Olivia Allison

The export market of privatized force from Russia and Ukraine differs significantly from markets in more commonly studied countries, such as the United States and the United Kingdom. Thousands of Russians and Ukrainians have worked as private contractors abroad in the past twenty years, primarily in minor conflicts. The market is characterized by its reliance on informal networks (most linked to official military and intelligence contacts), rather than the corporate structures used in Europe and North America. The Russian/Ukrainian export market of privatized force has not been studied in depth by academic or journalistic articles, most likely because of the isolated nature of the market. However, the personnel in the market have operated in brutal conflicts and civil wars, including reportedly acting as contractors for sanctioned regimes.

This chapter categorizes buyers and sellers of privatized force exported from Russia and Ukraine and aims to explain this market's causes and consequences. Hundreds of press articles, blogs, and websites have informed this chapter, as they provide examples of every type of transaction detailed below. The chapter is also based on research conducted in Russia and Ukraine in April and May 2009, which included twenty interviews with academics, private security firms, journalists, and international organizations. In most cases, the interviewees requested that their names be withheld because of the sensitivity of some of the discussions.

This chapter describes the attributes and causes of the exports of private force by military and security contractors and employees from Russia and

Ukraine. It does not address the domestic market for privatized force, concentrating instead on the externally focused export market in these two countries.[1] The two countries will be addressed as a single market for force because many of the informal networks that link buyers and sellers are based on Soviet-era military and intelligence connections. The examples below will also demonstrate that personnel from the two countries have been present and fought alongside each other in many of the same conflicts. There is also some degree of formal and informal cooperation and contact between Russian and Ukrainian security networks that allow the market to be treated as a single one. There are minor differences between Russian and Ukrainian exported force, and these gaps may grow. In the past twenty years that constitute the focus of this chapter, however, their differences were far less significant than their similarities.

The remainder of the chapter first discusses the characteristics of the market, with a focus on the relevant buyers and sellers. This is followed by an analysis of the causes underlying the existence and format of this market. The final section will address the consequences of this market for Russia's and Ukraine's monopoly on force and for security as a public good.

Structure of the Market

This is a neoliberal market, as defined by the typology developed in Chapter 11 of this volume: It is primarily organized around private business entities. In describing the structure of this market, this chapter analyzes the following aspects: (1) the services for sale, (2) the informal networks that define the transactions in the market, (3) the lack of regulation of the market, and (4) the key actors—its sellers and buyers. The discussion below highlights how the Russian and Ukrainian markets for exported force differ from the neoliberal market of the United States and United Kingdom—or the "Anglo Saxon model," as Carlos Ortiz refers to it in Chapter 4—that is most frequently discussed in the academic literature. It similarly highlights the main causes by illustrating how personal and informal networks have produced specific characteristics of transactions in this market.

The first characteristic of this market structure is the services that personnel provide, especially piloting Russian and Soviet planes and, to a lesser degree, acting as armed guards in conflict zones. Aircraft pilots and experts are by far the personnel most commonly contracted from Russia and

Ukraine because of the wide military export network of the Soviet Union and, more recently, Russia and Ukraine. In addition, there are reports that Russians and Ukrainians have worked as armed guards, and occasionally as hired or volunteer fighters, in conflicts in the Balkans and in Africa. For both types of services, this chapter only considers those that contribute to the most lethal end of the force spectrum, in keeping with this volume's focus on the most lethal aspects of each market studied. Therefore, references to transport pilots and unarmed guards have been omitted.

The second key characteristic of this market's structure is that the services in this market are generally bought and sold through informal networks, in contrast with the more formal corporate structure used by the major companies in the Anglo Saxon model defined by Carlos Ortiz in this book. The export of force from Russia and Ukraine relies heavily on informal—and often personal—networks. In the immediate aftermath of the Soviet Union's collapse in the 1990s, this could be seen in the number of sellers and buyers who were heavily dependent on ties and networks forged during the Cold War. For example, Moscow had developed a network of client states and allies around the world, often providing a wide variety of military technology to them. Soviet military and transport planes and helicopters were among those exported widely. In countries where buyers lacked a competent Air Force or trained pilots, these contracts were generally accompanied by agreements to either train the purchasing country's pilots or to provide Soviet personnel to operate the planes (interview with Russian military analyst, Moscow, April 8, 2009). The Soviet Union's demise did not mean that such training and piloting missions ceased. Instead, they either continued to be carried out by national arms companies as an addendum to an arms contract, or former and current security services personnel forged new private contracts.

These informal networks operate even when individual private military and security personnel are interacting with formal international networks. This is more marked in Ukraine, which has participated in NATO trainings and has increased cooperation with foreign military and police trainers ("Ukrainian Bodyguards Take Lessons" 2006). Because of this, several of the interviewees who participated in this study noted anecdotal evidence that these contacts had led to individual soldiers' recruitment into international security companies—in a few cases, into large multinational companies. This is logical, considering the reliance of market actors on informal networks rather than formal commercial structures. In Ukraine's case, for example, integration with NATO gives personnel access to the languages and technical skills that have enabled them to participate in international operations. The fact that Ukraine is consistently one of the top contributors of peacekeeping forces to international operations will improve its soldiers' networks with foreign militaries as well (Klimovich 2008). This causal factor will also be important if Russia continues to gradually expand its extremely limited cooperation with NATO. NATO's use of the Northern Distribution Network, a supply route that crosses the territory of several former Soviet countries, is one example of this cooperation (Nichol 2011). There is also growing use of Russian aircraft in supply operations in Afghanistan as a result of Russia's cooperation with NATO.

Third, the market has been shaped by the lack of domestic regulation or state control in either Ukraine or Russia. In theory, Russian entities (people and companies) are prohibited from participating in a foreign war to which Russia is not a party, according to Article 359 of the Russian Criminal Code, which defines these activities as *naemnichestvo* (mercenary). Russia's higher parliamentary body, the Federation Council, theoretically has the right to investigate reports and accusations of mercenarism, but no notable sanctions or investigations have occurred in the past (Dzhemal 2009). This is despite the proliferation of press reports of both companies and individuals undertaking these activities abroad. Mercenarism is defined in the Ukrainian Criminal Code (Article 447) in accordance with the Geneva Convention[2] (the same basic definition as in the Russian Criminal Code). Nonetheless, Ukrainian authorities generally deny that Ukrainian pilots or fighters are working as mercenaries overseas (Litvinenko 2009). These Russian and Ukrainian definitions of "mercenarism" are wider than that in international law,[3] and indeed many of them would not fit the international law definition of "mercenaries."

There are no other major domestic laws governing the prohibited or allowed activities for Russian and Ukrainian private military and security personnel overseas because the markets for privatized force—both internationally and domestically—emerged haphazardly as a result of the collapse of the Soviet Union and the sudden explosion of low-level and organized criminality in the region. The suddenness of this transition and lack of state control meant that "privatization of security and law enforcement in the region was driven mostly by ad hoc initiatives and short-term political and other considerations" (Juska 2009: 229). Because post-Soviet officials did not plan for this change (ibid.), they have not developed the regulatory base to control it.

The remainder of this chapter describes the key actors in this market: its sellers and buyers. The sellers are generally individuals or small companies, although the buyers range from foreign states to international governmental organizations to private individuals. There are no official estimates of the size of the export market, either in terms of personnel or revenue, but the presence of Russian and Ukrainian private soldiers has been an important part of the literature on private force since the 1990s. Data is particularly difficult to obtain concerning the number of individuals from the former Soviet Union fighting in foreign conflicts in the 1990s. However, reports from the UN Special Rapporteur on the Use of Mercenaries from the 1990s list Russian and Ukrainian citizens found or believed to have been fighting as private soldiers in conflicts in Georgia, Armenia, Tajikistan, Congo, Serbia, and Bosnia. Since the early 2000s, the Russian press reports have estimated the number between 5,000 and 10,000 contract personnel involved in transport—and sometimes conflict—activities. In the past decade, this has almost certainly continued to grow, but no more recent reliable estimates were found.

The downsizing of military and security forces has been a significant factor in determining which people become sellers of exported force and in influencing their reliance on informal networks. The Soviet Union had used a large proportion of its budget to sustain a vast military and improve its military technology. After the Cold War ended, the Soviet military and security forces were downsized, and their personnel lost their jobs. For example, one article notes that the number of pilots from the former Soviet Union fell from a Cold War height of 69,000 people to 19,000 within a few years (Serkov and Nadezhdin 2005). Further layoffs in the late 2000s included proposals to reduce the number of military officers by 61 percent between 2008 and 2013 ("Reform of the Russian Armed Forces" 2009). This has meant that, by far, the most frequent sellers of private force abroad on the Russian and Ukrainian market for force are individuals formerly employed by security forces (intelligence and law enforcement) and former Soviet military personnel. This has been the case because of both layoffs and early retirement associated with force modernization programs. Even personnel who have kept their employment face low salaries and frequent delays in payment (interview with private security provider, Kyiv, Ukraine, April 24, 2009).

The buyers of private force from Russia and Ukraine (and individuals from those countries) can be divided into the following two categories: (1) foreign governments; and (2) companies and individuals in foreign wars.

Many of the companies hiring Russian and Ukrainian individuals' services—particularly piloting services—are fly-by-night temporary companies set up to ship goods in contravention of UN arms embargoes and/or to work as subcontractors for large international or U.S.-based private military contracting firms such as Kellogg, Brown, and Root or General Dynamics (Shuster 2009).

Notably, this list of buyers does not include international governmental organizations (IGOs), although there are numerous reports that Russian and Ukrainian pilots fly supply missions for them. They have been excluded because of this volume's primary focus on those operations that require use of deadly force. However, it is important to recognize that these operations are important to each country's overall exported force sector because the supply contracts provide this sector with the access to international military networks that can contribute to each country's ability to expand its exported force industry.

Finally, this section summarizes the characteristics of each category of buyer and the causes underlying their involvement in the market and provides examples of each. Given the informal and personal nature of the trade, this is intended to be illustrative rather than an exhaustive list of all occasions when Russia and Ukraine have exported force.

The first category of buyer is foreign governments, primarily in Africa, and this constitutes the category of buyer that the English- and Russian-language press have covered most extensively. Foreign governments that hire private military and security personnel from Russia and Ukraine tend not to have received significant post–Cold War military aid from the United States. This has typically been because the country is involved in a conflict that the United States or United Nations have condemned and/or sanctioned or because it is perceived to be not strategically significant enough to the United States to justify significant spending.

Another unifying feature is that most of the personnel sought and hired by foreign governments abroad, particularly in Africa, are aircraft pilots. This industry continues to form one of the more significant areas of military export from the post-Soviet region, and it is the one that requires the most human expertise. Among the activities Ukrainian citizens participate in are technical assistance, training, and, "in a number of cases, [acting as] pilots for aircraft in service with the armed forces" (Holtom 2011: 8). Russians and Ukrainians are, therefore, not usually hired by other governments to carry out general fighting or combat missions but are specifically sought for their technical expertise.

Foreign government buyers have sought personnel to conduct missions along the full range of military force, from supply to combat missions. It would be an extremely difficult task to fully confirm whether any single contract is for supply or combat, and the informal nature of the trade impedes definition of the types of contracts that have been used or efforts to quantify how many people have been hired. There are some unofficial statistics, however: An article in the Russian newspaper *Kommersant* in 2001 stated that approximately 7,000 people had gone abroad in search of work in military and transport activities since the fall of the Soviet Union. It stated that an estimated 400 pilots had gone to Africa and that half of them had since disappeared (Drantsov et al. 2001). If true, this high statistic could point to a significant casualty and injury rate that might indicate the participation of many in intense conflict activities. Alternatively, this statistic may simply reflect the difficulty in keeping track of these contractors when companies with questionable reputations hire them under relatively informal contract mechanisms.

Because this volume focuses on the most lethal spectrum of force being sold on the market, this chapter focuses on countries where there have been reports that Russians and Ukrainians have provided a military service, rather than (or in addition to) a supply function. The following are the principal buyer countries (all in Africa) in which Russian and Ukrainian military activities are reported in the press: Angola, Chad, Democratic Republic of Congo (DRC), Ethiopia, Eritrea, and Sudan.

Many of the reports of Russian and Ukrainian involvement in these conflicts only generally refer to Russians' and Ukrainians' presence. In other cases, their military activities are mentioned more specifically, but no details of buyers' or sellers' locations or identities are given. For example, reports concerning Chad state that contracted Ukrainians control "the Chadian unit of operating Su-25 combat aircraft, and Mi-24 and Mi-17 helicopters" (Holtom 2011).

Other articles have provided general statistics about the number of personnel involved in a specific conflict. For example, a journalist wrote that 400 people—mostly tank specialists and pilots—were employed by Ethiopia during its war with Eritrea, while Eritrea employed approximately 100 foreign fighters. Both sides' private fighters were reportedly from the former

Soviet Union and the Balkans (Shteynberg 2004). Other articles about the same conflict note that Ethiopians tended to hire Russians more, while Eritrea more frequently hired Ukrainians (Klimovich 2008). An article about Angola stated that there were more people from the former Soviet Union fighting there in 2004 than anywhere else in Africa.[4]

In other cases, press reports provide the most detail when personnel are killed in a conflict. The most specific report about Angolan military activity focused on a plane shot down by the militant group National Union for Total Independence of Angola in the late 1990s. Three men from the post-Soviet region, referred to in press pieces as "soldiers of fortune," were killed in this incident ("Еще раз о наемниках" 2007).

Similarly, reports of Russians' and Ukrainians' participation in DRC conflicts have been forthcoming for ten years (Klimovich 2008), but a 2001 crash of an Antonov-28 provides additional insight into the identities and activities of personnel there. The incident killed the Russian and Kazakh crew on board (Drantsov et al. 2001). In another report, a man claimed that he went to fight in the DRC in 2000 after he was fired from the Russian military. He said he received USD 3,000 per military flight (Dzhemal 2009).

Russian press coverage of private contractors' missions in Sudan has been under more consistent scrutiny since six Ukrainians were killed when an Ilyushin-76 plane crashed in 2005. Reports stated that they had been flying the MiG-29s because there were "significant problems in the effectiveness of Sudanese MiG pilots" (Serkov and Nadezhdin 2005). This scrutiny remained even years later, and in 2008 Russian articles stated that "Sudanese President Omar Bashir was using former and current Russian Air Force to fly Khartoum's fleet of MiG-29 fighter-jets" and that they had "participated in operations against rebels in both the Darfour province as well as around Khartoum in May 2008" ("Russian Pilots Fly Sudan MIGs" 2008).

Press reports thus far have contained very few details about how the missions were arranged at an international political level. For example, none of the military contracts in Sudan appear to have been officially sanctioned by the Russian or Ukrainian government, but an interview with the Russian ambassador to Sudan in 2010 indicates that he was aware of the presence of Russian private military contractors in the country (Durnovo 2010). In a rare instance in which Russian government complicity is claimed to have occurred, a Russian article states that in 2004 a man claimed he had worked in the Ethiopian army, instructing two battalions in a mission to storm the Somali capital Mogadishu. He claimed that the Russian Ministry of Defence had been paid USD 2 million from the assistance it had received from the U.S. State Department for this mission (Dzhemal 2009).

In addition to these combat activities, Russian and Ukrainian counter-terrorism and military trainers work with foreign governments. These activities are not nearly as widespread as those of U.S. and European trainers, whose work around the world has been documented elsewhere. However, this may be an area of growth for regional private military and security exports in the future. Large international military and police training firms collaborate widely with military trainers from around the world and host trainings for international personnel. One example of this is the International Law Enforcement Training Agency (ILETA) in the Crimean region of Ukraine, which ran a counterterrorism training course in preparation for the Euro 2012 football final that took place in Poland and Ukraine ("В Крыму в рамках подготовки к Евро-2012" 2010).[5]

This category of buyer—companies and individuals recruiting for foreign wars—is more secretive and differs from the previous category in that the connections linking these buyers to the Ukrainian and Russian personnel are more informal. Therefore, its global presence is fairly difficult to assess. In the examples presented below, the recruiting company appears to have been a relatively small private company, albeit with global capabilities.

The two most significant cases reported in the press involve recruitment of Russian and Ukrainian citizens to work as private contractors in Iraq. In September 2004, the General Prosecutor of Ukraine stated that it had investigated four foreign citizens from Greece, Iraq, and Pakistan who had been attempting to recruit 100–150 former military personnel "to participate in armed conflicts on the territory of other states," specifically Iraq (Tsaplienko 2005). It is not clear what functions the citizens were being recruited to perform, and the outcome of the case was not reported.

Similarly, a *Russian Newsweek* report claimed in 2009 that three companies had been working in Iraq to provide private security services since 2004. So far, the Russian Criminal Code's ban on receiving funds for participating in a war that Russia is not party to has been interpreted as a ban on Russian companies and individuals earning money from military or security contracting abroad. Therefore, the key firms mentioned in the Russian press—Tigr Top-Rent Security, Orel-Antiterror, RSB Group, Centre-Alfa, and Redut Anti-terror—were run by Russians but were registered either as "training centers" in Russia or incorporated in the British Virgin Islands to avoid prosecution (Dzhemal 2009). According to the article, these companies' services had been utilized by the Russian Engineering Company, the United Nations, the Tourism Department of Iraq, Russian embassies abroad, the Government of Sri Lanka, and shipping companies. A 2009 report indicated that Orel-Antiterror was training Russian soldiers for Iraq, although it was not clear when or where such soldiers would be deployed or the specific functions they would be performing ("Former Russian Soldiers Ready" 2009). A 2011 press release on RSB Group's website, rsb-group.ru, stated that it would be providing armed guard services for the Sri Lankan shipping industry, supported by the Ministry of Defense. Interviews produced other anecdotal information about American recruiters who were teaming up with Ukrainian businessmen to carry out similar activities in Afghanistan, but no official evidence of this has been reported (interview with IGO official, April 23, 2009). Several of these companies appeared to be active at the time of writing; Anti-Terror Orel, RSB, and Centre-Alfa had functional websites with new press releases posted as of August 2013.

Consequences of This Market Structure

The previous section described the structure of the market for force in Russia and Ukraine as a neoliberal market that is based on informal networks and has little government regulation or official oversight. The sellers tend to be individuals or small companies who either pilot Russian and Soviet planes or act as armed guards. There is a wide range of buyers, including foreign states, IGOs, and private individuals or small foreign companies.

This market structure has led to the following consequences: (1) increased insecurity for the sellers in the market; (2) state institutions are undermined; (3) a lack of clarity concerning the separation of private and public exported force. These are described in more detail below.

First, this market structure increases insecurity for the sellers in the market. The lack of direct regulation and the informal nature of the contracting system has resulted in a lack of legal and organizational clarity, especially muddled terminology and contracting procedures. For example, the Russian term *kontraktniki* (contractor) legally only refers to contract soldiers in the Russian military; other terms such as "private guard" and "private guard company" (abbreviated as *ChOP* in Russian) refer to domestic armed (or unarmed) guards. The legal uncertainty over all other force activities has resulted in press reports referring to contracted personnel interchangeably as *kontraktniki* and *naemniki* (mercenaries), but neither term is based on its legal definition. There have been no reports concerning the structure and nature of the contracts under which personnel are contracted, either as pilots or as guards, but it is more likely that their contract terms are general consulting terms, rather than explicit references to exported force. There were also no references found to employment or other court cases based on these contracts, and it is not clear how (or whether) they are enforced.

For the individuals involved, this lack of legal certainty has meant that there is no safety net for them if they face problems—safety or contractual—while working in a military or security capacity abroad. For example, postings on a popular Russian-language aviation website contain at least one story in which a Russian citizen claimed he had been held against his will in Sudan and forced to work for unfair contract terms. This person claimed that when he and his colleagues escaped and approached the Russian Embassy in Khartoum for help, diplomats were unwilling to jeopardize the bilateral relationship to assist them. The men claim they eventually escaped to Egypt, although the story has not been independently verified (Serkov and Nadezhdin 2005). Because of such stories, many advice columns and online posts advise potential recruits to only apply to companies and organizations in which they have a trusted personal contact (Petrenko 2008).

Second, the market structure—particularly the lack of oversight and the market's informality—undermines state institutions. First, it contributes to the declining professionalization of the military by providing an opportunity for trained soldiers to earn larger salaries working for private companies and foreign governments overseas. The stated aim of the Russian and Ukrainian militaries' downsizing has been to make these militaries more professional. The process itself has conversely contributed to the view among military personnel that their best options for a military career lie in contracting privately.

Similarly, Ukrainian and Russian personnel have been recruited to undertake private force activities abroad through their official interaction with foreign international military networks, including training exercises with NATO and other foreign governments. This fact undermines the formal relationships between Russia and Ukraine and the international military networks and organizations.

Finally, this market structure contributes to a lack of clarity concerning government and private exported force. For example, there is evidence that the trade exists in collaboration with or supplementation to large arms sales.

In one report, this unofficial collaboration has even included falsified contracts with implicit permission from government agencies, whereby Russian state companies acting abroad utilize accounting fraud to obscure their participation in private military and security activities (Dzhemal 2009). The techniques for this may include using offshore or other apparently unrelated companies to earn a portion of the fees for training or exported force, although the companies effectively represent official interests.

This lack of clarity was also reflected in legal debates in 2012–13, which indicated that Russia was considering setting up and using private military companies overseas. In April 2012, then–President-elect Vladimir Putin responded to a question about these companies from a parliamentary deputy, saying that "such companies are a way of implementing national interests without the direct involvement of the state" (Bogdanov 2012) and "should be considered" ("Putin Backs Private Defense" 2012). Several months later, Deputy Prime Minister Dmitry Rogozin said that private military companies could be set up by the Russian Military Industrial Commission, in order to protect Russia's economic interests abroad (Peleschuck 2012).

In addition, as of August 2013, there was a draft law under consideration that would allow the major state-controlled oil and gas companies to use private security companies to protect their assets. The law, On Amendments to Some Legislative Acts of the Russian Federation to Establish Departmental Security to Ensure the Safety of the Fuel and Energy Complex, was introduced in March 2013 and passed its first reading in the Duma (lower house of parliament) in June 2013. The draft current in August 2013 would allow companies in the strategic energy industry (which would include Gazprom, Rosneft, Transneft, and others) to used lethal force and rules of engagement to defend transport, production, and extraction assets.

Combined, these two trends could significantly amplify the lack of clarity between private and government interests already evidenced in the market structure. If both of these events occurred, for example, there may be government investment in private companies that work to protect Russia's publicly traded but government-controlled oil and gas industry overseas.

All of these consequences demonstrate that the shape of the market for exported force from Russia and Ukraine contributes to an erosion of the monopoly on force in these countries. The lack of definition and formal contracting structure gives the market a semi-legal (or semi-illegal) nature that is largely uncontrolled by the state. Similarly, the erosion of state institutions and the blurring of the boundary between state and private force erodes the government's monopoly on force by making it unclear who is responsible for and in control of these exports.

Conclusion

This chapter describes the neoliberal market for force exported from Russia and Ukraine. This market has exported thousands of aircraft pilots and armed guards who have carried out combat activities in civil wars and conflicts. It is based far more on informal networks than corporate structures because of the uncertain legality of the export of private force from these countries and because of the politically sensitive nature of many of the activities carried out by these personnel.

The export of private force by Ukrainian and Russian actors has demonstrated and contributed to an erosion of the state's monopoly on force and the provision of security as a public good in the countries where these actors operate. This is primarily evident in the differences between Russia and Ukraine in the country's authority over force and its authority over the mode of allocating force. Russia remains more authoritative in both than Ukraine does. Moscow is perceived as having far more authority to determine when and where force is used than Ukraine; indeed, one interviewee said that the government was directing the exports to a large degree. Many of Ukraine's exports have links to the state-owned arms export company or other government officials, but the central government lacks such control. However, although Russia is more authoritative in determining the mode of violence that is exported, both countries ultimately use a semi-controlled market allocation based on informal networks to allocate force abroad.

This distinction highlights how the state's monopoly on force is eroded by the informal nature of the market: The more sellers in this market have interacted and/or integrated with private security companies and international military structures, the more their home country has lost authority over the type of force exported and its mode of allocation. Ukraine and Russia differ in this sense. Ukraine has integrated into the international defense community slightly more than Russia has, and as a result, its personnel have been able to contract independently in conflicts abroad, while Russia is perceived as having greater control over its exports of private force services. The impact of the Russian and Ukrainian market for exported force has been far less in the mode of their control over the means of violence.

Finally, the exported force market has had little impact on domestic security as a public good (that is, within Russia and Ukraine), as it has had no observable impact on domestic security overall. This study found no evidence that the lack of control over means of violence used in exported force undermined the control over force domestically in Russia and Ukraine. In a similar way, the existence of the exported force market has little impact on Russian and Ukrainian security as a public good. The effects of this market are more important for the recipient countries, but such concerns fall outside the scope of this volume.

Notes

Research for this chapter was supported in part by a grant from IREX (International Research & Exchanges Board) with funds provided by the United States Department of State through the Title VIII Program. Neither of these organizations is responsible for the views expressed herein.

1. This concentration on the externally focused export market is due to this volume's overarching focus on the most lethal segments of the market for force in each of the cases studied.

2. The full name of this protocol is Protocol Additional to the Geneva Conventions of 12 August 1949, and relating to the Protection of Victims of International Armed Conflicts (Protocol I), 8 June 1977.

3. The most commonly referenced definition of "mercenary" in international law is found in Additional Protocol I of the Geneva Conventions, which entered into force in 1977. Article 47.1 of this convention dictates that mercenaries do not benefit from prisoner-of-war (POW) status if captured. Article 47.2 develops a comprehensive and frequently referenced definition of a mercenary as any person who

   a. is specially recruited locally and abroad in order to fight in an armed
       conflict;
   b. does, in fact, take a direct part in hostilities;
   c. is motivated to take part in the hostilities essentially by the desire for
       private gain and, in fact, is promised by or on behalf of a Party to the
       conflict material compensation substantially in excess of that promised or
       paid to combatants of similar rank and functions in the armed forces of
       that Party;
   d. is neither a national of a Party to the conflict nor a resident of territory
       controlled by a Party to the conflict;
   e. is not a member of the armed forces of a Party to the conflict; and
   f. has not been sent by a State which is not a Party to the conflict on official
       duty as a member of its armed forces.

See Protocol Additional to the Geneva Conventions of 12 August 1949, and relating to the Protection of Victims of International Armed Conflicts (Protocol 1; Adopted on June 8, 1977; Entry into force December 7, 1979). Notably, *each* of these six provisions must be fulfilled in order for the person in question to qualify as a mercenary. Many analysts argue that this definition is inapplicable to modern private security contractors and is generally "unworkable" due to the six cumulative conditions (Cameron 2006: 578; Percy 2007: 367).

4. Although the war had ostensibly finished by that time, many fighters from the former Soviet Union were still there, including some who were reportedly being kept there against their will by employers (Shteynberg 2004).

5. On its website, the company also claims to have cooperated with the King Abdullah II Special Operations Training Center in Amman, Jordan (ILETA n.d.).

References

"В Крыму в рамках подготовки к Евро-2012 военнослужащие из 10 стран проходят курс контртеррора [In Crimea in Preparation for Euro2012 Military Personnel from 10 Countries Participate in Training]." 2010. *KIANews*, August 12. http://www.kianews.com.ua/node/22679.

Bogdanov, Konstantin. 2012. "Russia May Consider Establishing Private Military Companies." *RIA Novosti* (April 13). http://en.ria.ru/analysis/20120413/172789099.html.

Cameron, Lindsey. 2006. "Private Military Companies: Their Status Under International Humanitarian Law and Its Impact on Their Regulation." *International Review of the Red Cross* 88(863): 573–98.

Drantsov, Kirill, Leonid Zavarskiy, Elena Miklashevskaya, Andrey Smirnov, Andrey Sheptitskiy, Gul'chachak Khannanova, and Roman Golubev. 2001. "Воздушные наемники [Air Mercenaries]." *Kommersant Dengi* 35(339).

Durnovo, Aleksey. 2010. "Судан глазами консульского работника [Sudan in the Eyes of a Consulate Worker]." Ekho Moskvy on *Voyna i Mir* website, March 13.

Dzhemal, Orkhan. 2009. "НАЛИЧНЫЙ СОСТАВ [Available Personnel]." *Russian Newsweek*, December 2.

"Еще раз о наемниках и частных армиях в горячих точках [One Again About Mercenaries and Private Armies in Hot Spots]." 2007. *Mir* (October 22). Accessed August 2010. http://vybory.org/articles/1098.html.

"Former Russian Soldiers Ready to Take on Blackwater in Iraq." 2009. *Russia Today*, December 11. http://rt.com/news/russian-soldiers-blackwater-iraq.

Holtom, Paul. 2011. *Ukrainian Arms Supplies to Sub-Saharan Africa*. Stockholm: Stockholm International Peace Research Institute (SIPRI).

ILETA. n.d. *Partners*. Accessed June 20, 2011. http://ileta.vg/rus/index.php.

Juska, Arunas. 2009. "Privatisation of State Security and Policing in Lithuania." *Policing and Society*: 226–46.

Klimovich, Sergey. 2008. "Казаки-наемники [Cossack-Mercenaries]." *Podrobnosti. ua*, March 21. http://podrobnosti.ua/power/security/2008/03/20/506277.html.

Litvinenko, Andrey. 2009. "Украина тайно поставляет пилотов для войны в Афганистане [Ukraine Secretly Supplies Pilots for the War in Afghanistan]." *Novaya*, July 22. http://novaya.com.ua/?/articles/2009/07/20/222505-13.

Nichol, Jim. 2011. *Russian Political, Economic, and Security Issues and U.S. Interests*. Washington, D.C.: Congressional Research Service.

Peleschuck, Dan. 2012. "Private Military Companies May Appear in Russia—Rogozin." *RIA Novosti*, September 19. http://en.ria.ru/crime/20120919/176067373.html.

Percy, Sarah. 2007. *Mercenaries: The Histroy of a Norm in International Relations*. Oxford: Oxford Univeristy Press.

Petrenko, Ustin. 2008. "Украинские наемники во Франции: верность за 1000 евро в месяц [Ukrainian Mercenaries in France: Loyalty for 1000 Euros per Month]." *UNIAN News Agency*, January 18. http://www.unian.net/world/89347-ukrainskie -naemniki-vo-frantsii-vernost-za-1000-evro-v-mesyats.html.

"Putin Backs Private Defense Company Idea." 2012. *RIA Novosti*, April 11. http://en.ria .ru/military_news/20120411/172754492.html.

"Reform of the Russian Armed Forces." 2009. *RIA Novosti*, April 12. http://en.ria.ru /infographics/20091204/157098191.html.

"Russian Pilots Fly Sudan MIGs in Darfour Missions." 2008. *World Tribune*, May 29. http://www.worldtribune.com/worldtribune/WTARC/2008/af_sudan0189_05 _29.html.

"Ukrainian Bodyguards Take Lessons from Foreign Trainers." 2006. *KyivPost*, June 22. http://www.kyivpost.com/content/ukraine/ukrainian-bodyguards-take-lessons -from-foreign-tra.html.

Serkov, Dmitriy, and Igor Nadezhdin. 2005. "Itogi: Гастарбайтеры небес [Migrant Workers' Heaven]." Usenet Aviation Newsgroup, March 1. http://aviation.kryshi.net.

Shteynberg, Mark. 2004. "Спецназ в аренду. Наемники из СНГ пользуются спросом . . . для свержения африканских лидеров [Special Forces for Rent. Mercenaries from CIS Are in Demand . . . For Overthrowing African Leaders]." *Nezavisimoe Voennoe Obozrenie* [Independent Military Review], August 27.

Shuster, Simon. 2009. "New Job for Ex-Soviet Pilots: Arms Trafficking." *Time*, December 17. http://content.time.com/time/world/article/0,8599,1948398,00.html.

Tsaplienko, Andrey. 2005. "Украинские наемники [Ukrainian Mercenaries]." *Podrobnosti.ua* (September 13). http://podrobnosti.ua/projects/arch/2005/09/13/243664 .html.

CHAPTER 7

The Markets for Force in Afghanistan

Jake Sherman

The use of private security in Afghanistan has emerged as both a substitute
for weak public security forces and, in an increasingly volatile environment,
as a supplement to them. Its primary function is to offer protection to government institutions and officials; to international military, diplomats, and
aid officials; and to private businesses across the country. This protection is
intended to enable the conduct of military operations, delivery of aid, and
engagement in vital economic activities, as well as the training of Afghanistan's police and armed forces.

The long-term objective of international engagement in Afghanistan
since September 11, 2001 is stability—a public good from which the vast majority of Afghans and foreign nationals in the country would benefit.[1] However, the means of achieving stability—specifically, the establishment and
use of private security providers (PSPs)—is not a clear public good. On one
hand, the use of PSPs has enabled civilian reconstruction activities in areas
where they would otherwise not be possible, resulting in infrastructure and
other economic development projects.[2] On the other hand, the direct benefit
of private security (the provision of security itself) is largely restricted to a
particular group (i.e., those individuals and institutions that contract private
security). Certainly, there are exceptions. The presence of private security
providers at institutions such as banks, supermarkets, and shopping centers
provides a measure of security to the small segment of the urban population
that uses them. More broadly, the skills transferred to public security institutions by international private security companies like Dyncorp International
have increased their competency and professionalism (ACSOR 2010).

The market for force in Afghanistan is characterized by a diversity of international, national, and subnational providers, and it has evolved over time. This makes broad characterization of private security in the country difficult. Nonetheless, the activities of private security companies in Afghanistan have emerged as a significant point of tension between Afghan President Hamid Karzai and the coalition of governments that have supported him against a widening Taliban insurgency. Viewed from this perspective, the public perception of private security in Afghanistan is that it has a detrimental impact on public security and is an excludable good.

The absence of effective oversight and control of private security providers employed by the international community undermines the credibility—and the effectiveness—of the Afghan government, international military forces, and reconstruction organizations. It hinders the development of the public security sector in Afghanistan by strengthening alternative power structures and by diverting resources from the police.

Indeed, the burgeoning private security sector in Afghanistan has posed a dilemma. PSPs have fulfilled a need for which, until recently, there was no clear, immediate alternative. There are too few Afghan National Police (ANP) to provide protection to the staff, premises, and projects of the international community—and too little confidence in their ability among most internationals to entrust them with protection responsibilities. Better government regulation, monitoring, and enforcement by international consumers of private security would have helped ensure that it enabled, rather than hindered, the stabilization of Afghanistan. This chapter briefly examines the diversity of PSPs that make up the market for force in Afghanistan. It then reviews the environmental factors, including the weakness of state security providers and the regulatory environment, that have shaped the market for force. Finally, it analyzes the consequences for the state's monopoly on force and provision of security as a public good.

Characteristics of the Afghan Market for Force

Since 2001, the international military forces, reconstruction and development contractors, embassies, international organizations, and businesses operating in Afghanistan have extensively utilized private security. These entities have encompassed a wide range of PSPs, from international and national private security companies (PSCs) operating with or without the required Afghan licensing permits, to outlawed militias hired as "armed support groups" by U.S. and allied military forces, to an Afghan state–owned "public protection force."

According to U.S. Central Command, as of fourth-quarter fiscal year 2012 there were 18,914 private security personnel (including unarmed personnel) on U.S. Department of Defense (DoD) contracts (U.S. DoD 2012; see Table 7.1).

The main services offered by PSCs in Afghanistan span a wide range of nonlethal and lethal security services: static guarding of premises, construction projects, and mining operations; close protection; escorting convoys; security assessment and training; intelligence and risk management; electronic security and surveillance; and quick reaction forces. PSPs have also been contracted for de-mining, poppy eradication, supporting the electoral process, and training Afghan security forces. Although there is limited public information, incidents like the December 30, 2010 suicide bombing of a Central Intelligence Agency base in Khost province that killed six agents and two private contractors from Xe, the firm formerly known as Blackwater, also suggest the use of private security providers for "black ops," including detention and interrogation (Oppel and Tavernise 2010).

The International Security Assistance Force (ISAF) and U.S. Special Forces, which operate outside of the ISAF chain of command, have employed a range of PSPs to provide services toward the more lethal end of the force continuum to augment their security. Employment of PSPs has enabled more troops to be sent out on patrol to interact with the local population and on combat operations (although historically, base security in other theaters has been performed by military police). Although ISAF and U.S. contingents employ licensed security companies in some locations, the use of unregistered companies and armed support groups operating outside the legal framework, with little oversight or accountability, appears to have been widespread.

Two former UN officials separately estimated that there are also as many as 1,000 to 1,500 illegal armed support groups that have been employed,

Table 7.1. Number of Private Security Contractors in Afghanistan, Fourth Quarter, FY 2012

	Total	U.S. Citizens	Third Country Nationals	Local/Host Country Nationals
DoD PSCs	18,914	2,014	1,437	15,413

trained, and armed by ISAF and Coalition Forces to provide security to forward operating bases, escort supply convoys, and perform other functions, as well as by development agency contractors and provincial reconstruction teams to protect assistance projects. The UN estimated in 2005 that there were nearly 5,000 militias nationwide—upward of 120,000 armed individuals. By one estimate, fewer than 10 percent of these militia groups had been disarmed or their members arrested. At the time of writing, in most districts, local commanders still remain in power and beyond the law (Anonymous, pers. comm.).

The following are examples of unregistered private security companies and armed support groups employed by international military forces:

- In Parwan province, Bagram Airbase has employed a private security company run by Asil Khan, a former Northern Alliance commander allied with Haji Almas, a member of parliament from Parwan and also a former Northern Alliance military commander.
- Another company, Afghanistan Navin, also has had contracts with Bagram, and its 500 guards have provided convoy escorts to and from the airbase to Kunduz and Ghazni. Navin is owned by former mujahideen commander Lutfullah (Sadeq Azad 2010).
- The use of militia groups for security services is not confined to international military forces: In the best-documented case of a private security company employing militia, U.S. Protection and Investigations (USPI) partnered with Northern Alliance military commanders like General Din Mohammad Jurat to provide their foot soldiers to the company. USPI—the American owners of which have been federally indicted for fraud in the United States— has held contracts with the U.S. Agency for International Development, the World Bank, the Japan International Cooperation Agency, the United Nations, and private businesses (Schmeidl 2007; Schulman 2009).

These security providers have frequently been run by former military commanders with ethnic, political, or kinship ties to serving and former government officials and other Afghan elite. Many are responsible for human rights abuses and are involved in the illegal narcotics and black market economies. In the south of Afghanistan, there is also a tribal dimension. PSPs are associated with the tribe of their leader—for instance, Kandak

Amnianti Uruzgan in Uruzgan (commanded by Matiullah Khan) is associated with the Popalzai. In Kandahar, there have been Popalzai- and Barakzai-affiliated PSPs (e.g., those linked to the Karzai family and Gul Agha Shirzai, respectively).

In keeping with the focus of this volume, the remainder of this chapter focuses primarily on PSPs providing services toward the lethal end of the force continuum, to the extent that it is possible to separate those actors from actors who provide solely nonlethal services.

Contextual Causes of This Form of Market

One of the main reasons underlying the growth of the market for force is the weakness of the Afghan National Security Forces (ANSF). They are not at the level, either in number or competence, that the U.S. military estimates is necessary to stabilize Afghanistan and permit withdrawal of foreign forces (U.S. Government Accountability Office 2011). The counterinsurgency strategy and plans for the handover to Afghan security forces require more national soldiers and police officers who can complement and take over from international military forces to clear and hold reclaimed territory.

U.S. military strategy aims to increase the capacity and size of the Afghan National Army (ANA) and Afghan National Police (ANP). Donors and the Afghan government steadily agreed to increase the ANA from an initial target of 50,000 troops in 2001 to 195,000 by October 2012, a target achieved in May 2012. The ANP, likewise, expanded from a goal of 82,000 police to 149,208 police by May 2012 (Bumiller 2010; NATO 2012).

The ANA has demonstrated increasing operational capability and independence. Afghanistan's police, however, suffer from a lack of public trust, due to incompetence and corruption, and from an inability to protect themselves from insurgent attacks, due to inadequate leadership, training, and equipment. More Afghan police than soldiers die fighting insurgents.[3] David Kilcullen has described the problem with the Afghan police this way: "We have built the police into a less well-armed, less well-trained version of the Army and launched them into operations against the insurgents. Meanwhile, nobody is doing the job of actual policing—rule of law, keeping the population safe . . . civil and criminal law enforcement—the Taliban have stepped into this gap" (Packer 2008).

The Focused District Development (FDD) program addressed some of the problems that plagued earlier police reform.[4] Yet, although the FDD worked to effectively transform the ANP into a paramilitary force capable of standing up to insurgents in targeted districts, other policing skills necessary for upholding the rule of law remain underaddressed.

Without effective public security forces, peace is impossible. Yet maintaining and expanding the ANSF is prohibitively expensive for Afghanistan, which had an annual revenue of USD 2.25 billion in fiscal year 2010–11. According to the U.S. DoD, expanding the ANA alone will cost between USD 10–20 billion over a seven-year period; recurrent costs have been calculated at USD 2.5 billion per year for the ANA and USD 1 billion per year for the ANP. Foreign donors, principally the United States, supply the overwhelming share of financial support for ANSF (Ball, Byrd, Middlebrook, and Ward 2009).[5]

Faced with weak Afghan government security institutions—and, relative to counterinsurgency doctrine, insufficient numbers of their own forces—the United States and its allies have sought alternatives to fill the gap. This has resulted in reliance on the market for force.

Co-opting former Afghan military commanders as anti-Taliban allies has been a centerpiece of international military operations in Afghanistan since the 2001 military intervention. The United States armed and funded military commanders—many with egregious human rights records—in the initial war to overthrow the Taliban. The existing system to protect U.S. forces dates from this period. As there was effectively no government—and hence no public security service—commanders' private militias were hired for security. During the 2003–6 period, these commanders and their militias were supposedly dismantled,[6] and state security forces were established. But, at the time of writing, many of the same military commanders still lead the same armed men in the form of armed support groups and private security companies, licensed and unlicensed. As private security became a lucrative form of business, Afghan elites sought to enter—and subsequently dominate—the legal market, in contravention of national regulations.

Regulatory Causes of This Form of Market

Although the private security industry in Afghanistan grew apace with demand, regulation has been more reactive than proactive. In mid-2007, at least eighteen domestic and fifty-seven international private security companies were operating in Afghanistan (Schmeidl 2007). In February 2008, the Ministry of Interior (MoI) Disarmament and Reintegration Commission introduced an interim licensing procedure for existing PSCs (Government of the Islamic Republic of Afghanistan/MoI 2008a) in an effort to limit the transformation of illegal armed groups (i.e., private militias) into private security companies and to prevent their involvement in trafficking arms and narcotics, as well as other criminal activity (ibid.: 2).

Initially, MoI issued operating licenses to thirty-nine international and Afghan-owned PSCs, a move that was intended to cap the size of the industry. The number of licensed PSCs nonetheless steadily expanded in response to increased demand. In late 2009, PSCs employed between 19,260 and 23,000 security personnel (Government of the Islamic Republic of Afghanistan/MoI 2008a; Zucchio 2009), the majority of whom were locally hired Afghan personnel working in Kabul (Anonymous, pers. comm.). By October 2010, fifty-two security companies had been licensed by the MoI, employing some 40,000 armed security guards (Vogt and Faiez 2010). This number reached a peak in January 2011, when fifty-five licensed companies were operating.

From the outset, the licensing initiative faced several obstacles. First, the licensing process required that each PSC provide extensive documentation on its operations, the identity of its management and personnel, and its vehicles and weapons. However, the system was centralized in Kabul and the transfer of files to the provinces limited by technology. Because provincial officials had difficulty accessing the information, their investigations into possibly illegal PSC activity were often inconclusive. A participant at a July 2009 closed-door workshop on international private security regulation efforts described a meeting in which provincial authorities in Nangarhar stated their belief that they would be unable to trace weapons belonging to PSCs back to those catalogued by the MoI's registry in Kabul. The waiting period for a response to a request for hard copies of PSC registration records could take up to five months, if responded to at all.

Second, there was no political will for the licensing initiative to succeed because Afghan elites had a vested interest in the market. Holding companies and other means were used to obscure the true ownership of PSCs. According to interviews with UN and MoI officials, close relatives of senior officials—including President Karzai and Defense Minister Abdul Rahim Wardak—are previously documented owners and partners in companies, but they often removed their names from licensing documents despite indications of continued ownership, though not day-to-day management.

On August 17, 2010, the Afghan government issued Presidential Decree 62, which ordered that all PSCs, with the exception of those guarding embassies and consulates, would have to be disbanded by December of that year. Following initial closures, the president delayed the deadline in response to international—particularly U.S.—objections, providing more time to find an alternative. During this time, the government placed renewed regulatory scrutiny on private security firms, closing fifty-four (mostly unregistered) companies—but in December 2010, backed off plans for further closure of the remaining predominantly Afghan licensed firms after it became apparent that government security forces would be unable to fill the resulting gap ("Karzai Abandons Plan" 2010).

On March 15, 2011, the government again publicly attempted to phase out PSCs with the Bridging Strategy for the Implementation of Presidential Decree 62, which outlined conditions and procedures for a phased disbandment of PSCs suited to the timetables and requirements of international stakeholders. Notably, the Bridging Strategy identified seven PSCs to be disbanded within ninety days due to violation of the provisions of the 2008 regulation banning company links to senior government officials, including NCL Security, established by Hamed Wardak, the son of then–Afghan Minister of Defense Rahim Wardak; Strategic Security Solutions International (SSSI), which has connections to Hasseen Fahim, the brother of First Vice-President Mohammad Fahim; Watan Risk Management, with which Ahmad Wali Karzai, the president's brother, was associated until his assassination in July 2011; Elite, owned by Sadeq Mojadedi, the son of Hazrat Sibghatullah Mojadedi, leader of the Meshrano Jirga (the upper house of parliament) and chairman of the National Commission for Peace in Afghanistan; and the Asia Security Group, founded by Heshmat Karzai, the president's cousin (Van Bijlert 2011).

The Bridging Strategy also extended the deadline for PSC activities pending the establishment of the Afghan Public Protection Force (APPF), a state-owned enterprise run by the MoI to provide the security functions of PSCs. Accordingly, international development sites, military convoys, and commercial security had to transition to the APPF by March 2012. Military bases and construction projects were given a further year, until March 2013. PSCs were also authorized to become "risk management companies," providing security advisory services, including training and management of APPF employees, to those entities required to use APPF. As of mid-2012, the APPF had 10,000 guards, and was slated to increase to 25,000 by March 2013. Recruitment and training of a sufficient number of APPF guards to take over the services provided by PSCs, as well as overall management of the entity by the MoI, remained key tests of the viability of the APPF at the time of writing.

The Consequences of the Market for Force for the Afghan State's Monopoly on Violence and the Provision of Security as a Public Good

As noted at the beginning of the chapter, the establishment and use of private security providers to achieve stability in Afghanistan is not a clear public good. The benefits of private security are largely restricted to a particular group. One reason for this is that many of the PSPs operating in Afghanistan are armed support groups (ASGs)—illegal, private militia groups employed by foreign armed forces.

The challenge posed by these groups to Afghan state authority was demonstrated on June 29, 2009, when forty-one Afghan nationals employed by an armed support group run by U.S. Special Forces out of Camp Gecko in Kandahar killed the chief of police of Kandahar province and five other police officers. The incident occurred during a gun battle inside a government compound after the ASG sought the release of one of their members arrested earlier that day. When the provincial attorney general refused and called the ANP, the firefight broke out. U.S. Special Forces claimed they could not be held responsible for the actions of the ASG, but the incident raised the question of how forty-one heavily armed men and their vehicles could simply drive out of a U.S. Special Forces–run base. President Hamid Karzai responded to the killing, stating, "Such incidents negatively impact the state-building process in Afghanistan" and "weaken the government" (Oppel 2009; Anonymous, pers. comm.).

The consequence of the use of PSPs in Afghanistan is the provision of security as an excludable good and a decrease in the state's monopoly on force. Six different ways in which the market for force leads to these overarching consequences for the Afghan state can be identified: creation of future spoilers, undermining institutions, diversion of resources from ANSF development, diversion of resources to insurgents, increased cost of reconstruction, and insecurity.

Creation of Future Spoilers

The mandate of the Coalition Forces and ISAF is to support the Afghan government and the ANSF. However, by employing illegal militias, the international community strengthens their power relative to Afghan government institutions. The authority wielded by the heads of many PSPs surpasses that of provincial governors and police chiefs because they are better armed and funded. PSPs, especially unlicensed security companies and armed support groups, are dependent on short-term contracts with foreign entities and have no prospect of sustainability. Hence, when the foreign entities eventually leave or terminate their contracts, these entities are likely to refocus on illegal economic activities and will fight among themselves for market share—better trained and better armed than before.

Undermining Institutions

Many PSPs continue to serve as ready-made militias that compete with the state or otherwise protect the power and interests of their commanders. Employees for many private security companies, particularly registered companies headquartered in Kabul, are hired through an open recruitment process and, in theory, vetted by MoI's Criminal Investigation Department. Yet, PSPs are a relatively well-paid, readily available option open to former combatants that have either been excluded from—or failed by—the international community's disarmament, demobilization, and reintegration initiatives. Many have been lured back to PSPs, including those led by their former commanders.

Diversion of Resources from ANSF Development

There are visible indications that the private security arena is better armed and better paid than their counterparts in the ANP.[7] Although there are no concrete figures on the amount of money spent on private security, as contracts are either confidential or cannot be substantiated, several sources within the private security sector and the Afghan government estimated that 10–20 percent of reconstruction funding is spent on security. This would amount to USD 300–600 million per year, based on 2011 Official Development Assistance figures; however, this figure does not reflect the full scope of contracts from international military forces, embassies, nongovernmental organizations, and the private sector. One senior Afghan government official privately estimated the total value at three times that spent on the police and ANA salaries (Anonymous, pers. comm.). If correct, this would amount to USD 6–10 billion.

Diversion of Resources to Insurgents

Drug trafficking and other criminal activities in which commanders may be involved—and for which their militias provide security—is a lucrative source of illegal revenue that can then be used to bribe government officials and buy influence, strengthening shadow structures of authority. Taxation of PSPs escorting convoys and other scams on private transport and security are also an important source of funding for corrupt police and insurgents. The Kandak Amnianti Uruzgan, for example, secures protection "by paying a hefty toll to the policeman in charge of the road" (Kelly 2009).[8] Although transportation and construction companies, both international and national, are the main source of "protection" revenue, private security escorts also pay Taliban not to be attacked. According to a senior Afghan intelligence official, there are examples of PSPs paying as much as 60 percent of their gross profits from convoy security to the Taliban and other insurgent-cum-criminal groups for protection. An international analyst and a private security manager based in Afghanistan thought the usual rate was likely much lower, but did not discount the practice.

Increased Cost of Reconstruction

Private security also adds to the cost of reconstruction in Afghanistan, though it is a necessary cost of undertaking civilian reconstruction efforts in a highly insecure environment. According to the World Bank, contracted security increased the cost of highway reconstruction projects by between 3 percent and 15 percent (Ball et al. 2005: 29). Security concerns are routinely cited as the main impediment to implementation of development and reconstruction projects, effectively stunting the flow of aid (SIGAR 2009b). At the same time, amid worsening insecurity, maintaining the delivery of reconstruction assistance across the country—and the willingness of governmental, nongovernmental, and private reconstruction organizations to deploy staff to Afghanistan—depends upon the protection services of a range of private security entities.

Insecurity

Symbolically, ongoing abuses by—and lack of accountability of—PSPs demonstrates to the Afghan public that their security and well-being is not a priority for international forces or the Afghan government. Local commanders and their militias are a primary source of insecurity for Afghan citizens because they violate basic human rights with impunity (Ayub, Deledda, and Gossman 2009).

Conclusion

The majority of Afghans cannot afford private security. The existence of a credible and accountable public security force, sized and trained commensurate to the scale and nature of insecurity in Afghanistan, would mitigate the need for international donors to spend billions of dollars on the private security industry—above all on unaccountable illegal companies and armed support groups. Investing a greater share of current private security expenditure on the ANP would help break the cycle of insecurity and insurgency by better resourcing the police, disempowering illegal militias and weakening competitors to the state, and building public trust in public security.

Nonetheless, building a credible public security sector is a long-term process, one that will not address the immediate security needs of international and national stakeholders in Afghanistan. Nor, in the longer term, will it completely replace the market for PSCs. The role of the ANA and ANP is not to provide static and convoy security; placing them in that role would detract from their essential task of safeguarding public security and safety—and deteriorate their performance of these responsibilities. The goal, therefore, should be a private security sector that is better regulated and controlled by the government of Afghanistan and, critically, by the international community that constitutes their primary source of contracts and revenue.

Notes

1. There is, of course, a minority of the Afghan and foreign population who do benefit from instability—not least individuals who profit from the licit and illicit markets created or facilitated by armed conflict. Private security in the country falls well within the bounds of this category.

2. Many of these projects are necessary public goods—roads, schools, power stations—but others, undertaken in an effort to win "hearts and minds," have arguably fueled instability (Fishstein and Wilder 2012).

3. Between 2007 and 2009, 1,504 ANP were killed in action, compared to 568 ANA soldiers ("Factbox: Afghanistan National Security Forces" 2009).

4. To rectify this situation, police units were retrained through the Focused District Development program, which had shown promising results as of mid-2012. In February 2009, the U.S. Department of Defense assessed 19 percent of retrained units as capable of conducting missions on their own and 25 percent as capable of doing so with outside support. But, again, without enough trainers, rolling out the program countrywide will be impossible (U.S. GAO 2009).

5. In 2005, Afghanistan spent 56.5 percent of GDP on the security sector. Eighty percent of overall security expenditure in Afghanistan was directly executed by donors or their contractors through the external budget, instead of going through the core budget process of the Ministry of Finance (Ball et al. 2005: 23). These figures do not represent the authorized increase in the size of the ANA and ANP; as a result, the percentage of external expenditure has likely increased.

6. After the fall of the Taliban, Northern Alliance militia groups were organized into the Afghan Military Force, which nominally organized these disparate groups and brought them under the umbrella of the Ministry of Defense. In practice, however, the militias continued to operate independently, loyal to and serving the interests of their respective commanders. Viewed as a threat to the stability of Afghanistan and the post-Taliban Afghan state by the international community, the AMF was the target of disarmament, demobilization, and reintegration under the Afghanistan New Beginnings Program (ANBP), which ran from 2003 to 2006. ANBP was succeeded by the Disbandment of Illegal Armed Groups (DIAG) program, which targeted any independent militias—now considered illegal—that remained.

7. Following pay reforms, the salary for ANP patrolmen as of March 2009 was USD 100–110 per month (U.S. GAO 2009: 37); private security personnel on basic guard duty earn USD 200–300 per month (private security officer, Kabul, e-mail comm.).

8. According to Kelly (2009), Matiullah receives "at least $1700 USD . . . a truck to ensure each convoy arrives at its destination safely"; with about 200 trucks a month going to Tarin Kowt, this was worth nearly USD 340,000 per month in 2011.

References

Afghan Center for Socio-Economic and Opinion Research (ACSOR) Surveys. 2010. *Police Perception Survey*. Kabul: UNDP-Afghanistan.

Ayub, Fatima, Antonella Deledda, and Patricia Gossman. 2009. *Vetting Lessons for the 2009–10 Elections in Afghanistan*. New York: International Center for Transitional Justice.

Ball, Nicole, William Byrd, Peter Middlebrook, and Christopher Ward. 2005. *Improving Public Financial Management in the Afghan Security Sector*. Report No. 34582-AF. Washington, D.C.: World Bank.

Bumiller, Elisabeth. 2010. "U.S. General Cites Goals to Train Afghan Forces." *New York Times*, August 23.

"Factbox: Afghanistan National Security Forces." 2009. Reuters, March 27.

Fishstein, Paul, and Andrew Wilder. 2012. *Winning Hearts and Minds? Examining the Relationship Between Aid and Security in Afghanistan*. Medford, Mass.: Tufts University, Feinstein International Center.

"Karzai Abandons Plan to Scrap Private Security Firms." 2010. *BBC News*, December 6. http://www.bbc.co.uk/news/world-south-asia-11925855.

Kelly, Jeremy. 2009. "The Long Road to Tarin Kowt." *Australian*, April 28.

North Atlantic Treaty Organization. 2012. *Afghan National Security Forces (ANSF): Training and Development. Media Backgrounder*. Brussels: Public Diplomacy Division.

Oppel, Richard, Jr., and Sabrina Tavernise. 2010. "Strike Aimed at Militant in Pakistan, Officials Say." *New York Times*, January 15.

Oppel, Richard Jr. 2009. "Afghan Security Guards Are Blamed in a Gun Battle That Killed a Police Chief." *New York Times*, June 30.

Packer, George. 2008. "Kilcullen on Afghanistan: 'It's Still Winnable, but Only Just.'" *New Yorker*, November 14.

Sadeq Azad, Malyar. 2010. "Top Leaders Tied to Security Companies." Killid Group, August 21.

Schmeidl, Susanne. 2007. *The Privatization of Security in Afghanistan: When Nobody Guards the Guardians*. Bern, Switzerland: SwissPeace.

Schulman, Daniel. 2009. "The Cowboys of Kabul." *Mother Jones*, July 27.

United States Department of Defense. 2012. *Contractor Support of U.S. Operations in the USCENTCOM Area of Responsibility, Iraq, and Afghanistan, 4th Quarter FY 2012 Contractor Census*. Washington, D.C.: Government Printing Office.

United States Government Accountability Office. 2009. *Afghanistan Security: U.S. Programs to Further Reform Ministry of Interior and National Police Challenged by Lack of Military Personnel and Afghan Cooperation.* Washington, D.C.: Government Printing Office.

United States Government Accountability Office. 2011. *Afghan Army Growing, but Additional Trainers Needed; Long-term Costs Not Determined.* Washington, D.C.: Government Printing Office.

United States Office of the Special Inspector General for Afghanistan Reconstruction (SIGAR). 2009b. *January 30, 2009 Report to Congress.* Washington, D.C.: Government Printing Office.

Van Bijlert, Martine. 2001. "The Survival of the Private Security Companies." *Afghanistan Analysts Network Blog,* March 27. http://aan-afghanistan.com/index.asp?id=1582.

Vogt, Heidi, and Rahim Faiez. 2010. "Afghan Starts to Close Private Security Firms." Associated Press, October 3.

Zucchio, David. 2009. "Deadly Contractor Incident Sours Afghans." *Los Angeles Times,* August 13.

CHAPTER 8

China's Managed Market for Force

Jennifer Catallo

In 2004, the private security guard was officially listed as a legitimate occupation in the Chinese city of Shenzhen, "launching the so-called 'professionalization' of security service personnel" (Zhong and Grabosky 2009a: 14). The Chinese government's signing of the *Montreux Document*,[1] a document that contains rules and good practices relating to private security companies operating in armed conflict, further signals the government's legitimation of the private security industry (PSI). In signing the *Montreux Document* and listing private security as a legitimate occupation, the Chinese government has clearly accepted the PSI. Despite this evidence of liberalization in the market for security services, the Chinese case is by all accounts counterintuitive: The PSI in China is largely owned by subsidiaries of local branches of China's police force (public security bureau, or PSB) and—having retained a monopoly on force—the PSB provides both command and control for the market for force. In essence, China's market for force is distinct in that it is a managed quasi-private market for force. It thus defies the assumptions held about private/public categorizations, establishing a kind of "hybrid" market for force.[2]

However, evidence continues to mount forecasting a change in the structure of China's market for force. Until recently, foreign security firms were excluded from the Chinese market. However, the Chinese State Council enacted the Security Service Management Regulation Act on January 1, 2010, which opened the market for foreign firms. Seeking the opportunity, international private security companies like G4S consider the Asian market to be the way of the future, insisting that China is one key area for future market growth (G4S International 2007). This potential influx of foreign providers also changes the role of the PSB from helmsman to regulator. Only time will tell whether the government will effectively regulate China's market for force.

In the remainder of this chapter, I first examine how China's market for force developed partly in response to domestic security needs and in direct response to international privatization trends. I go on to establish the characteristics of China's market for force and identify the important role played by China's PSBs in controlling, operating, managing, and supervising China's market for force. Turning to the types of security providers participating in China's market for force, I examine the recent move toward privatization and the corresponding growth of domestic and international firms working to gain access to China's domestic market for force. With the increased presence of the Chinese government and (primarily extraction-based) companies working internationally in unstable regions, I investigate the security options available to these companies and the extent to which Chinese security companies have entered the international market. In the final section of the chapter, I examine the consequences of China's market for force domestically (i.e., the consequences for the Chinese state and its monopoly on force) and internationally (how China's market for force will fare when faced with competition). Acknowledging the unique character of China's managed market for force, I explore the benefits and potential drawbacks of this model.

Causes and Characteristics of China's Market for Force

This is not the first time that a market for force has developed within China. The historical record suggests that a market for force existed in China far more often than not throughout Chinese history. However, when the Chinese communists took power in 1949–50, they imposed such a strict monopoly on the use of force that the market for force ceased to exist in China (Bradshaw 2009). China's contemporary market for force is, therefore, a child of modern times, developed during the last three decades of economic reform (Zhong and Grabosky 2009a; Trevaskes 2007; Dutton 2005) and continuing to flourish as a consequence of the move toward privatization and a socialist market economic system.[3]

Today's market is characterized by its large size, its strict state control and ownership, its intentions to make social profits, and limited access for foreign firms. Each of these facets of the current Chinese market for force will be discussed below.

In early 2010, the Chinese government officially earmarked more than USD 50 million to combat internal threats, assigning a portion of this internal budget to the PSI (Moore 2010). In 2006, approximately four million authorized private security personnel operated throughout China, marking a 100 percent increase in personnel over the previous year (Trevaskes 2007: 38). Of the four million authorized private security personnel, Trevaskes maintains that 930,000 personnel worked for companies owned directly by China's PSBs, while the remaining three million personnel worked for "private companies," which are monitored and managed by the PSB (ibid.).

An important factor driving the industry's size in China was the increase in private foreign-owned enterprises' demand for private security companies. Foreign investors wanting to secure their enterprises did not want the "communist mass-line security forces," preferring instead "another form of security more in keeping with international business practice. The result was the development of a private security company system" (Zhong and Grabosky 2009a). Facilitating the need of the private sector for security was the fact that the economic reforms created economic and social strains, which led to growing tension between soaring crime and public resources (Trevaskes 2007: 40), requiring the development of extensive security services that could not be met exclusively by public sources. PSCs flourished in China because "the growth in crime . . . far outweighed the amount of public resources put into the public security regime" (Trevaskes 2007: 40).

However, this development was far from an unintended consequence of the privatization trend. The Chinese government had gathered experience with PSCs in 1985 in the Shenzhen special economic zone (SEZ). The Shenzhen SEZ was established by China's central government to serve as a laboratory for piloting policies associated with market-oriented reforms (Guo and Feng 2007: 6). The experiences of the Shenzhen SEZ showed that fast economic growth generated a series of benefits from employment, improved living standards, and reduced poverty (ibid.), yet also created the need for more security. This, in turn, resulted in the establishment of the first Chinese private security firm. Because it could be expected that the introduction of economic reforms on a broader scale would be accompanied by a rising demand for security that could not be met by the state alone, Premier Li Peng "publicly encouraged the development of private security firms" as early as 1986 (Liu 2005: 6).

A second important factor driving the growth of the private security sector in China is public demand. Part of the explanation for the growth of the private industry in the West is the turn of states' armed forces toward the market to provide various services (see Singer 2003; Avant 2005; Kinsey 2006; Carafano 2008; Isenberg 2008). China's People's Liberation Army (PLA) is not an exception to this trend. Chinese armies have historically participated in subsistence commerce; however, with the economic reforms, that "subsistence transformed into big business." Running more than 20,000 companies across all sectors in the Chinese economy, the PLA has been dubbed "PLA Inc." (Dietrich 2000).

As such, there are several contextual causes of force privatization in China. As a direct result of the PLA's privatization move, it has undergone complete modernization. In the area of logistics, the PLA has shifted from managing barracks and building maintenance to civilian companies (Payne 2008). The PLA is progressing toward privatizing procurement, transportation, and building construction. Another important driver for privatization was the need to keep pace with U.S. military transformation. The privatization of several components of PLA logistics is similar to how the U.S. military shifted many of its own logistics responsibilities to private sector vendors (ibid.). The PLA is also increasingly engaging in cyber/strategic information warfare, which requires expertise offered by the PSCs in technically sophisticated areas such as the operation of complex weapons systems, logistics, personal protection, and intelligence gathering (Deschamps 2005: 37).

Quasi-Private Managed Market for Force with Intentions to Make Social Profits

Officially, private security companies are classified as state-owned assets and are hierarchically organized under the control of PSBs. PSBs directly and indirectly control the thirty general parent companies established in each of China's thirty provincial jurisdictions that oversee the set-up and management of many private security companies (Trevaskes 2007: 44). Staffing appointments and management roles across these parent firms are controlled and must be approved by PSBs (ibid.). While maintaining a monopoly over the management, regulation, and establishment of private security companies via general parent companies across provincial jurisdictions, PSBs operate under the guidance of the Ministry of Public Security. In 2000, the Ministry of Public Security defined private security companies as "a force that operates under the direct leadership and management of the public security organs that protect public order, and prevents and controls illegal and criminal activities" (as cited in Trevaskes 2007: 43). The Chinese government defines security as a public good and expects the PSI to protect this public good.

Another link between the government and PSCs is the China Security and Protection Industry Association (CSPIA). CSPIA is a trade association for the security industry. It was founded in 1992 by the governing body of the Ministry of Public Security for China and considers itself a bridge between governments and enterprises.[4] The association maintains strong links with the government and acknowledges the importance of a strong relationship between PSCs and government to improve safety and security.

Although private security companies often work at the behest of China's PSBs, Chinese private security companies act as for-profit enterprises, funded through private investment and contracted to provide specific tasks for monetary reward. Chinese private security companies function within a market economy, with both public and private customers contracting out their services. The services offered range from guarding, surveillance work, patrolling venues, and providing bodyguard services, to armed guard transportation and security consulting.

This particular relationship between the for-profit industry and the PSB constitutes a hybrid security industry. The reason for this particular organization is a noteworthy idiosyncrasy of the Chinese market for force. According to the Chinese government, private security companies play a dual role. Acting as for-profit enterprises tasked with seeking monetary reward, private security companies in China are also required to *make social profits*, that is, to maintain social order and prevent crime (Liu 2005: 25–27). The emphasis placed on making social profits is stipulated across a range of government regulations that deal with the PSI (see Liu 2005; Zhong and Grabosky 2009a). The stipulation for making both social and traditional profits demonstrates that China's PSCs are largely influenced by the country's socioeconomic make-up and cultural norms and that security is considered to be a public good according to those cultural norms. Private security companies are expected to serve the needs of the Chinese police and Chinese society as a whole. Xiamen Security Services Company, for example, assists the Xiamen PSB with special crackdowns and anti-vice raids by dispatching twenty quality security guards free of charge perennially (Zhong and Grabosky 2009a: 8).

However, the grip of the state bureaucracy is not as tight as it appears at first sight. First, the PSC market is not only hierarchically organized, but also *vertically* organized across municipalities. It is this vertical organization that renders the total authority of PSBs questionable. Across municipalities there continues to be an influx of private security companies spreading to an "unchecked degree." According to Zhong and Grabosky (2009a: 15), a "substantial number of localities have made their own laws on the security service industry." Some even allow private enterprises, not only public security organs, to establish security service companies.

Second, there is a growing black market beyond the control of the Chinese government. Many companies are failing to meet the PSB and Ministry requirements. In Guangxi province, for example, the Guangxi government has made various efforts to respond to the increasing concerns over the high number of black market companies in its region (Trevaskes 2007: 51). Another example is seen in Hunan, where "limited liability companies" have been established to deal with the increasing growth of companies that do not conform to the PSB hierarchical structure and to quell the potential growth and further development of a private security black market. There have also been attempts to create joint ventures with firms such as the Xi'an Transportation Company (Zhong and Grabosky 2009a: 18). Finally, some companies in Yunnan have moved toward a complete detachment from public security organs (ibid.). It is not surprising that a shift in the market for force has occurred that requires the government to take less of a monopolistic role and more of a regulative one.[5]

I maintain that the Chinese government attempts to simultaneously privatize and control private force, characterizing the market for force in the country as a hybrid market and making it difficult for foreign firms to enter the market. The international trends toward privatization have influenced the move by the Chinese government to open up the private security market. Opening the industry has been an effort on the part of the Chinese government to be in line with China's WTO agreement.[6]

The PSB's deliberate shift within the last ten years into a supervisory role had a significant impact on the domestic market. Zhong and Grabosky (2009a: 18) describe the changing role of the PSB as being from "rowing" to "steering." The shifting role of the PSB is most clearly evident in the 2008 Ordinance on the Management of Security Services issued by the Legislative Affairs Office of the State Council. The Ordinance removes the preconditions that limit the establishment of private security companies via PSBs and shifts the preconditions for establishing a security service company. Applicants now can obtain a license from city and provincial public security organs to provide security services (ibid.: 19). The intention is to move away from a monopoly on private security, with the Chinese government intending to play a supervisory and regulatory role in the face of increasing demands for private security (see Wang 2006; "Security Legislation Has Been Completed" 2006).

However, this legislation suffers from many shortfalls. At the time of writing, application forms for security licenses and the government departments necessary to process these licenses had not yet been created, and the general Chinese bureaucracy was limiting the ease with which to access these licenses in the interim (Anonymous, pers. comm.). When asked about the new Chinese legislation, a sub-Asian regional program manager for a multinational private security company acknowledged that the "implementation of private security legislation is not progressing because as with many things in China implementation is . . . frequently thwarted, diluted or twisted . . . by the various regions, districts and localities" (ibid.). Furthermore, although the legislation is meant to limit the public security organs to regulators, many continue to retain an interest in private security companies, partly because of their previous connections and partly because of their personal investments. Zhong and Grabosky (2009a: 15) maintain that across Chinese government policy documents pertaining to the PSI from as early as 1988 up to the most recent 2010 regulations, the government is explicit that security service companies and the public security police must retain independence from each other (particularly in finance and accounting systems). Yet, there is a "glaring disjuncture" between the Chinese government's policies and regulations and what occurs on the ground, as a survey of twenty-six provinces shows. In some provinces in 2007, 10 percent of the turnover of security service companies and 70 percent of their profits were taken away by public security organs (ibid.). In addition, a "revolving door" effect further contradicts official policy, as many senior officers from China's PSB are retiring and moving into the business (Bardsley 2011).

Another important step to further liberalization was taken on January 1, 2010, when the Chinese State Council enacted the Security Service Management Regulation, which opened the market for foreign security firms. However, foreign firms are also affected by the lack of an application procedure for security licenses and, in addition, are limited to owning only general security service companies, which offer services like guarding offices and residential complexes. They "cannot work with organizations or institutions related to national security or state secrets" (Yanrong 2010). The new legislation has received mixed receptions from the security industry.

Some have expressed skepticism about future opportunities in the market. The Public Affairs Director for a large multinational private security company commented that the situation may not be as conducive as one might expect with the changing regulations (Anonymous interview, 2010). Having initially created private security companies while leaving foreign companies out of the market, the local police still retain jurisdiction (both through a licensing regime and investment options). Each local police bureau has set out how to regulate foreign private security companies with quite different stipulations and requirements, which frustrates foreign companies because of the navigational costs associated with these often diverse stipulations. Even if foreign private security companies have taken the appropriate steps to complete applications for a license in China, as of the time of writing no licenses had been publicly granted. According to this official, the main problem is that there is little incentive for the local police to facilitate foreign security licenses or investment (ibid.).

However, the bulk of industry representatives do not seem to share this skepticism. The CEO of the Danish security firm G4S assures investors of the potential for market growth within China. He compares the situation with the position when his company first entered India eighteen years ago. "We started from scratch and we've now got 120,000 staff doing all sorts of services, ranging from security and cleaning to chauffeuring and catering" (cited in Petrie 2008: 36). The expansion of G4S in China seems to have proven him right. Despite the licensing problem, G4S teamed up with Beijing Security, which has 110,000 security officers and was the only provider of security for the 2008 Beijing Olympics. Through the arrangement, G4S was able to operate in China and could direct some of Beijing Security's staff on its behalf.

Alf Goeransson, CEO of the Swedish security service provider Securitas, considers the possibilities in China to be fantastic. "There are plenty of market opportunities, plenty of customers. The problem for us right now is getting personnel, getting the guards licensed. They must be licensed and that's not so easy with the Chinese bureaucracy" (cited in Kinnander 2010). Already Securitas employs hundreds of guards in China and is looking to pursue—and compete with G4S for—more security contracts in China.

It appears to even be possible to break into the closely guarded military security market. Take, for instance, ADEN Services, which offers a range of services in China including close protection services, risk management, and maritime security "with a team of former Navy Soldiers ready for individual missions" (ADEN Services 2014).

In short, many firms consider it worthwhile to enter the Chinese market, as it appears to be booming. Although private security has expanded globally, the expansion of the industry in China has been particularly marked. In Hong Kong, there are about four times as many private security guards as there are police officers, greater than the typical proportion for most countries of two to three private security personnel for each officer. Additionally, the Ministry of Public Security has indicated that there are 2,767 registered companies generating USD 1.2 billion annually (cited in Bardsley 2011). With private security being used to protect commercial buildings and wealthy individuals in addition to being mandated by the Chinese government to protect schools (from elementary to universities), more options will be needed than those offered by the PSB. Because almost every enterprise is in need of some kind of security service, the government alone cannot meet market demand.

Consequences: The Future of
China's Managed Market for Force

As noted above with regard to the stipulation that Chinese PSCs must make both social and traditional profits, China's PSCs are clearly influenced by the country's socioeconomic make-up and cultural norms, and security is considered to be a public good according to those cultural norms. However, as China's market for force shifts, with government as regulator rather than helmsman, there is likely to be a slight shift in the control of force away from the state. That is, as the PSCs follow the "unsteady path of globalization, where demand and supply are not so easy to control" (Trevaskes 2007: 51), the responsibility for public order (i.e., social control) may shift to the unsteady hands of the market. Because the industry is profit driven, only those who can afford the industry's services may be provided with the advantages of the industry. In other words, the provision of security as a public good may decrease, furthering divisions across Chinese society.

This has not occurred as of yet, though it is a distinct possibility in the future. China's market for force is still managed by the state to a substantial extent, which allows the government continued (though not complete) control to exercise power over the market. Therefore, issues of accountability concerning the PSI may be offset because of the institutionalized role of the government in China's market for force. Although the market appears to have had a fairly neutral impact on the state's monopoly on force and the provision of security as a public good up to the present, balancing the role of the market and the state will be instrumental to the success of China's market for force in the future.

The Chinese government may continue to own and invest in private security firms. Yet, if it refrains from separating the private and public security organs, PSB firms will likely continue to retain a monopoly over the PSI, which will, in turn, facilitate less competition, ensure fewer incentives for high standards in areas like training, and provoke growth in black market private security companies able to meet the growing demand for security. Commentators have acknowledged that the market for force in China may itself be a source of insecurity, especially when the media frequently reports crimes committed by security guards accused of working with organized crime groups to illegally detain protestors in "black jails" (see Jingjing 2010). News reports further describe guards as undisciplined, poorly trained, and often used as heavies hired to assist in winning disputes (see Foreman 2009; Zhong and Grabosky 2009a: 16). Furthermore, security companies continue to operate in a legal gray zone between public and private sectors, either in cooperation with the PSB or as part of the private security black market. The move to open the PSI to foreign and domestic enterprises and the new role played by government as regulator may provide the necessary competition to ensure better trained personnel, more transparency, and less abuse across the industry. Opening the PSI to foreign enterprises is perceived by the PSB as threatening to its interests, limiting the extent to which it has come to embrace its new role as regulator. The move to separate the PSI from public security both in terms of finance and management will likely be instrumental in facilitating a competitive, transparent, and accountable PSI in China.

Since the opening of China's market for force provides Chinese firms with the option to render their services overseas, enterprising private eyes in China—many of them military veterans or former police officers—are in a position to invest in China's domestic and international market for force. With state-owned enterprises working in conflict and post-conflict areas around the world and suffering from attacks, kidnappings, and general instability, there is a potential advantage to both entering the international PSI and using the services offered by home-based companies. The problem, of course, is that smaller Chinese firms and individual entrepreneurs who work in conflict and post-conflict areas will be unable to afford private security for even an advisory relationship, thus exacerbating inequality as security becomes less and less of a public good.

Conclusion

China's turn to a socialist market economy with its extensive economic reforms has created an opportunity for a Chinese PSI to develop and flourish. Officially classified as a for-profit service industry, China's PSI is required to seek economic profits and to also make social profits by maintaining social order and assisting in the prevention of crime (see Trevaskes 2007: 40; Zhong and Grabosky 2009b: 447). Security, originally provided by public institutions including the PSB, is now provided by a hybrid market for force. Although public institutions remain and compete with private institutions, the future structure of China's market for force will include a regulatory role for the government and a for-profit service industry role for private firms. Balancing these two roles will be instrumental to the success of China's market for force.

The opening up of the PSI to foreign and domestic firms further pushes China toward a managed market for force. Obstacles abound, ranging from the lack of infrastructure available to approve license applications to the continued embedded interest of the PSB. Although such obstacles will likely make entering the Chinese market difficult at best, overcoming those obstacles will be instrumental to future market growth for the PSI. The hybrid market for force, with an administrative and regulative capacity already in place via the government, may prove to be capable of overcoming issues often associated with unregulated markets, such as lack of quality personnel training and accountability. Therefore, although security is still very much envisioned to be a public good even as the Chinese PSI grows, the growth of this market has the potential to diminish the public nature of security in this country. Whether the Chinese government is able to maintain some control over the use of force will determine the extent to which security becomes a private good in China. Chinese history, culture, and norms all indicate that the government may, indeed, be able to retain some degree of control over the use of force, while contextual and legislative/ regulatory factors point to continued challenges to the state's monopoly on force.

Notes

1. The full title is *Montreux Document on Pertinent International Legal Obligations and Good Practices for States Related to Operations of Private Military and Security Companies During Armed Conflict.* The document's signing occurred four years after the private security guard was officially listed as a legitimate occupation in the Chinese city of Shenzhen.

2. It is noteworthy that, similar to the Czech Republic case in Chapter 5, force in the context of the Chinese market is "officially" at the lower end of the force spectrum and usually not deadly or lethal. Chinese citizens and private security personnel are prohibited from even owning firearms, with the exception of security companies providing transportation security (Zhong and Grabosky 2009a: 13). However, this has not stopped PSCs from purchasing and using arms in their daily business (ibid.). Cases of excessive force occur (Trevaskes 2007: 45), and companies "even promote [the sales of] guns through public advertisements" (Zhong and Grabosky 2009a: 13). Thus, unofficially, the Chinese market for force stretches across both the nonlethal and lethal spectrums of force.

3. The maritime sector also drives demand for PSCs in Asia. Employed to secure commercial vessels, offshore energy installations, and container terminals and ports, PSCs are said to fill an important void in the protection against rebels, terrorists, and/ or piracy. An in-depth exploration of the demand for PSCs in the maritime sector is beyond the scope of this chapter, but the reader can consult Carolin Liss 2005.

4. This is an additional indication that even privately provided security has been considered a public good in China. For further details, see the CSPIA website (http:// english.21csp.com.cn).

5. The Beijing PSB now requires all private security companies to be registered. This registration is, in part, a response to efforts made by some private security companies to illegally detain citizens who legally petition the Chinese government (Brown and Smith 2012). Petitioning exists to provide a channel for citizens to present their grievances to government officials, and citizens often use the petitioning system to seek redress for perceived wrongs (i.e., issues in local corruption and land compensation). A private security company, Anyuanding, was exposed for being under contract by local governments to block petitioners from petitioning to central authorities in Beijing (ibid.). This company was accused of employing a variety of methods, including "coercion, pressure, abduction, detention in 'black jails' [extralegal detention

facilities] for extended periods of time, and beatings" (ibid.). In response, the Beijing municipal PSBs launched an official six-month crack down on illegal detentions of petitioners by private security companies (ibid.).

6. In December 2001, the Chinese government instituted a series of broad reforms and accession commitments required by the WTO. China's commitments range from significant reductions in tariffs to opening up critical service sectors like banking, insurance, and securities to international and domestic investors (for further details, see Lardy 2001).

References

ADEN Services. 2014. "Yacht and Marina Security." Accessed May 12, 2014. http://security.adenservices.com/en/yacht-marina-security.

Avant, Deborah. 2005. *The Market for Force: The Consequences of Privatizing Security.* New York: Cambridge University Press.

Bardsley, Daniel. 2011. "China's New Wealthy on Guard." *National Online,* January 17.

Bradshaw, Richard. 2009. "A Review of *Mercenaries: The History of a Norm in International Relations,* by Sarah Percy." *Mercenary Matters,* January 25.

Brown, Senator Sherrod, and Representative Christopher Smith. 2012. *Beijing Cracks Down on Private Security Companies Used to Detain Petitioners.* Washington, D.C.: Congressional-Executive Commission on China.

Carafano, James Jay. 2008. *Private Sector, Public Wars: Contractors in Combat—Afghanistan, Iraq, and Future Conflicts.* Westport, Conn: Praeger.

Deschamps, Sebastian. 2005. *Toward the Use of Private Military Companies in the United Nations Peacekeeping Operations.* COTIPSO thesis, Peace Operations Training Institute.

Dietrich, Chris. 2000. "The Commercialization of Military Deployment in Africa." *African Security Review* 9(1): 3–17.

Dutton, Michael. 2005. "Toward a Government of the Contract: Policing in the Era of Reform." In *Crime, Punishment and Policing in China,* ed. Borge Bakken, 189–233. Toronto: Rowman & Littlefield.

Foreman, William. 2009. "Security Guards a Source of Insecurity in China." Associated Press, September 4.

Guo, Wanda, and Yueqiu Feng. 2007. *Special Economic Zones and Competitiveness: A Case Study of Shenzhen, the People's Republic of China.* PRM Policy Note, Series No. 2. Manila: Asia Development Bank.

G4S International. 2007. *Opening Up in China.* Accessed September 20, 2009. http://www.g4s.com.

Isenberg, David. 2008. *Shadow Force.* Westport, Conn.: Praeger.

Jingjing, Xuyang. 2010. "Black Jail Company Chiefs Allegedly Detained by Cops." *Global Times,* September 27.

Kinnander, Ola. 2010. "Securitas Seeks Purchases for Push into More Markets." *Bloomberg Business Week Online,* May 27.

Kinsey, Christopher. 2006. *Corporate Soldiers and International Security: The Rise of Private Military Companies*. New York: Routledge.

Lardy, Nicholas R. 2001. *Issues in China's WTO Accession*. Testimony Before the U.S.-China Security Review Commission, May 9. Washington, D.C.: Brookings Institution.

Liss, Carolin. 2005. *Private Security Companies in the Fight Against Piracy in Asia*. Working Paper No. 120. Perth: Murdock University, Asia Research Centre.

Liu, Shanxun. 2005. *Bao'an Qinwu* [The Work of Private Security]. Beijing: Renmin Gongan Daxue Chubasnshe.

Moore, Malcolm. 2010. "China Spends Record Amount Targeting Domestic Security Threats." *Telegraph*, March 29.

Payne, Captain David. 2008. "Chinese Logistics Modernization." *Army Logistician: Professional Bulletin of United States Army Logistics* 40(4):10–11.

Petrie, Anne. 2008. "Nick Buckles Interview." *Business Voice* (April): 34–38.

"Security Legislation Has Been Completed, Private Person Can Establish Bodyguard Company." 2006. *Qingdao Evening News*, December 15.

Singer, Peter W. 2003. *Corporate Warriors: The Rise of the Privatized Military Industry*. Ithaca, N.Y.: Cornell University Press.

Trevaskes, Susan. 2007. "The Private/Public Security Nexus in China." *Social Justice* 34(3–4): 38–55.

Wang, D. D. 2006. 保安服务业管理条理即将破茧 [Security Service Regulations Ready to Come]. Accessed September 24, 2008. http://www.ycwb.com/myjjb /2006-09/28/content_1229496.htm.

Yanrong, Zhao. 2010. "China Unlocks Door to Foreign Security Firms." *China Daily*, January 28.

Zhong, Lena Yueying, and Peter Grabosky. 2009a. *The Changing Role of the State in the Private Security Industry in China: From Rowing to Steering*. Working Paper. Canberra: ARC Centre of Excellence in Policing and Security.

Zhong, Lena Yueying, and Peter Grabosky. 2009b. "The Pluralization of Policing and the Rise of Private Policing in China." *Crime, Law and Social Change* 52: 433–55.

CHAPTER 9

The Canadian Market for Force

Christopher Spearin

Near the turn of the last century, then–Canadian Prime Minister Jean Chrétien asserted that Canadians were "boy scouts" best suited to peacekeeping
(cited in "East Timor Troops Need More Power" 1999: A1). However, the
international strategic shift instigated by the terrorist attacks against the
United States a few years later increasingly placed the exclusivity—and perhaps even the political utility—of this orientation in doubt. The Canadian
Forces (CF) became more robust, and the Canadian government applied
them in activities found toward the higher end of the conflict spectrum. For
the domestic audience, the Canadian government instigated this shift, in
part, in the hope of ensuring the security of Canadians at home. For international audiences, this shift was to enhance the strategic relevance of Canada and to display Canada's bona fides as a reliable and responsible actor. In
this vein, to help advance Canada's stature further, the Canadian Department of Foreign Affairs and International Trade (DFAIT) and the Canadian
International Development Agency (CIDA), alongside the CF and the Canadian Department of National Defence (DND), attempted to become more
integrated actors in their execution of whole-of-government policies in unstable environments.

One should view the contemporary Canadian market for force with its
neoliberal contours in this context. This chapter argues that the security politics of the 1990s, which featured declining budgets and military personnel
rosters and the adoption of neoliberal economic initiatives, instigated the Canadian government's turn toward privatization. The increasing reliance on
potentially lethal private military and security company (PMSC) services co-
incided with the aforementioned desire to have a greater impact on the world

stage, despite the CF's quantitative limitations. Indeed, the Canadian government has relied on both foreign and Canadian PMSCs to protect CF, DFAIT, and CIDA personnel in many parts of the world, and especially in Afghanistan. In providing additional options to the CF and the Canadian government as they seek to project Canadian power abroad, the Canadian market for force has increased Canada's ability to apply the use of force. Nevertheless, there are some negative implications regarding this monopoly and the provision of security as a public good that Canadian officials have attempted to address through financial, managerial, and regulatory policy measures.

Characteristics of the Canadian Market for Force

To begin, the Canadian market for force has five distinct features. First, there is a noncorporate segment. To be more specific, there are a number of Canadian security personnel available for hire in the country's labor market. However, many of these security specialists do not work for Canadian PMSCs, but for U.S.- and U.K.-based PMSCs. Second, there is a corporate market segment, in that there are Canadian PMSCs. Globe Risk International, for instance, is based in Canada. Other firms, like Tundra SCA, have Canadian-Afghan ownership. There are also larger conglomerates, like Garda, contributing to the Canadian market for force. In recent years, Garda has purchased other firms, such as Kroll Security International and Vance International. Such acquisitions increased Garda's workforce to 50,000. They also brought with them high-profile contracts, such as the provision of security for British diplomats and USAID personnel in Iraq.

Third, Canadian regulations governing Canadian PMSCs are minimal and untailored. This conforms to a free and open neoliberal marketplace. For Canadian firms, only general regulations like the Canada Business Corporations Act and the Income Tax Act cover them; no specific regulations exist that identify the unique qualities of these firms or the potential implications of their operations (Maidment 2008: 10–11). Similarly, the Export and Import Permits Act includes Canada's Export Control List and Canada's Area Control List, which cover both exported defense goods and intended recipients. This act, however, focuses primarily on hardware; it pertains only to services associated with exported equipment.

Fourth, Canadians and Canadian PMSCs serve a wide variety of international clientele. This is in keeping with the economic desires of Canada's wider defense and security industry to service more than just Canadian requirements. In particular, this Canadian industry is based upon access to American clientele (Spearin 2005: 1106).

Last, as for Canadian usage, arguably the most important driver behind the Canadian market for force is the Canadian government. In Afghanistan, the CF employed PMSCs to protect installations, forward operating bases, convoys, and road construction projects and to provide security details after incidents involving CF personnel. For base security specifically, it contracted five firms during combat operations—including the aforementioned Tundra SCA, which earned approximately CAD 5.3 million. Other assessments contend that in Afghanistan, DFAIT and DND employed eleven PMSCs from 2006–2011 at a cost of CAD 41 million ("Canada Spends $41M on Hired Guns" 2011). This included American firms such as Blue Hackle and British companies such as Saladin Security, Hart Security, and ArmorGroup. As for CIDA, it utilized the Canadian PMSC Globe Risk International and Watan Risk Management, an Afghan-based PMSC, to provide security for the Dahla Dam project, one of the Canadian government's signature initiatives. Outside of Afghanistan, DFAIT contracted Garda in September 2010 to provide security for Canadian embassy and diplomatic staff in Haiti, an important country to Canada for both domestic and international political reasons. Similarly, PMSCs also provide security for Canadian embassies in Central America.

The remaining discussion of the Canadian market for force will focus mainly on the significant segment of the market catering to the Canadian government.

Causes and Development of the Canadian Market for Force

The initial development of the Canadian market for force with its neoliberal characteristics is rooted in the security politics of the Canadian government in the early 1990s. On the financial side, DND's budget dropped by 23 percent and its real purchasing power declined by 30 percent during the 1990s. These reductions, some of the largest among NATO members, led to the decline or elimination of CF capabilities. On the manpower side, the 1994 Defence White Paper dropped the CF from 88,000 to 60,000 personnel. In fact, by the early 2000s, the CF's effective military strength was 52,000. Yet from 1996 to 2001, despite the funding drop, the government deployed double the number of CF personnel abroad for six months or longer than it did from 1990 to 1996 (Cohen 2003: 53). Afterward, with considerable commitments both in Bosnia and Afghanistan at the start of 2002, the government had to significantly downgrade the CF's involvement in Afghanistan in order to regenerate forces (Granatstein 2004: 171–72). What is more, subsequent quality of life issues impacted recruitment and retention efforts negatively; these were already under strain given the way DND instituted the quick decrease in manpower.

At the same time, the government's overcommitting of the CF adversely affected training. With the CF focused more on operations, trainers were not always available for established units, thus forcing the cancellation of exercises and training programs. The lack of personnel and resources affected recruit intake and basic training systems as well, thus prompting many applicants to leave the CF prematurely (Cohen 2003: 52; Wattie 2003: A10; Blanchfield 2008: A4; O'Neil 2007: A13; Canada Standing Committee on National Defence 2006). Hence, in 2002, the Council for Canadian Security in the 21st Century rightly assessed that "because cuts in the CF establishment were not matched by cuts in operational tempo, 'leaner' did not translate into 'meaner' and the military became more thinly stretched than ever" (23).

In order to mitigate these challenges, DND embraced Alternative Service Delivery (ASD). Like neoliberal economic policies followed in other countries, ASD pertained to the cost-effective spending of limited tax dollars through, among other initiatives, privatization, contracting out, and public-private partnerships (Detomasi 2002; Cohen 2003: 47; DND 1994: ch. 7).

Collectively, DND's responses during the 1990s and into the twenty-first century led to a number of private military training and logistical support arrangements. For instance, several air training programs—NATO Flying Training in Canada, Contracted Flying Training and Support, and Contracted Airborne Training Services—became the purview of companies such as L-3 Communications, Phoenix Air, Bombardier Aerospace, Kelowna Flightcraft, and Top Aces (now Discovery Air Defence Systems). ATCO-Frontec, as another example, maintains and operates the Northern Warning System that feeds information directly into the North American Aerospace Command. The CF employs U.S. firms to help teach parachute skills at Canadian Forces Base (CFB) Trenton. As well, DND has sought private contractors to train CF personnel on the LAV-III armored vehicle at CFB Gagetown.

Although the CF's use of private companies provides the extra manpower to train both incoming and current personnel and to relieve operational strains, it does present challenging implications. This approach runs somewhat contrary to ASD in that the goal is to compensate for limited resources and not necessarily to economize. In 2006, the then–Chief of the Land Staff, Lieutenant-General Andrew Leslie, offered this reflection on private trainers to the Standing Parliamentary Committee on National Defence: "With regard to privatization of certain activities within the military, when it makes sense to do so and it's only a function of money, then I am absolutely in favor of it, so that we can free up soldiers to do the soldier activities for which they're trained" (cited in Canada Standing Committee on National Defence 2006).

The desire of the Liberal and later Conservative governments of the 2000s to respond to Canada's strategic decline was an important factor shifting the Canadian market for force toward lethality. To expand, they sent the CF to Afghanistan to participate explicitly in ground combat operations for the first time since the Korean War. In fact, compared to other NATO allies, Canada shouldered a considerable amount of risk over a longer period of time; Afghanistan was Canada's "longest war." As well, Prime Minister Stephen Harper's Conservative government, in particular, put more weight on the CF's participation in NATO operations rather than on those directly under the United Nations.[1] Furthermore, though funding was cut in 2012 due to austerity measures, the Conservative government did introduce the largest increase in defense spending in twenty years.

For Canadian military officials, the government's call was an opportunity to remake the CF's image for domestic and international audiences alike; the CF were to be seen as well-resourced and robust fighters rather than as underfunded peacekeepers. General Rick Hillier, Canada's Chief of Defence Staff (2005–8), who referred to the 1990s as the CF's "decade of darkness," suggested that the CF could "offer our government more options to pile on in such a way that we get the profile and we get the credit for it" (cited in Geddes 2006). General Hillier was also blunt about how the CF could contribute as a unique Canadian actor: "We're not the public service of Canada; we're not just another department. We are the Canadian Forces, and our job is to be able to kill people" (cited in "The Essential Rick Hillier" 2008). As for Afghan insurgents, the general employed very "unpeacekeeper-like" language: "These are detestable murderers and scumbags. . . . We're not going to let these radical murderers and killers rob from others and certainly we're not going to let them rob from Canada" (cited in Leblanc 2006: A1). In fact, among NATO allies, General Hillier was insistent on the CF's 2005 operational shift from relatively safe Kabul to more dangerous Kandahar (Saunders 2006: A12).

This is not to suggest, however, that the shift from peacekeeper to war fighter means that the CF and the Canadian government do not wish to promote security as a public good overseas. Instead, the CF is to do so in a robust manner. Advancing security as a public good is to come about through the CF's operations on its own terms and by helping to implement the agendas of the CF's whole-of-government partners.

Continued manpower challenges, however, confront this shift even with recruitment efforts. For instance, approximately 80 percent of CF manpower in Afghanistan has come from the Canadian Army, an organization that in 2009 was short by 700 officers and 700 noncommissioned officers. Thus, in recent years, CF recruitment has targeted combat arms positions in the army's infantry and armored units. As well, Prime Minister Paul Martin's government wanted to increase the CF by 5,000 and Prime Minister Harper's government, upon its 2006 election, announced the CF would be 75,000 strong. Nevertheless, the CF has had to reassess and lengthen the timelines regarding its ability to increase its ranks, and the government has had to reduce its expansion plans to 70,000. Even then, 2009 government budgetary documents indicated that developing a 70,000-strong CF may take until 2028 (Brewster 2009).

In this context, the Canadian market for force offers some much-needed relief. By 2011, some Canadian Army personnel were on their fifth rotation into Afghanistan—an incredibly taxing institutional commitment (Blanchfield 2009: A3). On the one hand, Prime Minister Harper has asserted that such a commitment reveals Canadian mettle on the world stage and garners Canada international acclaim: "Countries that cannot or will not make real contributions to global security are not regarded as serious players . . . . They may be liked by everybody. They may be pleasantly acknowledged by everybody. But when the hard decisions get made, they will be ignored by everybody" (cited in Clark 2008). On the other hand, Canada's specific commitment to Afghanistan would not have been as robust without PMSC participation. Given the CF's limitations, Brigadier-General Denis Thompson, the commander of Task Force Kandahar in 2008, observed that "without private security firms it would be impossible to achieve what we are achieving here. . . . We just don't have the numbers to do everything" (cited in Galloway 2008).

"Not doing everything" also fits well with recasting the CF's image; employing PMSCs for defensive purposes leaves CF personnel free to conduct offensive activities. As discussed elsewhere, the PMSC industry has increasingly emphasized its defensive credentials for both normative and commercial reasons (Spearin 2010). A CF spokesperson keenly upheld this distinction in 2007: "The Canadian Forces does not use any private security contractors to conduct offensive operations. . . . Using private security contractors for specific tasks permits Canadian Forces personnel to focus their efforts on those duties where they bring the greatest value to the mission" (cited in Mayeda 2007: A5). In 2009, another spokesperson similarly observed that PMSCs "are integral to the security of Canadian personnel and enable the Canadian forces to focus their efforts on those duties where they provide the greatest value to the mission" (cited in Galloway 2009).

Consequences of the Canadian Market for Force

The Canadian market for force has increased the options available for the projection of force and is one of the elements helping to augment Canada's international presence. At the same time, the Canadian government's use of the market for force has not yet been as extensive as, for instance, the use of the market by the governments of the United Kingdom or United States (see Chapters 4 and 10). As such, private market actors have not challenged the authority of Canadian military commanders to the extent seen in some other countries.

There are, nevertheless, two challenges related to state authority and/or promoting security as a public good. One relates to the neoliberal marketplace. Just as the government freely enters into, and thus helps to substantiate, the Canadian market for force, former CF personnel can easily enter into the marketplace, either working for Canadian firms or, more likely as noted above, for foreign companies. Given the industry's longstanding reliance on special operations forces (SOF) as identified elsewhere, there has been a drain on the CF's SOF in recent years, especially its elite unit JTF-2 (Spearin 2007; Pugliese 2005). This has come at a time when the Canadian government has increasingly relied upon the CF's SOF capabilities, particularly in Afghanistan. As such, the shift from public to private caught the attention of the Canadian Senate and catalyzed remuneration and benefit increases in order to maintain both overall manpower levels and small unit cohesion. Though the activities and interworkings of Canadian SOF are notoriously secretive, one can argue that manpower challenges would affect whether the Canadian government could apply force in order to obtain various policy objectives abroad. Additionally, Canadian SOF still have North American responsibilities, from domestic counterterrorism efforts to helping to secure major international events (e.g., the 2010 Olympic Winter Games in Vancouver). Though the CF and its SOF are not the only or primary providers of security as a public good domestically, manpower challenges along with multiple operations pull at the fabric.

Second, and returning to the international context, the Canadian market for force has, arguably, contributed to a mixed record regarding promoting security as a public good in Afghanistan. As a consumer of security services in Afghanistan, Canada experienced many of the negative consequences identified in Chapter 7, especially those linked to employment of Afghans by PMSCs. As I have noted elsewhere, the Canadian government was initially concerned with how the CF and other government partners could promote security as a public good, to the neglect of considering its reliance on the market for force (Spearin 2008). In fact, utilizing Afghans in private security roles was a way to employ idle men and hopefully prevent them from joining the Taliban. However, as the CF over time placed greater emphasis on training Afghan security sector personnel, the zero-sum effects of the public/private divide became evident. Indeed, Canadian Major-General Michael Ward, who served as Deputy Commander for Police Development and Training of the NATO Training Mission, identified that "if they're all going across the street to earn more money [with] a competitor who can afford to pay more . . . it becomes a losing venture around which [the Afghan government is] trying to insert larger control" (cited in Rennie 2010).

In the face of this second batch of challenges, one notes some constriction in Canada's neoliberal approach. To explain, DFAIT, since the turn of the last century, has been concerned with markets for force writ large. Initially, DFAIT's focus was on the safety of humanitarian aid workers and on how PMSCs might present positive and negative operational implications for humanitarian efforts. Later, DFAIT expanded its push for regulations in order to (1) advance civilian protection; (2) respond to developments in Afghanistan and Iraq; and (3) "be ahead of the curve" in light of the expanding

PMSC presence (correspondence with DFAIT official, August 9, 2013). These elements underscored Canada's efforts in the process leading to the *Montreux Document* (Canada was one of the initial signatories) and in the development of the International Code of Conduct for Private Security Service Providers.

The constriction comes through DND's response, one which takes into account these international endeavors and reflects upon Canada's usage of PMSCs: the *National Defence Directive on the Selection and Use of Private Military and Security Contractors on Deployed Operations* (in draft form at the time of writing). From one standpoint, the directive is a tool for risk assessment. Factors such as value for money and the availability of CF capabilities are to be balanced against international humanitarian law and human rights requirements. As well, the contracting decision is to be balanced against the risk of hampering operational and strategic goals. The directive identifies six areas upon which PMSCs may have a negative effect:

1. The development of local national security forces
2. Disarmament, demobilization, and reintegration efforts
3. The proliferation of small arms
4. The general stability of the area of operations, including consideration of the possibility that illegal armed groups may re-emerge as PMSCs
5. The acceptability of PMSCs in the local environment
6. The CF's relationship with the local population resulting from the association with a PMSC (DND n.d.: 4)[2]

These factors relate, in part, to promoting security as a public good in operations abroad. Because they are primarily employed abroad, however, Canada's use of PMSCs has had virtually no effect on the provision of security as a public good domestically in Canada.

From another standpoint, the directive's language engages to a stronger degree Canada's "bureaucratic center." During its operations in Afghanistan, DND/CF assumed the risk regarding contracting and security clearances for the PMSCs it employed. To facilitate security arrangements, CF commanders could approve contracts valued up to CAD 1 million. It is clear in the directive, however, that other prominent actors usually involved in government contracting practices will now be increasingly engaged (i.e., Public Works and Government Services Canada and the Canadian Industrial Security Directorate). The directive also states explicitly that senior DND/CF leaders, up to the Chief of Defence Staff and the Deputy Defence Minister, may become involved in contracting decisions, depending on requirements and the level of risk assessed.

Conclusion

The neoliberal Canadian market for force has helped to present a different "Canadian" face on the world stage, a face dissimilar to the one Prime Minister Chrétien offered at the Afghan campaign's start: "Of course, we do not want to have a big fight there. We want to bring peace and happiness as much as possible" (Canada House of Commons 2001). Today, the Canadian government has rejuvenated the CF and allowed it to fight. Hence, the Canadian market for force has provided personnel and allowed for task allocations that have both compensated for the CF's manpower limitations and permitted the CF to promote its fighting credentials. This market, however, instigated some negative effects related both to CF capacity, in terms of SOF, and to the promotion of security as a public good abroad. In response, the government has not shunned PMSC usage, but instead it has developed policies to help mitigate risk. Put differently, the government has introduced some measures to better manage the effects of a neoliberal marketplace. Future analysis should consider these measures' efficacy because though the Canadian market for force is smaller than many of the other markets examined in this book, in a relative way this market has catalyzed effects that are no less profound.

Notes

1. Canada, for instance, turned down the opportunity to lead the U.N. mission in the Congo and has eschewed substantial CF participation in Sudan. Also, since 2003, the government has reduced the funding for the Pearson Peacekeeping Centre to the degree that the organization terminated its operations in Cornwallis, Nova Scotia, in June 2011. This distancing from the peacekeeper image was likely one of the reasons contributing to Canada's failed attempted to win a nonpermanent seat on the United Nations Security Council in October 2010 (York 2010: A1; Pugliese 2011; Stairs 2011).

2. Among the finer points in the directive's criteria is the need to be particularly diligent regarding the contracting of armed private personnel who "provide mobile services" (Canada n.d.: B-2/2). According to Allison Stanger (2010: 1–2), in looking at

the U.S. context, private personnel of this type perform "inherently governmental functions" and are more likely to use their weapons.

References

Blanchfield, Mike. 2008. "Brass Questions 'Bench Strength' of the Military." *Edmonton Journal*, June 3, A4.

Blanchfield, Mike. 2009. "Army to Consider One-Year Pause by 2011." *Ottawa Citizen*, March 10, A3.

Brewster, Murray. 2009. "Forces Beef-Up to Take 20 Years." *Halifax Chronicle Herald*, May 25.

Canada Department of National Defence. n.d. *National Defence Directive on the Selection and Use of Private Military and Security Contractors on Deployed Operations.* Draft.

Canada Department of National Defence. 1994. *1994 White Paper on Defence.* Ottawa: Supply and Services Canada.

Canada. House of Commons. 2001. *Legislative Debates (Hansard).* 37th Parliament, 1st Session, No. 114 (November 19). Ottawa: Supply and Services Canada.

"Canada Spends $41M on Hired Guns in Afghanistan." 2011. *Canadian Press*, February 6.

Canada. Standing Committee on National Defence. 2006. *Evidence.* 39th Parliament, 1st Session (November 20). Ottawa: Supply and Services Canada.

Clark, Campbell. 2008. "Compromise on Afghanistan Muffles Election Drumbeat." *Globe and Mail*, February 22.

Cohen, Andrew. 2003. *While Canada Slept: How We Lost Our Place in the World.* Toronto: McClelland & Stewart.

Council for Canadian Security in the 21st Century. 2002. *Peoples' Defence Review,* September 11.

Detomasi, David. 2002. "The New Public Management and Defense Departments: The Case of Canada." *Defense & Security Analysis* 18(1): 51–73.

"East Timor Troops Need More Power: Axworthy." 1999. *National Post*, September 14, A1.

"The Essential Rick Hillier: Facts and Quotes." 2008. *CTV*, April 15. http://www.ctv.ca.

Galloway, Gloria. 2008. "Military Investigating How Canadian Soldier Died." *Globe and Mail*, August 9.

Galloway, Gloria. 2009. "Canada Spending Millions on Private Security in Afghanistan." *Globe and Mail*, November 27.

Geddes, John. 2006. "Bullets Fly. Ottawa Ducks." *Macleans*, August 25.

Granatstein, J. L. 2004. *Who Killed the Canadian Military?* Toronto: HarperCollins.

Leblanc, Daniel. 2006. "JTF2 to Hunt al-Qaeda." *Globe and Mail*, July 5, A1.

Maidment, Erica. 2008. *A New Governance Strategy for Canadian Private Military Policy.* Paper presented at the Conference of Defence Associations Institute Graduate Student Symposium, Kingston, Ontario, October 31–November 1.

Mayeda, Andrew. 2007. "MPs Seek Cost of Private Contractors." *Ottawa Citizen*, November 26, A5.

O'Neil, Peter. 2007. "Troop Demand Leaves Forces 'Struggling' to Train." *Ottawa Citizen*, June 14, A13.

Pugliese, David. 2005. "Soldiers of Fortune." *Ottawa Citizen*, November 12, A17.

Pugliese, David. 2011. "Cash-Strapped Peacekeeping Centre Closing Nova Scotia Office." *Vancouver Sun*, June 9.

Rennie, Steve. 2010. "Afghanistan to Regulate Private Security: Canadian General." *Toronto Sun*, January 25.

Saunders, Doug. 2006. "NATO Chief Defends Afghan Mission." *Globe and Mail*, March 7, A12.

Spearin, Christopher. 2005. "Not a 'Real State'? Defence Privatization in Canada." *International Journal* 60(4): 1093–1112.

Spearin, Christopher. 2007. "SOF for Sale: The Canadian Forces and the Challenge of Privatized Security." *Canadian Military Journal* 8(1): 27–34.

Spearin, Christopher. 2008. "What Manley Missed: The Human Security Implications of Private Security in Afghanistan." *Human Security Bulletin* 6(1): 8–11.

Spearin, Christopher. 2010. "The International Private Security Company: A Unique and Useful Actor?" In *Modern War and the Utility of Force: Challenges, Methods and Strategy*, ed. Jan Angstrom and Isabelle Duyvesteyn, 39–64. New York: Routledge.

Stairs, Denis. 2011. *Being Rejected in the United Nations: The Causes and Implications of Canada's Failure to Win a Seat in the UN Security Council—A Policy Update Paper*. Ottawa: Canadian Defence & Foreign Affairs Institute.

Stanger, Allison. 2010. *Testimony on "Are Private Security Contractors Performing Inherently Governmental Functions?"* Hearing Before the U.S. Commission on Wartime Contracting in Iraq and Afghanistan, House of Representatives, 110th Cong. Washington, D.C.: U.S. Government Printing Office.

Wattie, Chris. 2003. "Too Many Generals Spoil the Forces." *National Post*, December 3, A10.

York, Geoffrey. 2010. "Our Tradition, Our Specialty, Our Future?" *Globe and Mail*, October 29, A1.

CHAPTER 10

The Market for Force in the United States

Scott Fitzsimmons

The post–Cold War emergence of a market for force in the United States is a significant milestone in the history of American foreign policy. Indeed, the emergence of multiple American corporations with the capacity to deploy heavily armed combat units in foreign conflict zones has, for the first time in its history, provided the U.S. government with the option to legally and overtly supplement or even supplant its public armed forces with thousands of private troops. This basic point is well recognized in the existing literature on the contemporary private military industry (Carafano 2008; Geraghty 2009; Isenberg 2009). In contrast, the structure, development, and consequences of the American market for force remain poorly understood. This chapter, accordingly, engages a number of previously unanswered questions about the American market for force: First, what are the structure and distinguishing characteristics of the market for force in the United States? Second, why has this market evolved into its current form? And finally, what consequences have the structure and characteristics of this market had for the U.S. government's monopoly on force and the provision of security as a public good?

This chapter provides a comprehensive introduction to the market for force in the United States, with a primary focus on the market's operations during the first decade of the twenty-first century in Iraq and Afghanistan. This market is dominated by a relatively small collection of firms, including Academi (formerly Xe Services and before that Blackwater), DynCorp, USPI, and Triple Canopy. Employing deadly force on a regular basis, these firms provide robust combat services to their clients in an attempt to safely shepherd convoys and government officials or other high-profile customers along the streets and highways of active conflict zones and defend stationary facilities from any perceived threats (Avant, Boot, Friedrichs, and Friesendorf 2009). Driven by a fortuitous combination of largely unplanned processes and unintended circumstances, the firms that make up the American market for force have emerged as perhaps the most capable and willfully independent private armed forces in the world, which have regularly ignored regulations imposed by their chief client: the government of the United States.[1] It is, therefore, unsurprising that their behavior during Operation Iraqi Freedom and Operation Enduring Freedom in Afghanistan has undermined the United States' monopoly on force and the provision of security as a public good in its operations abroad.

The Structure and Distinguishing Characteristics of the Market for Force in the United States

The market for force in the United States is structured as a neoliberal market and bears several distinguishing characteristics. Of perhaps greatest importance, legally established private corporations, which have been labeled variously as "private security contractors (PSCs)," "military provider firms," "private military companies," and "private security firms," serve as the primary service providers in this market (Singer 2003: 45; Isenberg 2009: 4). This characteristic of the American market for force helps distinguish it from the market for force in certain other countries, such as Afghanistan, where the service providers are not always or even usually private corporations. This characteristic also distinguishes the contemporary American market for force from the market that existed prior to the end of the Cold War, when the chief American service providers were often ad hoc groups of filibusterers and freelance mercenaries who usually offered their services covertly through an informal and illegal black market (Nimkar 2009: 4; Singer 2003: 46; Isenberg 2009: 4).

Although American PSCs have provided security services for international organizations and foreign governments, including the governments of Iraq and Afghanistan, the U.S. government serves as the primary direct and indirect client of these firms (Committee on Oversight and Government Reform 2007; Schumacher 2006: 168; Carafano 2008: 67). Most PSCs based in and/or employed by the United States provide services in foreign countries. Iraq and Afghanistan, as unstable conflict zones that fall within the United States' current area of influence, were, at the time of this writing, the primary operating environments for these firms. In these contexts, the U.S. Departments of Defense and State as well as the U.S. Agency for International Development (USAID) have employed American PSCs through direct contract actions, in which the private security contactors involved work directly for a government department or agency, and indirect contract actions, in which PSCs work for an organization, such as a nongovernmental organization or a private corporation, which is performing tasks that have been financed by the American government (Office of the Special Inspector General for Iraq Reconstruction 2008: 1; Thurnher 2008: 79).

PSCs employed by the U.S. Department of Defense have tended to guard military facilities in Iraq and Afghanistan and provide mobile security teams to defend supply convoys and senior military officials as they traveled within Iraq and Afghanistan (Office of the Special Inspector General for Iraq Reconstruction 2008: 1; Thurnher 2008: 71–77). The U.S. Department of State, similarly, has employed PSCs to protect American ambassadors, members of Congress and other American government officials, and the Department's facilities in these conflict zones (Thurnher 2008: 64, 78; Terlikowski 2008: 44). During long periods of the wars in Iraq and Afghanistan, this responsibility largely fell to three American firms: what was then Blackwater/Xe Services, DynCorp, and Triple Canopy (Committee on Oversight and Government Reform 2007; Carafano 2008: 67; Isenberg 2009: 30). USAID paid directly for similar security services from private security contractors until 2005, but then it began relying on the Department of State to manage its security needs (Office of USAID Inspector General 2010: 1, 15; Thurnher 2008: 79).

Belying the sense of permanence conveyed through the conventional corporate structure of those private security contractors based in or employed by the United States, the low-level employees of these organizations may be hired and fired in short order as a firm acquires and loses contractors over time (Tarzwell 2009: 186; Terlikowski 2008: 37). These firms, which usually employ no more than a few thousand security personnel at a time, rely on databases containing the names and contact information of thousands of people who have indicated their interest in security work, rather than maintaining a large number of tenured employees (Terlikowski 2008: 44).

The employees of private security firms based in or hired by the United States need not be American citizens (Nimkar 2009: 5; Schwartz 2010: 3; Geraghty 2009: 187). Rather, these firms routinely employ citizens of the country they are operating in (such as Iraqis and Afghans), as well as "third country nationals," meaning citizens from any country other than the United States and the country the firm is operating in. Americans and third country nationals made up a substantial proportion of the total employees of American security firms operating in Iraq for the duration of that conflict; in contrast, these groups made up less than 10 percent of the total in-country employees of firms operating in Afghanistan as of mid-2010 (Schwartz 2010: 10). Regardless of their citizenship, the employees of American private security contractors tend to be veterans of military, police, or militia forces (Tarzwell 2009: 186; Terlikowski 2008: 37).

As with most other American corporations, the firms that make up the American market for force are profit-driven entities (Singer 2003: 46; Carafano 2008: 77; Isenberg 2009: 19). This characteristic has proven especially important because it has encouraged American PSCs to prioritize the provision of security to their client—the person or organization providing their revenue—above the security concerns of other actors in their operating environment, including civilians, other PSCs, and state-based security forces. Put differently, PSCs in the American market for force, as profit-driven and client-centric organizations, provide security as an excludable good in the areas where they operate and lack the concern for maintaining public security that state-based security forces are often assumed to possess. This characteristic is not, however, unique to the American market for force.

Finally, the firms that make up the American market for force provide robust combat services for their clients. Some scholars have maintained a problematic distinction between the largely defensive uses of deadly force by these actors and "combat," which they have improperly limited to offensive uses of deadly force (Pelton 2006: 5, 109; Geraghty 2009: 186). In contrast, this chapter considers any use of deadly force by armed actors in a conflict zone to be a form of "combat" behavior. A tactic utilized by U.S.-hired PSCs relatively early in the conflicts in Iraq and Afghanistan was to shoot at "threatening" pedestrians and vehicles, regardless of whether the target was carrying a visible weapon (Pelton 2006: 145, 202; Schumacher 2006: 170, 177–78, 207). Although rules of engagement were eventually developed to reduce the frequency with which such a tactic was practiced, another common tactic involved the use of counter-assault teams, or CATs, which are vehicle-borne squads of private infantry that travel behind the other vehicles in a security convoy and launch attacks against insurgents that threaten the convoy. In effect, CATs were to engage insurgents with deadly force in order to disrupt their attacks so that the rest of the convoy could escape. This could involve a combination of machine gun attacks against insurgents to either kill them or force them to flee and, in cases involving vehicle-borne insurgents, ramming the insurgents' vehicles to disable them or kill the occupants (Schumacher 2006: 172; Pelton 2006: 220–21). By most traditional conceptions of warfare, employing these tactics would constitute combat.

Moreover, data on the American PSCs that protected U.S. State Department personnel in Iraq suggest that their employees used deadly force on a regular basis. For example, according to a 2007 memorandum issued by the Congressional Committee on Oversight and Government Reform,

> Incident reports compiled by Blackwater reveal that Blackwater has been involved in at least 195 "escalation of force" incidents in Iraq since 2005 that involved the firing of shots by Blackwater forces. . . . In addition to Blackwater, two other private military contractors, DynCorp International and Triple Canopy, provide protective services to the State Department. . . . All three companies shoot first in more than half of all escalation of force incidents.

Taking this into account, it is not surprising that American private security contactors have both suffered and inflicted numerous casualties in the course of their security operations (Geraghty 2009: 187).

The Development of the Market for Force in the United States

A combination of bureaucratic, legal, and military factors have, together, driven the development of what is now perhaps the premier market of private combat service providers in the world. There is considerable agreement within the existing literature on the American market for force that the recent emergence of multiple U.S.-based PSCs offering combat services to their (usually American) clients was largely driven by two interrelated processes. The first is the process of downsizing the U.S. military after the end of the Cold War, and the second is the process of outsourcing an ever-greater range of tasks that have traditionally been performed by the U.S. military to private firms. Much of the literature has, however, mischaracterized the role played by these processes in the development of the American market for force, which, in reality, was less direct than is commonly assumed.

Scholars have drawn a direct link between the elimination of hundreds of thousands of positions in the U.S. Armed Forces during the late 1980s and early 1990s and the rise of U.S.-based PSCs. A popular rationale is that, when the U.S. military began downsizing, the civilian economy was flooded with thousands of trained soldiers, some of whom wanted to continue earning a living with their military skills (Ortiz 2010: 36; Terlikowski 2008: 36). This labor pool not only allowed for the establishment of multiple American PSCs, but also provided these firms with the capacity to deploy security forces numbering in the thousands to overseas conflict zones. To support this rationale, scholars often point to the fact that some of the founders of leading U.S.-based private security contractors, such as Blackwater and Triple Canopy, were veterans of U.S. special operations units, such as the U.S. Navy SEALs and the U.S. Army Special Forces (Nimkar 2009: 6).

This explanation for the development of the American market for force is plausible but problematic. For instance, the relationship between downsizing the U.S. Armed Forces and the emergence or growth of U.S.-based PSCs is largely assumed rather than supported by clear evidence. The fact that Triple Canopy and Blackwater only began offering combat services during the first decade of the twenty-first century, several years after the downsizing process had largely ended, suggests that the post–Cold War downsizing process did not directly lead to the development of American combat service firms. Moreover, scholars have not presented evidence to support the notion that the founders of these firms, or a substantial proportion of their employees, left the U.S. military because their positions had been eliminated through the downsizing process (Isenberg 2009: 59; U.S. Special Operations Command 2008: 5–13).

Similar problems afflict the existing literature's largely uncritical attempt to use initiatives to outsource some of the U.S. military's traditional functions to private firms during the 1980s and 1990s to explain the development of the American market for force. The most frequently referenced logic is that because the United States government believed that the private sector could provide some services more efficiently than the Department of Defense, the government outsourced many traditional military tasks to private firms, which led to the development of American private security contractors (Ortiz 2008: 4–5). Of course, the notion that several traditional functions of the U.S. military have been outsourced is undeniable. Moreover, although the U.S. military has received assistance from private corporations offering logistical and support services since the First World War, the process of outsourcing these services has certainly expanded since the 1985 creation of the Logistics Civil Augmentation Program (LOGCAP). However, attempts to draw a direct causal link between planned outsourcing initiatives, like LOGCAP, and the rise of American PSCs mischaracterize the scope of the American military's planned outsourcing initiatives. These outsourcing initiatives were confined to support functions such as logistics and intelligence analysis and were not intended to include "core" functions related to combat and the use of weapons in conflict zones—that is, the tasks performed by American PSCs (Nimkar 2009: 6). Regulatory documents, such as Army Regulation 715–9, "Contractors Accompanying the Force," affirm that the U.S. government did not intend for contractors to perform "inherently governmental functions" such as those requiring "military training for their proper execution," which would certainly include combat functions (Department of the Army 1999: 21). As Major Jeffrey S. Thurnher, a U.S. Army lawyer, put it, the U.S. Department of Defense "did not significantly plan for the use of PSCs when troops first entered Iraq in March 2003. . . . Contractors were not expected to perform inherently governmental functions, such as security in a complex battlefield" (Thurnher 2008: 72).

This is not to suggest that downsizing and outsourcing played no role in the development of the American market for force. Rather, while still important, the role played by these processes was less direct than is commonly assumed: They helped drive the expansion of *other* sectors in the private military industry, such as the American market for military logistics and support services, which helped legitimize a social role for private sector institutions in the United States' overseas military operations. To put it in another way, outsourcing and downsizing helped drive the growth of American military support firms, like KBR and its former parent company, Halliburton. This, in turn, established a legitimate social role for private corporations seeking to support the work of the U.S. Department of Defense and the United States' other government departments and agencies operating in foreign conflict zones (Kidwell 2005: 16, 21). Although indirect, outsourcing and downsizing still played a critical role in the development of the American market for force. If these processes had not taken place, then the U.S. government would likely not have deemed it appropriate to allow U.S.-based security firms to openly sell their services in conflict zones like Iraq and Afghanistan, let alone become the primary client of these firms.

In addition, the American market for force could not have evolved in the absence of a relatively unrestrictive legal and regulatory environment that would permit firms offering robust combat services to develop and flourish. At first glance, the American employees of PSCs appear to be subject to a number of U.S. laws that should constrain their behavior and enable the prosecution of security contractors who commit homicide or other serious felonies while operating overseas. These include, but are not limited to, the Military Extraterritorial Jurisdiction Act of 2000, the Uniform Code of Military Justice, the Special Maritime and Territorial Jurisdiction Act, the U.S. Arms Export Control Act of 1976, the War Crimes Act of 1996, and certain provisions of National Defense Authorizations Acts from 2007 onward (Elsea 2010: 14–29; Hurst 2008: 1314–16).

However, the constraining effect of this legislation is, at best, highly questionable. For example, although the Military Extraterritorial Jurisdiction Act unambiguously applies to contractors who are "employed by" the U.S. Armed Forces abroad, it is unclear whether it also applies to contractors who are merely "accompanying" U.S. military personnel on overseas operations but working for another agency of the U.S. government or any one of several other potential clients (Doyle 2012: 1–2). Regardless, these laws have rarely been applied to the employees of U.S.-based or U.S.-hired PSCs (Terlikowski 2008: 47–48; Kidwell 2005: 4). As Human Rights First noted in a 2008 report, "If used, these laws would cover most of the serious violent crimes committed by contractors in Iraq and Afghanistan. By law, authority to prosecute . . . cases [involving American PSCs] is shared by the Justice and Defense Departments. In practice, however, *neither* of these federal agencies is aggressively investigating, nor prosecuting, contractors" (Human Rights First 2008: 3).

The most prominent exception to this was the U.S. Department of Justice's prosecution, utilizing the Military Extraterritorial Jurisdiction Act, of five Blackwater contractors for their alleged involvement in a deadly shooting incident in Baghdad's Nisour Square in 2007. A U.S. District Court judge dismissed all charges in this case in December 2009 on the grounds that it largely rested on testimony that was improperly obtained from the accused in exchange for a promise of immunity from prosecution. The case was subsequently reopened on appeal and had not yet been decided at the time of publication. Lingering ambiguity over this issue prompted Senator

Patrick Leahy and Congressman David Price to introduce bills to create a Civilian Extraterritorial Jurisdiction Act in 2010. If this legislation had been enacted, it would have permitted the U.S. Department of Justice to prosecute contractors "employed by or accompanying any department or agency of the United States other than the Department of Defense" for a wide range of crimes, such as murder, assault, theft, and fraud, committed outside the United States (Doyle 2012: 5). This bill was reintroduced in 2014, but as of the time of writing, it has not been enacted, nor has any American employee of a U.S.-based PSC ever been convicted on charges pertaining to human rights violations or the use of military force during an operation in an overseas conflict zone.

These shortcomings in the application of U.S. domestic laws and regulations pertaining to PSCs have been mirrored by the application of laws and regulations pertaining to these firms by the governments of Iraq and Afghanistan. For much of the Iraq War, American PSCs operated with few legal restrictions. Indeed, following a post-invasion period when contractors enjoyed near-complete legal ambiguity in Iraq, the Coalition Provisional Authority (CPA) issued Order 17 in June 2004, which officially exempted contractors from prosecution under Iraqi law for actions committed in the course of discharging their contracts. In practice, this provided legal immunity to non-Iraqi PSCs for any use of deadly force during their security operations (Hurst 2008: 1312–13; Terlikowski 2008: 47; Avant et al. 2009: 41).

CPA Order 17 did, however, grant the Iraqi Ministry of the Interior the power to issue and revoke operating licenses for PSCs (Hurst 2008: 1313–14). Nevertheless, although the Ministry of the Interior threatened to strip Blackwater of its operating license following the deaths of seventeen Iraqi civilians at the hands of the firm's employees in the aforementioned Nisour Square incident, the firm continued to operate in Iraq until 2009. On January 1, 2009, the Iraqi government gained legal authority over American and other foreign PSCs under the Status of Forces Agreement of November 2008 (Elsea 2010: 12–13; Avant et al. 2009: 41). This agreement should, at least in theory, have afforded the government of Iraq "primary jurisdiction" over U.S.-based and/or U.S.-hired PSCs and their employees and should have allowed prosecution of these actors in Iraqi courts for actions deemed, by the Iraqi government, to be criminal. In practice, however, these legal powers have rarely been applied to American PSCs.

PSCs operating under U.S. contracts in Afghanistan have, similarly, enjoyed few tangible restraints under Afghan law. The United States concluded an agreement with the government of Afghanistan in 2002 that extended to American PSCs "a status equivalent to that accorded to the administrative and technical staff" of an American embassy under the 1961 Vienna Convention on Diplomatic Relations (Elsea 2010: 13–14). In practical terms, this means that U.S.-hired PSCs enjoy immunity from prosecution under Afghan laws for any actions performed in the course of discharging their contracts. As in Iraq, the general lack of legal restrictions on the actions of private security contractors employed by the United States has encouraged firms operating in Afghanistan to believe that they can use as much force as they deem necessary to protect their clients' personnel and cargo from perceived threats.

The government of the United States has recently indicated support for the development of international agreements, sets of standards, and codes of conduct designed to regulate the use and behavior of PSCs. The 2008 Montreux Document highlights several existing legal obligations of states, PSCs, and their personnel and recommends good practices to follow when states decide to hire firms (International Committee of the Red Cross 2008). The 2010 International Code of Conduct (ICoC) for Private Security Service Providers puts forward a set of standards to help PSCs comply with international humanitarian and human rights law (Swiss Federal Department of Foreign Affairs 2010). As of September 1, 2013, 708 PSCs were signatories to the Code, including a number of prominent American firms, like Academi, DynCorp, and Triple Canopy. Finally, the ANSI/ASIS PSC series of standards, which was completed in 2013, builds on both the Code and the Montreux Document by articulating an administrative mechanism that may be used by PSCs and their clients to help them adhere to the provisions contained in these earlier initiatives (ASIS International 2012).

It remains to be seen whether these initiatives will significantly influence how the government of the United States employs and governs the use of American PSCs. Its direct involvement in the development of these initiatives may be taken as a sign of strong support for their provisions. However, none of these initiatives imposes new *legal* constraints on either the United States or the firms that make up the American market for force. Moreover, many of the best practices promoted in these initiatives, such as "to take into account, within available means, the past conduct of the PMSC, and its personnel" when determining whether to hire a particular firm, are rather commonsensical and, therefore, should already have guided the United States' use of PSCs (International Committee of the Red Cross 2008: 17). Ultimately, the practical effect these initiatives will be largely determined by whether the government of the United States and American PSCs deem it to be in their interest to live up to the provisions and the related national and international laws regarding the use of force and human rights.

Finally, perhaps the most important factor that has influenced the evolution of the American market for force is the particular military context in which this market developed. This context is the American-led war on terror, which, from its origins in the fall of 2001, has been marked by U.S. military capacity shortages and the extended and repeated deployment of U.S. troops. Several major American PSCs, including Blackwater, Triple Canopy, and Custer Battles, rose to prominence within this context and sought to capitalize on their government's desperate need for additional combat personnel in Iraq and Afghanistan (Schwartz 2010: 5; Schumacher 2006: 26). Using PSCs to undertake tasks that had initially been performed by the U.S. military allowed the U.S. government to effectively increase the number of "boots on the ground" without suffering the political fallout that probably would have occurred if it had significantly increased its "official" troop levels. As Sarah Percy put it, "it is possible to imagine that, had the war in Iraq gone differently, then the private security industry would still look very much as it did before 2003, with a focus on training and policing" but not combat (Percy 2009: 62–63).

The Consequences of the Market for Force in the United States for the United States' Monopoly on Force and the Provision of Security as a Public Good

The development of the American market for force has had profound consequences for the U.S. government's monopoly on force and the provision of security as a public good in the states in which American PSCs have operated. Indeed, the structure and characteristics of the American market for force have significantly eroded the United States' monopoly on force and contributed to the provision of security as an excludable good in overseas conflict zones. This assessment stands in contrast to those put forward in this volume by Carlos Ortiz and Chris Spearin, both of whom contend that the markets for force in the United Kingdom and Canada, respectively, have not undermined either the British or Canadian governments' monopoly on force or the provision of security as a public good. Four different ways in

which the American market for force has led to these overarching consequences can be identified.

Creation of Political Spoilers

The use of violence by American PSCs has undermined relations between
U.S. government entities and both leaders and ordinary civilians in Iraq and
Afghanistan. The profit-driven nature of American PSCs motivated them to
prioritize the provision of security to their clients above the security concerns of other actors inhabiting their operating environments (Petersohn
2008: 46). Put differently, American PSCs, as profit-driven and client-centric
organizations, lacked the broader incentive to provide security as a public
good that state-based security forces are commonly assumed to possess
(Kidwell 2005: 1; Singer 2003: 46). Employees of U.S.-based and/or U.S.-
hired PSCs have, at times, followed these profit-driven incentives to their
ultimate end by engaging any threat—confirmed or merely perceived—with
deadly force in an effort to ensure the security of their clients. This behavior
proved highly problematic in the context of the U.S. counterinsurgency
missions in Iraq and Afghanistan by undermining the U.S. Armed Forces'
efforts to "win the hearts and minds" of civilian populations and by strain-
ing diplomatic relations between the United States and the Iraqi and Afghan
governments (Kidwell 2005: 4; Avant et al. 2009: 46).

Undermining the Political Control over the Use of Force

The U.S. government's extensive use of PSCs has also undermined its political
control over the use of force. Ortiz and Spearin, in contrast, conclude that the
U.K. and Canadian governments maintain a good degree of political control
over the use of force by their respective PSCs. In the American context, the
so-called "authority dimension" of the monopoly on force that comprises the
focus of this volume, also known as "political control," refers to the capacity of
the U.S. Armed Forces to determine when and how force will be used in a
conflict zone (Avant 2005: 5–6; Petersohn 2008: 3). When a state's public
armed forces lose political control, their military commanders will not be able
to determine when and how the various actors operating in a conflict zone use
force. This is influenced by the degree to which a state's public armed forces

are dependent on PSCs. This dependency is, in turn, influenced by the scope of the military capabilities that have been outsourced to PSCs, the necessity of these capabilities to produce security, and the state's capacity to replace a defective PSC if it performs poorly (Petersohn 2008: 9; Mulrine 2009).

The American market for force has undermined the U.S. government's political control over the use of force in Iraq and Afghanistan because American military commanders have seen their capacity to determine when and how force is used impaired by the presence of well-armed and willfully independent U.S.-based PSCs in theater (Petersohn 2008: 48). PSCs operate according to the terms of their contracts, rather than according to orders handed down through the U.S. military's hierarchical chain of command. PSCs are, consequently, inherently harder for an American military commander to control than his or her own soldiers. Control issues are further compounded when a U.S.-based PSC is working for an organization other than the U.S. Department of Defense. Indeed, these clients, whose specific interests may differ from those of the American military, can issue requests to their security providers—regarding, for instance, which areas of a conflict zone they wish to travel to and which routes they wish to take—that contradict the preferences of U.S. military commanders.

The most visible consequence of this loss of political control is that PSCs employed by U.S. entities have used force with a frequency and in a manner that not only contravened the preferences of U.S. military commanders, but also caused considerable problems for them. For example, the *New York Times* documented an incident when Blackwater employees used tear gas at a crowded U.S. military traffic checkpoint in May 2005. An American soldier who was quoted by the reporter described Blackwater's actions as "very, very dangerous" to the safety and security of the soldiers who were exposed to the gas (Risen 2008a). A *Washington Post* article included similar statements made by General Karl R. Horst, deputy commander of the U.S. Army's 3rd Infantry Division, who argued that American PSCs "run loose in this country and do stupid stuff. . . . They shoot people, and someone else has to deal with the aftermath. It happens all over the place" (Finer 2005).

Increased Cost of Reconstruction and Occupation

Paying for the services of PSCs also increased the financial costs incurred by the U.S. government for reconstructing and occupying Iraq and Afghanistan. This government spent an estimated USD 13.3 billion on private security companies in Iraq and Afghanistan between fiscal year 2001 and fiscal year 2009 (Center for Strategic and International Studies 2009: 1–2). U.S. spending on PSCs, therefore, accounted for approximately 9 percent of its USD 153.3 billion in spending on the civilian contractors that supported its reconstruction and occupation efforts in Iraq and Afghanistan during this period. Blackwater, DynCorp, and Triple Canopy alone received an estimated USD 7.5 billion from the government of the United States for security services in Iraq and Afghanistan during this period, primarily through contracts with the U.S. State Department (ibid.: 2). As discussed earlier, the U.S. government's reliance on PSCs was driven, in part, by a need to increase the number of combat personnel in Iraq and Afghanistan without suffering the probable political costs associated with deploying sufficient state-based troops to handle every essential security task. Bearing this in mind, deploying thousands of additional U.S. troops for several years would, of course, have also cost billions of dollars and likely led to the deaths of additional U.S. military personnel. Therefore, while certainly notable, the financial costs associated with U.S. spending on PSCs during the Iraq and Afghan Wars may have been offset or even exceeded, both financially and politically, if it had forgone the widespread use of these actors and, instead, relied more heavily on its own state-based armed forces.

Insecurity

In contrast to Ortiz's conclusion that the market for force in the U.K. has had a positive or, at minimum, neutral effect on the provision of security as a public good, the provision of excludable security by the firms that make up the American market for force has helped to undermine the provision of security as a public good. In theory, the police and armed forces of a state are supposed to provide security as a public good—that is, these actors are commonly assumed to provide security in a nonexcludable manner, in which the consumption of security and benefits enjoyed by some citizens do not undermine the ability of other citizens to consume and benefit from security. In contrast, PSCs provide security as an excludable good by restricting its consumption and benefits to a particular group—the firms' clients— rather than society at large. In fact, the attempts by American PSCs to provide excludable security for their clients have routinely resulted in lower security for many other actors in their operating environments, such as civilians and other security forces. In addition to the 2007 Congressional study of PSC behavior discussed earlier in this chapter, this aspect of the firms' behavior has been well documented in press coverage of their activities in Iraq and Afghanistan. For example, several articles in the *New York Times* and the *Washington Post* include accounts of American PSCs who are described as "reckless gunslingers charging around Iraq with impunity" and argue that they are often "quick to shoot" and "quick on the trigger" when they feel threatened (Tavernise 2007; Broder and Risen 2007; Broder and Johnston 2007; Risen 2008b; Raghavan, Partlow, and DeYoung 2007). One article accused an American firm of flaunting, "an aggressive, quick-draw image that leads its security personnel to take excessively violent actions to protect the people they are paid to guard" (Broder and Risen 2007). Another included a statement from an Iraqi policeman, who argued that U.S.-hired firms were "butchering" ordinary Iraqi citizens as a result of using excessive force in defense of their clients (Kramer and Glanz 2007).

Conclusion

The American market for force maintains a neoliberal market structure dominated by privately owned business entities that enter into contracts regulating for-profit exchanges of goods and services with the government of the United States and a range of other clients. In contrast to other neoliberal markets for force, such as those in Canada and the United Kingdom, the American market for force may be distinguished, in part, by the fact that a number of its major firms have provided robust combat services for their clients in overseas conflict zones. A combination of bureaucratic, legal, and military factors, including outsourcing and downsizing certain elements of the U.S. Armed Forces, a relatively unrestrictive legal and regulatory environment, and a desperate need for additional combat personnel in Iraq and Afghanistan during the first decade of the twenty-first century, together drove the development of this market.

The structure and characteristics of the American market for force have had profound consequences for the U.S. government's monopoly on force and the provision of security as a public good in the states in which American PSCs have operated. Indeed, the firms that make up this market have eroded the United States' monopoly on force and contributed to the provision of security as an excludable good in conflict zones like Iraq and Afghanistan. As profit-driven and client-centric organizations, American PSCs lacked the incentive to provide security as a public good and contributed to the high financial costs of reconstructing and occupying Iraq and Afghanistan. In addition, the violent and willfully independent nature of many American PSCs has made it difficult, at times, for American military commanders to maintain political control over the use of force in overseas conflict zones. Finally, attempts by American PSCs to provide excludable security for their clients have routinely undermined the level of security experienced by a range of other actors in their operating environments, such as civilians and other security forces. Notably, however, because virtually all of the American PSC operations referred to here occur outside of the U.S. homeland, they have had little to no effect on the provision of security as a public good *domestically* in the United States.

Note

1. For instance, incident reports produced by the U.S. State Department, Blackwater, DynCorp, and Triple Canopy indicate that security personnel who worked for these firms during the wars in Iraq and Afghanistan frequently ignored the State Department's escalation of force regulations, which called for private security personnel to issue multiple nonviolent warnings to a suspected threat, such as an approaching vehicle, before resorting to deadly force.

References

ASIS International. 2012. *ANSI/ASIS PSC1-2012: Management System for Quality of Private Security Company Operations—Requirements with Guidelines.* Alexandria, Va.

Avant, Deborah D. 2005. *The Market for Force: The Consequences of Privatizing Security.* New York: Cambridge University Press.

Avant, Deborah D., Max Boot, Jorg Friedrichs, and Cornelius Friesendorf. 2009. "The Mercenary Debate: Three Views." *American Interest* (May/June): 32–48.

Broder, John M., and David Johnston. 2007. "U.S. Military Will Supervise Security Firms." *New York Times*, October 31.

Broder, John M., and James Risen. 2007. "Blackwater Tops All Firms in Iraq in Shooting Rate." *New York Times*, September 27.

Carafano, James Jay. 2008. *Private Sector, Public Wars: Contractors in Combat—Afghanistan, Iraq, and Future Conflicts.* Westport, Conn.: Praeger Security International.

Center for Strategic and International Studies. 2009. *Contracting for Operations in Iraq and Afghanistan.* Washington, D.C.

Committee on Oversight and Government Reform. 2007. *Memorandum.* Washington, D.C.: United States House of Representatives.

Department of the Army. 1999. *U.S. Army Regulation 715-9: Contractors Accompanying the Force.* Washington, D.C.: U.S. Department of Defense.

Doyle, Charles. 2012. *Civilian Extraterritorial Jurisdiction Act: Federal Contractor Criminal Liability Overseas.* Washington, D.C.: Congressional Research Service.

Elsea, Jennifer K. 2010. *Private Security Contractors in Iraq and Afghanistan: Legal Issues.* Washington, D.C.: Congressional Research Service.

Finer, Jonathan. 2005. "Security Contractors in Iraq Under Scrutiny After Shootings." *Washington Post*, September 10.

General Accounting Office. 2005. *Rebuilding Iraq: Actions Needed to Improve Use of Private Security Providers.* Washington, D.C.: General Accounting Office, United States Congress.

Geraghty, Tony. 2009. *Soldiers of Fortune: A History of the Mercenary in Modern Warfare.* New York: Pegasus Books.

Human Rights First. 2008. *Private Security Contractors at War: Ending the Culture of Impunity.* New York.

Hurst, Michael. 2008. "After Blackwater: A Mission-Focused Jurisdictional Regime for Private Military Contractors During Contingency Operations." *George Washington Law Review* 76(5): 1308–26.

International Committee of the Red Cross. 2008. *The Montreux Document: On Pertinent International Legal Obligations and Good Practices for States Related to Operations of Private Military and Security Companies During Armed Conflict.* Geneva, Switzerland.

Isenberg, David. 2009. *Shadow Force: Private Security Contractors in Iraq.* Westport, Conn.: Praeger Security International.

Kidwell, Deborah C. 2005. *Public War, Private Fight? The United States and Private Military Companies.* Fort Leavenworth, Kans.: Combat Studies Institute Press.

Kramer, Andrew E., and James Glanz. 2007. "U.S. Guards Kill 2 Iraqi Women in New Shooting." *New York Times*, October 10.

Mulrine, Anna. 2009. "Obama to Confront Limits of America's Overstretched Military." *U.S. News & World Report*, January 16.

Nimkar, Ruta. 2009. "From Bosnia to Baghdad: The Case for Regulating Private Military and Security Companies." *Journal of Public and International Affairs* 20(Spring): 1–24.

Office of the Special Inspector General for Iraq Reconstruction. 2008. *Agencies Need Improved Financial Data Reporting for Private Security Contractors.* SIGIR Audit 09-005. Arlington, Va.

Office of USAID Inspector General. 2010. *Audit of USAID/Afghanistan's Oversight of Private Security Contractors in Afghanistan.* Manila, Philippines: United States Agency for International Development.

Ortiz, Carlos. 2008. "Private Military Contracting in Weak States: Permeation or Transgression of the New Public Management of Security?" *African Security Review* 17(2): 2–14.

Ortiz, Carlos. 2010. "The New Public Management of Security: The Contracting and Managerial State and the Private Military Industry." *Public Money & Management* 30(1): 35–41.

Pelton, Robert Young. 2006. *Licensed to Kill: Hired Guns in the War on Terror.* New York: Crown.

Percy, Sarah. 2009. "Private Security Companies and Civil Wars." *Civil Wars* 11(1): 57–74.

Petersohn, Ulrich. 2008. *Outsourcing the Big Stick: The Consequences of Using Private Security Companies.* Cambridge, Mass.: Harvard University, Weatherhead Center for International Affairs.

Raghavan, Sudarsan, Joshua Partlow, and Karen DeYoung. 2007. "Blackwater Faulted in Military Reports from Shooting Scene." *Washington Post*, October 5.

Risen, James. 2008a. "2005 Use of Gas by Blackwater Leaves Questions." *New York Times*, January 10.

Risen, James. 2008b. "Iraq Contractor in Shooting Case Makes Comeback." *New York Times*, May 18.

Schumacher, Gerald. 2006. *A Bloody Business: America's War Zone Contractors and the Occupation of Iraq.* St. Paul, Minn.: Zenith Press.

Schwartz, Moshe. 2010. *The Department of Defense's Use of Private Security Contractors in Iraq and Afghanistan: Background, Analysis, and Options for Congress.* Washington, D.C.: Congressional Research Service.

Singer, P. W. 2003. *Corporate Warriors: The Rise of the Privatized Military Industry.* Ithaca, N.Y.: Cornell University Press.

Swiss Federal Department of Foreign Affairs. 2010. *International Code of Conduct for Private Security Service Providers.* Bern, Switzerland: FDFA.

Tarzwell, Amanda. 2009. "In Search of Accountability: Attributing the Conduct of Private Security Contractors to the United States Under the Doctrine of State Responsibility." *Oregon Review of International Law* 11: 179.

Tavernise, Sabrina. 2007. "U.S. Contractor Banned by Iraq over Shootings." *New York Times*, September 18.

Terlikowski, Marcin. 2008. *Private Military Companies in the U.S. Stabilization Operation in Iraq.* Warsaw, Poland: Polish Institute of International Affairs.

Thurnher, Jeffrey S. 2008. "Drowning in Blackwater: How Weak Accountability over Private Security Contractors Significantly Undermines Counterinsurgency Efforts." *Army Lawyer* (July): 64–90.

U.S. Special Operations Command. 2008. *History of the U.S. Special Operations Command.* 6th ed. MacDill Air Force Base, Fla.

CHAPTER 11

The Causes and Consequences of Different Types of Markets for Force

Molly Dunigan and Ulrich Petersohn

As noted in Chapter 1, this volume takes as its starting point that the market for force is actually a conglomeration of different markets for force, rather than a single entity. The case study analyses in the preceding chapters illustrate the similarities and differences among a number of markets for force spanning various regions of the world. In this chapter, we first create a typology categorizing the markets explored in the previous chapters. In total, we identify three different types of market apparent in the preceding chapters: a neoliberal market, a hybrid market, and a racketeer market. We then determine the extent to which the markets' consequences for the state's authority over the use of force and the provision of security as a public good vary from case to case. Next, we inquire to what extent existing explanatory approaches can account for the variation in the markets' consequences. Finding these existing approaches to be incomplete, we move on to probe the explanatory power of our "market types" argument, exploring the consequences of each type of market for both the state's monopoly on force and the provision of security as a public good. Finally, in an effort to explain why the different market types affect the state's monopoly on force and provision of security as a public good in the manner that they do, we explore the conditions underlying the development of each type of market and outline the processes by which those conditions lead to various market consequences.

Our findings indicate that the "market types" argument does carry more explanatory and predictive power for the varying consequences of different markets for force than do the other explanations examined, at least in the cases explored in this volume. Indeed, racketeer markets, as defined below, tend to have the most negative effects for the state's monopoly on force and the provision of security as a public good, while neoliberal markets tend to have less harmful effects on both the state's monopoly on force and the provision of security as a public good. Hybrid markets' consequences vary depending on how the state exercises its capabilities to control and interact with the market. The chapter concludes by exploring the implications of these findings.

Types of Markets for Force

We identify three different types of markets from the case study data in the previous chapters: a neoliberal market, a hybrid market, and a racketeer market.

It is important to note that many of the markets examined in this volume display aspects of several of the types of markets identified here. Criminal actors, for instance, are not only present in racketeer markets, but also operate in other markets such as the Ukrainian, Russian, Chinese, and Czech markets. Although we recognize that some overlap exists, each market is categorized according to the most dominant aspect of the market as identified in the chapters of this volume.[1]

Neoliberal Markets

The basic characteristic of a neoliberal market is its organization around privately owned business entities. This is not to say that there are no state-owned firms, international organizations, or individuals participating in the market, but simply that privately owned firms are the main actors in the market. The basic logic of the neoliberal market for force is that clients and providers enter into legal contracts for the voluntary exchange of goods and services (Dewey 1926; Hansen 2010). In order for the market to be feasible, property rights must be guaranteed to enable transfer of ownership. A functioning state usually monitors these rights. The exchange in neoliberal markets is mainly determined by price, which is not fixed, but is subject to competition among sellers and buyers. Free competition is, therefore, a driving factor behind the dynamic of this type of market. Motivated by the prospect of profit, market actors seek to offer a competitive product for a preferable price to surpass an opponent's offer. The neoliberal market model is the most widespread among the cases examined in this volume, with the preceding chapters indicating the presence of this market model in the United States, Canada, the United Kingdom, the Czech Republic, Argentina, Russia,[2] and the Ukraine.[3]

Hybrid Markets

In the hybrid markets explored in this volume, the state is the dominant market actor, operating either through its own organs or through state-owned companies. In many ways, hybrid markets are the logical opposite of neoliberal markets, as the laws of the free market are defunct in these markets. Competition between companies is nonexistent because the state either owns or tightly controls each firm. Production does not occur spontaneously to meet demand, but only after state approval. Finally, clients' performance-based evaluation of providers is undercut in hybrid markets because only one true provider—the state—exists.

The Chinese market for force is a hybrid market producing mostly non-lethal guard services for domestic consumption. As Jennifer Catallo illustrates in Chapter 8, almost all private security companies in China are state-owned assets and are under the control of public security bureaus. Similarly, the state strictly regulates the export of services.[4]

We also consider the "military protection" markets discussed by both Kristina Mani (Chapter 2) and Maiah Jaskoski (Chapter 3) to be hybrid markets due to the state military's primary position as a market actor. However, in contrast to the Chinese market for force, the state does not act through the veneer of a company on the hybrid markets for force in Ecuador and Peru. Rather, in these two cases, state military units directly market their military services for private domestic consumption.[5]

Racketeer Markets

Third, our examination of the cases in this volume leads us to identify a racketeer market for force in which the roles of the state and legal system are marginalized. Force has replaced voluntary exchange on such markets, and customers cannot choose from among different providers; rather, they are faced with criminal organizations or warlords who have gained a monopoly over the use of force in an area by using force to eliminate all other competitors. These actors use their position to sell security services while simultaneously spreading insecurity and/or harassing those who are not willing to pay for security with threats of force.

Criminal force markets in Latin America fall into this category. For instance, as Kristina Mani points out in Chapter 2, criminal street gangs in Guatemala control parts of the country, and other criminal organizations buy protection (probably in a form similar to policing services). Although the Guatemalan market includes transnational actors buying services, it appears that the production of force is primarily for domestic consumption to protect against gang violence.

The Afghan market for force falls into the racketeer category as well. In Afghanistan, local warlords sell protective services (which fall at the military end of the force spectrum) to international actors—including coalition troops—in the country. Those who refuse to buy such services are more insecure and liable to be attacked than are those who purchase them. Additionally, for much of the duration of Operation Enduring Freedom, security services have been imported into Afghanistan. This import-oriented segment of the market resembles a neoliberal market much more than a racketeer market; this is not surprising, as the neoliberal markets in the United States, United Kingdom, and elsewhere exported their services to Afghanistan. However, Jake Sherman points out in Chapter 7 that the imported portion of the market appears to be relatively small, according to available data, with only 18,914 private security personnel working on U.S. Department of Defense contracts as of December 2012, compared to a 2005 U.N. estimate that 5,000 militias employing more than 120,000 individuals were operating in the country. During the middle years of Operation Enduring Freedom, at the very least, the market in the country appeared to be predominantly a racketeer market. This is true even if one considers the nonlethal side of the imported market for force in Afghanistan, which is not the focus of Sherman's chapter.[6]

Consequences of the Markets for Force

As stated in Chapter 1, one of the goals of this volume is to explore the consequences of the variations in the markets for force on the state's monopoly on force and on the provision of security as a public good. This goal was motivated by the longstanding debates in the literature regarding whether the privatization of force necessarily (a) decreases the state's monopoly on force and/or (b) hinders the provision of security as a public good, discriminating between those who can afford to pay for their own security and those who cannot.[7]

Tables 11.1 and 11.2 show the results of the case studies examined in the preceding chapters. We characterize the market's consequences for the state's monopoly on force as falling into five possible categories: positive, neutral, slightly negative, negative (indicated by *), and very negative (indicated by **). Positive consequences would entail an increase in the state's authority over when, where, and/or how force can be applied due to the existence of the market for force. The "neutral" category consists of all cases that did not display any change in the state's authority over the use of force despite the existence of a market for force in that state. The "slightly negative" category includes cases in which the state is restrained in exercising its authority, for instance through market actors' activities limiting the leeway of the state or tempting away government personnel. "Negative" consequences include the state losing a substantial amount of authority over decisions regarding the use of force—for instance, through market actors gaining a direct say in the use of force, deploying forces, or directly using government resources for their own purposes. Finally, the market has "very negative" consequences for the state's monopoly on force when the market yields new power

Table 11.1. Overall Effects of the Market on the State's Monopoly on Force

	Positive/Neutral	Slightly Negative and Negative	Very Negative
Monopoly on Force (Authority Dimension)	United Kingdom, Canada, China, Argentina	United States, Russia, Ukraine, Czech Republic, Ecuador*, Peru*	Guatemala**, Afghanistan**

Notes: United States (slightly negative): commander loses some measure of control over use of force on battlefield. United Kingdom (neutral): still enjoys decision making authority. Czech Republic (slightly negative): PSCs gain indirect authority over public policy. China (neutral): government has continued control over force. Afghanistan (very negative): additional power centers are generated. Argentina (positive): collaboration between market and state. Ecuador and Peru (negative): army captured by private interests. Guatemala (very negative): gangs hire other gangs, corrupt law enforcement. Russia and Ukraine (slightly negative): state lacks control over exports of force-related services.

centers that could directly compete with and challenge the state's authority. However, because the cases examined in the preceding chapters included only one case with positive consequences—Argentina—we collapsed the neutral and positive categories into a single category for the sake of simplicity.

The cases illustrate that the consequences of the market for the state's monopoly over the use of force have the potential to vary fairly broadly. Indeed, the market negatively affected the state's monopoly on force more frequently than it had a positive/neutral effect. However, the extent of the market's negative effect appears to vary to some degree as well, with the monopoly on force being negatively affected in five of the cases and *very negatively* affected in four others (see Table 11.1).

We employed the same four categories of "positive," "neutral," "negative," and "very negative" when assessing the markets' effects on the provision of security as a public good. If the market contributed positively to the provision of security as a public good, we expected to see an increased level of security for everyone as a result of the market. A neutral effect meant that the market did not have an impact on the overall security level provided to any particular group, while a negative effect meant that security was more excludable. The consequences of the market for force were considered to be

Table 11.2. Overall Effects of the Market on the Provision of Security as a Public Good

	Positive/Neutral	*Negative*	*Very Negative*
Security as a Public Good	United States, United Kingdom, Russia, Ukraine, China, Argentina, Czech Republic, Canada	Peru, Ecuador	Guatemala, Afghanistan

Notes: United States (neutral): no discernible effect on *domestic* security in the United States. United Kingdom (neutral): security remains public good. Russia and Ukraine (neutral): no impact on public security. Argentina (neutral): market correlated with positive effects on public good of security, but political culture of mobilization and resistance to repression drives positive outcomes in the provision of security as a public good, likely trumping purely market-based contributions. Czech Republic (neutral): possibility for negative effect in future, but neutral up to now. Canada (neutral): no discernible effect on domestic security in Canada. Peru and Ecuador (negative): reduction of public provision of security. China (neutral): security remains public good. Guatemala (very negative): poorly resourced police force, gangs control 40 percent of territory. Afghanistan (very negative): market actors produce insecurity.

"very negative" for the provision of security as a public good when market actors contributed additional security risks beyond what were present originally. As with the findings pertaining to the state's monopoly on force, there were no cases with exclusively positive market effects and, accordingly, we combined the positive and neutral categories into one for the purpose of our analysis.

The results again display no clear trend, indicating that there is a high potential for the consequences of markets for force to vary across different markets. The effects of the market on the provision of security as a public good were "neutral" in four cases, while they were "negative" in two cases and "very negative" in two other cases (see Table 11.2).

Market Types: Explaining Variation in Market Consequences

As briefly outlined in Chapter 1, previous scholarly analyses have argued that either the quality of the state, the strength of regulation, the type of commodity that is traded, or the question of whether the commodity is exported or consumed domestically explain any variation across markets in their effect on the state's monopoly on force and the provision of security as a public good. This volume, in contrast, argues that the *type* of market more powerfully explains this variation.

To prove this, we utilized tests of sufficiency and necessity to compare the relative explanatory power of these four alternative arguments with that of the "market types" argument. The details of this analysis are provided in the Appendix and summarized in Table 11.3. In sum, the existing explanations in the literature for the variation in the markets' effects on the monopoly on force and security as a public good fluctuate in their capabilities to accurately explain the markets' effects, at least with regard to the cases explored in this volume. Three of the four key arguments espoused by existing approaches offered neither necessary nor sufficient conditions leading to particular market effects, and they were unable to account for the markets' effects on the monopoly on force. Although the "state quality" argument is an exception to this, in its current dichotomous form it was only able to confirm the general direction of the trend and not the degree of variation in the outcome (i.e., whether the market had a weakly positive/negative or strongly positive/negative effect on the state's monopoly on force or provision of secu-

Table 11.3. Consequences of Particular Types of Markets as Sufficient/Necessary Conditions

	Sufficient Condition	Necessary Condition
Monopoly on Force		
Lethal/Nonlethal	—	—
Quality of State	Weak state quality is sufficient for negative effect.	Strong state quality is necessary for positive effect.
Regulation	—	—
Export/Domestic	—	—
Type of Market	Neoliberal market is sufficient for slightly negative effect. Hybrid market is often sufficient for negative effect. Racketeer market is sufficient for very negative effect.	Neoliberal market is often necessary for positive effect and necessary for slightly negative effect. Hybrid market is necessary for negative effect. Racketeer market is necessary for very negative effect.
Security as a Public Good		
Lethal/Nonlethal	—	Lethal market is necessary for negative effect.
State Quality	Strong state quality is sufficient for positive effect.	Weak state quality is necessary for negative effect.
Regulation	Regulation is often sufficient for positive effect.	—
Export/Domestic	Export is sufficient for positive effect.	—
Type of Market	Neoliberal market is sufficient for positive effect. Hybrid market is often sufficient for negative effect. Racketeer market is sufficient for very negative effect.	Neoliberal market is often necessary for positive effect. Hybrid market is necessary for negative effect. Racketeer market is necessary for very negative effect.

rity as a public good). Our argument focusing on the existence of different market types shows greater potential to provide necessary *and* sufficient conditions that are able to account for the variation in the markets' consequences.

The market types approach, in contrast to these other explanations, demonstrates predictive power. Indeed, among the cases examined in this volume, neoliberal markets are always necessary and sufficient for a *slightly* negative effect, hybrid markets are always necessary (though are not sufficient) for a negative effect, and racketeer markets are always sufficient and necessary for a *very* negative effect on the state's monopoly on force.

Furthermore, a neoliberal market is a sufficient and often a necessary condition for that market to have a positive effect on the provision of security as a public good. Hybrid markets are always necessary (though again, not sufficient) for a negative effect on the provision of security as a public good, and racketeer markets are sufficient and necessary for a very negative effect on the provision of security as a public good.

These findings are based on a relatively small number of case studies and should be viewed as preliminary and exploratory. Nonetheless, they provide support for the argument that the market for force is actually a heterogeneous conglomeration of different types of markets, each having different consequences for the state's monopoly on force and the provision of security as a public good. The fact that the markets' consequences relate so specifically to different types of markets is significant, indicating that the notion of different market types has significant explanatory power outweighing that of previously established arguments for the varying consequences of the market for force.

Causes of Different Market Types and How They Affect the Consequences of Each Market

These findings still beg the question of *why* and *how* the various market types have the effects that they do on the state's monopoly on force and the provision of security as a public good. To answer this question and develop a more complete explanation of the effects of the different types of markets, we take an in-depth look at the conditions that yield each of the distinct markets for force in the various cases studied, exploring the extent to which these conditions were consistent or varied across the different cases. As detailed in Chapter 1, such an examination of the conditions underlying the different types of markets is another goal of the volume, and it is useful in explaining why the various markets for force affect the state's monopoly on force and provision of security as a public good in the manner that they do.

As noted above, we recognize the danger in making far-reaching explanatory claims based upon a small number of comparative case studies. Yet, the cases examined in this volume do at least provide preliminary indications that it is the variance in the combination of the following conditions that yield the different market types: (a) the level of strategic security, (b) the capability and intention of the state to get involved in the market, and (c) the respective societal norms[8] (i.e., norms governing exchange and the role of armed private actors as a legitimate extension of the state's security-providing capacity).

When analyzing the cases, we see that free, developed states, where norms of state intervention in markets are less prevalent, tend to be correlated with neoliberal market structures. The fact that we find most of the neoliberal markets in this study to be located in North America and Europe, where the neoliberal economic model is a defining feature of the economy, can be read as supporting evidence for this claim. In contrast, we see that hybrid and racketeer markets appear to flourish in less developed and less free states, where norms of state economic interventionism prevail. This may explain why we find most of the hybrid and racketeer markets in Asia and Latin America, as less developed and less free states are much more common there than in Europe or North America (see Table 11.4).

We then turn our attention to considerations of the strategic security context underlying the particular markets in question. As Branovic and Chojnacki (2011: 559) point out when discussing the logic of security markets,

Table 11.4. Market Types in Context

	World Region	GNI per Capita	Freedom Index	Case
Neoliberal Market	North America, Europe (one exception in Latin America)	Very High and High (one exception is Low)	Free	United States, Canada, United Kingdom, Czech Republic, Argentina, Russia, Ukraine
Hybrid Market Racketeer Market	Asia, Latin America	Low and Very Low	Not Free and Partially Free	China, Ecuador, Peru. Afghanistan, Guatemala

Armed groups can strategically choose between the provision of security and the maintenance of insecurity. The more promising military and economic profits become, and the more uncertain a future. under the conditions of peace appears . . . , the higher the value of insecurity strategies should become. . . . Arbitrary violence and destruction of property are more probable in zones of strategic insecurity because of the asymmetric distribution of information and multiple material insecurities. . . . The ability to cause either security or insecurity (or both) becomes a political and economic resource, and hence an alternative source of power.

The convergence of neoliberal markets for force with zones of strategic security, and of racketeer markets for force with zones of strategic insecurity, is therefore not random, nor a mistake. Rather, it is the underlying security situation in the state or region that defines the utility of a market for force. Combined with the extent to which private security/force is considered "normal" or "legitimate" in the area in question, this defines the consequences that a particular market has on the state's monopoly on force and the provision of security as a public good.

Consider the Afghanistan case, where the underlying security situation is tenuous, weak, or an outright war zone, and the state's ability to generate security is minimal. As norms of free voluntary market exchange in general are not well entrenched in such states, new supply and demand streams are either incorporated into local exchange structures or form new arrangements making it easier for racketeer markets—as opposed to other types of markets—to flourish.[9] As the state has historically been weak, the practice of armed private security actors taking over state tasks is considered to be normal, and the use of force as a means of exchange on the market is already common. It is in these zones of strategic insecurity where racketeer markets are able to flourish, precisely because of the combination of state weakness and the absence of entrenched norms of voluntary exchange (see Figure 11.1). Because the security context in which racketeer markets tend to develop affords greater power to market actors when they detract from the state's monopoly and provide security only to the highest bidder in an exclusive fashion, racketeer markets are predisposed to lessen the state's monopoly on force and the provision of security as a public good.

Similarly, we see in neoliberal markets for force that corporations are heralded as legitimate economic actors; however, they nonetheless fulfill a

- **Security Situation:** Unstable
- **Role of State:** Potential Intent, But No Capability for Direct Involvement; State Chooses to Become Directly Involved in Market for Force
- **Societal Norms:** Armed Private Actors' Replacement of State Is Appropriate; Voluntary Exchange Not Well Entrenched; Force Is a Tool of Exchange

Racketeer Market for Force

Market detracts from the state's legitimate security-providing capacity and is provided primarily where profits can be made; it thus has a negative effect on the state's monopoly on force and provision of security as a public good.

Figure 11.1. Conditions underlying a racketeer market for force and its consequences.

role in support of state functions (see Figure 11.2). In part, this is due to the larger capability of the state and the more stable security situation in such areas allowing the practice of free market economic behavior. Because the neoliberal market model is the strongest and most established model in these states across all sectors of the economy, new demand and supply streams—such as those relevant to the market for force—are easily integrated. The norms of voluntary market exchange, the treatment of force as a commodity (and not as a means on the market), and the acceptance of free-market activities in general in such economies allow private security providers and other marketized forms of force to profit by increasing the provision of security as a public good. The same norms also allow neoliberal markets for force to have a relatively beneficial impact—or at least, a less negative impact than is seen in other markets—on the state's monopoly on force.

Hybrid markets are qualitatively different from either racketeer or neoliberal markets, primarily because they come in several different forms. The defining feature of a hybrid market is simply the state's direct involvement

- **Security Situation:** Stable
- **Role of the State:** Capability But No Intent for Direct Involvement: State Chooses Not to Become Directly Involved in Market for Force
- **Societal Norms:** Private Actors' Support for State Is Legitimate; Voluntary Exchange Is Well Entrenched

Neoliberal Market for Force

Market is seen as a legitimate extension of the state's security-providing capacity; it thus has a neutral/slightly negative effect on the state's monopoly on force and the provision of security as a public good.

Figure 11.2. Conditions underlying a neoliberal market for force and its consequences.

in the production of marketized force—yet, this can occur in a variety of ways. In the cases of hybrid markets explored in this volume, the state was either a direct provider of marketized force (i.e., offered its own forces for sale on the market, as in the Peruvian and Ecuadorian cases), or it tightly controlled all market interactions and private security actors (as in the case of the public security bureaus in China). Hybrid markets are similar to racketeer markets in that a layer of criminal activity both undergirds market activity and increases the demand for it, at least in the hybrid market cases examined in this volume.

Despite these similarities across hybrid markets, such markets can differ in their consequences for the state's monopoly on force and the provision of security as a public good. The effects of hybrid markets differ across the three hybrid market cases examined in this volume due to the role of the state interacting with the market. Where the state tightly controls the market, as in the Chinese case, it increases its monopoly on force and provision of security as a public good (see Figure 11.3). Where the state provides marketized forms of force in an effort to earn profits regardless of its own security interests, as in the Peruvian and Ecuadorian cases, it decreases its own

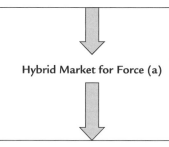

- **Security Situation:** Stable
- **Role of the State:** Capability and Intent for Direct Involvement: State Chooses to Become Directly Involved in Market for Force
- **Societal Norms:** Voluntary Exchange Not Well Entrenched; Market Exchange Is Tightly Controlled by the State

Hybrid Market for Force (a)

Market is seen as a legitimate extension of the state's security-providing capacity; it thus has a neutral effect on the state's monopoly on force. Market in China is specifically intended to create security as a public good, though this has the potential to change as the market becomes less state-controlled.

Figure 11.3. Conditions underlying a hybrid market for force and its consequences: the Chinese case.

monopoly on force and decreases the extent to which security is provided as a public good (see Figure 11.4). These markets are qualitatively different from both neoliberal and racketeer markets in that the state has both the *capability* and *intentions* necessary for it to become directly involved in the production of marketized forms of force, regardless of how it chooses to exercise that power.

Some might argue that the state strength argument defines the effects of various hybrid markets—with stronger states more capable of exercising direct oversight over the market and thus improving the market's consequences for the monopoly on force and provision of security as a public good, and weaker states unable to exercise direct oversight over the market and yet simultaneously motivated to utilize the market to generate profits for themselves (thus causing the market to have more negative effects on the monopoly on force and the provision of security as a public good). However, the state strength argument does not indicate *which* markets will become hybrid markets to begin with. Indeed—at least among the cases explored in this volume—both neoliberal and hybrid markets are found to flourish in

- **Security Situation:** Unstable
- **Role of the State:** Capability and Intent for Direct Involvement: State Chooses to Become Directly Involved in Market for Force
- **Societal Norms:** Voluntary Exchange Well Entrenched

Hybrid Market for Force (b)

Market detracts from the state's legitimate security-providing capacity and is provided primarily where profits can be made; it thus has a negative effect on the state's monopoly on force and provision of security as a public good.

Figure 11.4. Conditions underlying a hybrid market for force and its consequences: the Peruvian and Ecuadorian cases.

strong states, while both racketeer and hybrid markets are found to flourish in weak states. It is the development of state capability and intent to become directly involved in the market for force—borne out of the security situation and the societal norms in the area in question—that defines when a hybrid market will be created, as opposed to a neoliberal or racketeer market.

Implications of This Research

These findings are significant in the context of existing research on force privatization for several reasons. First, the case studies provide significant empirical material to a field suffering from a dearth of accessible data. This empirical material illustrates a wide range of situations in which the marketization of force both decreases and increases the state's monopoly on force and the provision of security as a public good, therefore providing ample material for future research on these issues. Second, and related to this, the lethality of services traded on a market, the export vs. domestically oriented nature of a market, state quality, and the level of regulation do not appear to be the only determinative variables driving the extent to which the commodification of force affects the state's monopoly on force and provision of security as a public good. Rather, the economic logic of exchange underlying the market—defined by the security and economic context in which the market is found, as well as the norms of "legitimate" market behavior in the society in question—appears to be able to predict the consequences of that market fairly accurately. More important, the market type is able to predict the *extent* of a market's consequences, allowing researchers and policymakers to predict with some specificity the degree to which the trade of security services in a particular market context will affect the state's authority over decisions to use force and the degree to which it will affect the provision of security in a nonexcludable manner to the public. These findings are particularly significant for governments considering the deployment of security contractors or other privatized forms of force to fulfill security force assistance and other missions in diverse areas of the globe, as they will enable governments to understand the potential risks and benefits of such deployments given each particular market configuration.

These conclusions also have significant implications for those seeking to regulate the private military and security industry. Of primary importance, they point to the particular market configurations that are most likely to maintain the state's monopoly on force and provide for the security of the public without prejudice toward one group or another. They also indicate where such market configurations are likely and/or unlikely to be found or succeed. Such knowledge suggests that attempts to regulate marketized forms of force must be specific to the logic of exchange underlying that particular type of market and that such regulations—if they are to be successful—should therefore vary from state to state and across different types of markets. This suggestion is supported by the fact that the level of regulation in each of the cases studied in this volume did not appear to have a consistent impact on either the state's monopoly on force or the provision of security as a public good. Clearly, therefore, it is necessary to take the type of market into account when developing regulatory initiatives to address the privatization of force. This will enable the use of targeted regulatory measures where they are likely to have the greatest impact.

Finally, while the intent of this volume is to elucidate the concept of different types of markets for force and to provide an in-depth examination of a number of case studies spanning multiple world regions, the findings speak to the need for additional research on this topic. Perhaps most important, given the breadth and depth of the markets for force across the globe, numerous cases of marketized force exist that were not within the scope of this study. Future research agendas might, therefore, usefully explore additional cases to test the arguments put forth here, either qualitatively or quantitatively.

Notes

1. It is similarly important to note that additional types of markets beyond those identified here may exist, as the relatively limited number of cases examined in this volume may have narrowed our scope such that we are only focusing on a few of many different types of markets for force. However, for the purposes of this study, our primary aim is simply to demonstrate conclusively that more than one type of market exists. We therefore leave it up to future research on the various different markets for force to identify additional types of markets.

2. Russia also displays characteristics of the hybrid market, in that the state-owned energy company Gazprom maintains its own security organization, the Gazprom Okhrana (Gazprom Guard). However, we consider this to be an exception rather than a defining characteristic of the Russian market, and therefore we categorize it as a predominantly neoliberal market.

3. In his chapter on the U.K. market for force, Carlos Ortiz refers to the similarities between the markets in these countries as an "Anglo Saxon Model." However, in the context of the entire body of cases explored in this volume, we thought it more appropriate to refer to this as a neoliberal model, as it encompasses several non–Anglo Saxon countries—such as Argentina and the Czech Republic—as well.

4. Some security services appear to be imported into China, but only to a very limited extent. For instance, Catallo notes in Chapter 8 that the international firm G4S is relatively active on the Chinese market.

5. It should be noted that although Kristina Mani usefully elaborates a number of market types in her chapter on the Latin American market for force, those types outline the specific conditions seen in the Latin American case. We therefore take a broader view here, elaborating several different types that share some similarities with Mani's typology, but that differ from it in important ways as well.

6. According to the Congressional Research Service, 90,339 private contractors operated on U.S. Department of Defense contracts in Afghanistan as of March 2011 (Schwartz and Swain 2011: 6). However, this number includes contractors providing services other than security, such as logistical and base operations support. Because we are focused here on the most lethal aspects of the market for force, such non-security contractors fall outside of the realm of our analysis.

7. With regard to the first of these, recall that we focus in this volume on the authority dimension of the state's monopoly on force, as mentioned in Chapter 1.

8. We define "norms" here in a standard sociological manner, as "collective expectations about proper behavior for a given identity." More specifically, the norms of

legitimacy discussed here are what are commonly known as "regulative norms," which "operate as standards for the proper enactment or deployment of a defined identity—like the standards defining what a properly conforming professor does in particular circumstances" (Jepperson, Wendt, and Katzenstein 1996: 54).

9. This is not to say that liberal economic policies are the only necessary prerequisites to stable societies, nor that they are necessarily correlated with stability in all instances; indeed, much of the literature on economic liberalism and security highlights additional variables for consideration (see, e.g., Ruggie 1982; Buzan 1984). Nonetheless, in the cases included in this volume, there does appear to be a correlation between instability and insecurity on the one hand and weak or closed economies on the other, as well as between stable/secure societies and open, free-market economies.

References

Branovic, Zeljko, and Sven Chojnacki. 2011. "The Logic of Security Markets: Security Governance in Failed States." *Security Dialogue* 42(6): 553–69.

Buzan, Barry. 1984. "Economic Structure and International Security: The Limits of the Liberal Case." *International Organization* 38(4): 597–624.

Dewey, John. 1926. "The Historic Background of Corporate Legal Personality." *Yale Law Journal* 35(6): 655–73.

Hansen, Robin F. 2010. "The International Legal Personality of Multinational Enterprises: Treaty, Custom and the Governance Gap." *Global Jurist* 10(1). Accessed November 28, 2011. http://www.bepress.com/gj/vol10/iss1/art9.

Jepperson, Ronald L., Alexander Wendt, and Peter J. Katzenstein. 1996. "Norms, Identity, and Culture in National Security." In *The Culture of National Security: Norms and Identity in World Politics*, ed. Peter J. Katzenstein, 33–75. New York: Columbia University Press.

Ruggie, John Gerard. 1982. "International Regimes, Transactions, and Change: Embedded Liberalism in the Postwar Economic Order." *International Organization* 36(2): 379–415.

Schwartz, Moshe, and Joyprada Swain. 2011. *Department of Defense Contractors in Afghanistan and Iraq: Background and Analysis*. CRS Report for Congress, May 13. Washington, D.C.: Congressional Research Service.

Testing the Relative Explanatory Power of the "Market Types" Argument

Ulrich Petersohn and Molly Dunigan

As noted in Chapter 11, we employed tests of sufficiency and necessity in line with Charles Ragin's qualitative comparative analysis (QCA) method to compare the relative explanatory power of the "market types" argument with that of four alternative arguments commonly found in the literature for the variation across markets in their effect on the state's monopoly on force and the provision of security as a public good: (1) the quality of the state, (2) the strength of regulation, (3) the type of commodity that is traded, and (4) whether the commodity is exported or consumed domestically. This Appendix describes that analysis in detail, illustrating how we arrived at the conclusion that the market types argument holds more explanatory power for the varied consequences of different markets for force on the state's monopoly on force and the provision of security as a public good.

First, a few methodological notes are in order. According to the QCA method, a cause is defined as *necessary* if it is always present when the outcome occurs. It should be noted that the cause can be present without the outcome occurring. A cause is defined as *sufficient* if the outcome is always present when the cause is present. In the case of sufficiency, the outcome can be present without the cause, but whenever the cause is present, the outcome needs to occur as well (Ragin 2000: 97). Significant for the below analysis, Ragin notes that all *combinations* of necessary and sufficient causes are meaningful (Ragin 1987: 99–100). Note that in some instances, there are not a sufficient number of cases falling within the "positive" or "negative" columns of the tables below to enable us to make accurate statements regarding sufficiency and/or necessity. In such instances, we rely upon correlational analysis to judge the relative adequacy of the alternative explanations for the variation in the markets' consequences.

In analyzing the data, we relax the absolute categories of "necessary" and "sufficient" slightly by not rejecting necessity or sufficiency in situations in which only one case deviates and the majority of cases indicate either necessity or sufficiency (or both). We therefore differentiate between the categories of "necessary" or "sufficient" (in which all cases support this categorization) and "often necessary" or "often sufficient," in which one case deviates from the categorization.[1]

It should be noted that because the four existing arguments mentioned above are usually discussed in a dichotomous fashion (lethal vs. nonlethal, export vs. domestic consumption, etc.), it is impossible for them to account for the entire range of variation delineated above. We therefore use slightly different measures to evaluate the four alternative arguments versus the market types argument. We consider the explanatory value of the alternative arguments to be confirmed if they correctly account for the direction of the effect—that is, positive or negative. We set the analytical bar higher with regard to the market types argument, considering the argument to only be sufficient if it is able to both account for the direction of the effect and shed light on the extent to which the effect is seen—that is, in terms of a difference ranging from *slightly* negative or positive effects to *very* negative or positive effects.

The Commodity Type Argument

Based on the examination of the individual markets in this volume, we found two cases—China and the Czech Republic—where only nonlethal services were traded, while lethal services were traded on the remaining markets. Table 11.4 in Chapter 11 displays the results of the effects of the type of commodity—that is, lethal or nonlethal force. The trade of lethal force often corresponds with a decrease in the state's monopoly on force in the cases examined. However, the market is not sufficient for a negative effect because the lethal force markets have neutral or positive effects as well. Moreover, it is not only lethal markets that decrease the state's monopoly on force. One of the two nonlethal markets examined in the preceding chapters—that of the Czech Republic—similarly decreased the state's monopoly on force.[2] Therefore, the trade of solely lethal services on a particular market is neither necessary nor sufficient for the market to affect the state's monopoly on force in a negative manner.

Likewise, nonlethal markets are not a sufficient condition for a positive or neutral effect on the state's monopoly on force. Although one has a positive/neutral effect, the other has a negative effect on the state's monopoly on the use of force. Moreover, the sale of nonlethal force on a market is not a necessary precondition for that market to have positive consequences for the state's monopoly on force because lethal markets are equally capable of having positive/neutral effects (see Table A.1).

Dissecting these results further, it appears from the case studies that lethal markets correspond with both negative and positive effects on the provision of security as a public good. Indeed, six lethal markets have neutral or positive effects on the provision of security as a public good, while four lethal markets have negative effects on the provision of security as a public good. This strongly suggests that the provision of lethal services in a market

Table A.1. Effects of the Type of Commodity Traded (Lethal vs. Nonlethal)

	Lethal	Nonlethal
Monopoly on Force		
Positive/Neutral	United Kingdom, Canada, Argentina	China
Negative	United States, Ukraine, Russia, Afghanistan[†], Guatemala[†], Ecuador*, Peru*	Czech Republic
Public Good "Security"		
Positive/Neutral	United States, United Kingdom, Russia, Ukraine, Canada, Argentina	China, Czech Republic
Negative	Peru*, Ecuador*, Guatemala[†], Afghanistan[†]	

*Cases in which the market's consequences for the state's monopoly on force is negative (slightly negative cases have no *).
[†]Cases in which the market's consequences for the state's monopoly on force is very negative.

is not a sufficient condition for that market to have a negative effect on the provision of security as a public good. The provision of lethal services is, however, a necessary condition for the market to negatively impact the provision of security as a public good. Yet, the trade of solely nonlethal force is not necessary for the market to have a positive effect on the provision of security as a public good, as lethal markets display this effect as well. All in all, the cases in the preceding chapters illustrate that the explanatory power of the commodity type argument is rather limited.

The Export Versus Domestic Consumption Argument

As outlined in Chapter 1, the existing literature often implicitly differentiates between export and domestic markets, suggesting that domestic markets have a positive effect on the state's monopoly on force and less favorable effects on the provision of security as a public good. Export markets, in contrast, are expected to have negative effects on the monopoly on force and positive effects on the provision of security as a public good.[3]

Like the commodity type argument, this argument does not adequately explain why there is such *variation* across different markets in their effects on the monopoly on force and the provision of security as a public good. Rather, the distinction between domestic and export-oriented markets is only able to differentiate between the negative or positive consequences of the markets. Indeed, the cases in the preceding chapters indicate no definitive relationship between domestic and export-oriented markets and the expectations of the literature regarding their effects on the monopoly on force. First, export markets appear to correspond with both positive and negative effects on the state's monopoly on force, with two cases displaying a positive effect and three cases displaying a negative effect. Hence, the export of private force is not a sufficient condition for a market to have a negative effect on the state's monopoly on force. Meanwhile, the domestic markets examined in the preceding chapters—in contrast to what the proponents of the export versus domestic consumption argument would expect—have both positive and negative effects on the monopoly on force. Indeed, this was the situation in five of the seven cases examined. Overall, neither domestic nor export markets are clearly sufficient or necessary to produce either a negative or positive effect on the state's monopoly on force (see Table A.2).

Table A.2. Effects of Export Versus Domestic Markets

	Export	*Domestic*
	Monopoly on Force	
Positive/Neutral	United Kingdom, Canada	China, Argentina
Negative	United States, Ukraine, Russia	Czech Republic, Guatemala[†], Afghanistan[†], Ecuador[*], Peru[*]
	Public Good "Security"	
Positive/Neutral	United States, United Kingdom, Russia, Ukraine, Canada	China, Argentina, Czech Republic
Negative		Ecuador[*], Peru[*], Guatemala[†], Afghanistan[†]

[*]Cases in which the market's consequences for the state's monopoly on force is negative (slightly negative cases have no [*]).
[†]Cases in which the market's consequences for the state's monopoly on force is very negative.

With regard to the market's effects on the provision of security as a public good, the export versus domestic consumption argument has fairly limited explanatory power. Export markets are clearly sufficient for positive/neutral effects on the provision of security as a public good. However, export markets are not necessary for a positive outcome, with four deviant cases. Domestic markets are neither sufficient nor necessary for negative effects on the provision of security as a public good, with four domestic markets having positive or neutral effects and four having negative effects. In sum, at least with regard to the issue of the provision of security as a public good, the export versus domestic consumption argument is not very well supported by the data in the case studies examined here.

The State Quality Argument

State quality is often considered to be a significant condition influencing the effects of the market for force.[4] The underlying logic of this argument suggests that weak state quality is problematic. Indeed, weak states in which force is traded as a commodity are predicted to experience negative effects from the market on the state's monopoly on force and the provision of security as a public good.

Yet, the cases in the preceding chapters indicate that strong state quality may not be sufficient for the market to have a neutral or positive effect on the state's monopoly on force (see Table A.3). Four strong states examined in this study contained a market that had positive or neutral effects on the state's monopoly on force, while two strong states had a negative effect. Strong state quality is apparently a necessary condition for a positive/neutral outcome, however. In the case of weak states, the results are clearer and more in line with the expectations of the state quality argument, as the markets in all of these had negative effects on the state's monopoly on force. Hence, from the data examined in this volume, state weakness appears to be

Table A.3. Effects of the Markets Controlling for State Quality

	Strong State Quality	*Weak State Quality*
Monopoly on Force		
Positive/Neutral	United Kingdom, Canada, China, Argentina	
Negative	United States, Czech Republic	Afghanistan[†], Ecuador[*] Ukraine, Russia, Guatemala[†], Peru[*]
Public Good "Security"		
Positive/Neutral	United States, United Kingdom, Canada, China, Czech Republic, Argentina	Russia, Ukraine
Negative		Afghanistan[†], Ecuador[*] Guatemala[†], Peru[*]

Note: We use the level of government effectiveness, as indicated by the Brookings Institution's 2008 *Index of State Weakness in the Developing World*, as a proxy for state quality (see Rice and Patrick 2008).
[*]Cases in which the market's consequences for the state's monopoly on force is negative (slightly negative cases have no [*]).
[†]Cases in which the market's consequences for the state's monopoly on force is very negative.

sufficient for the market to decrease the state's monopoly on force, indicating that state weakness is a possible explanation for the market to *negatively* affect the state's monopoly on force. On the flip side, however, the data also provide some support for the argument that state strength explains the *positive* effects of a market for force on the state's monopoly on force.

Meanwhile, strong state quality is sufficient for the provision of security as a public good. Strong state quality is not necessary for a market to have a positive effect on the provision of security as a public good; however, weak state quality was necessary for markets to negatively impact the provision of security as a public good. Yet, strong state quality also corresponded with markets that decreased the provision of security as a public good. In sum, the case studies included in this volume seem to indicate that the state quality argument does not adequately predict the market's consequences, at least not in every instance. As with the issue of the type of commodity traded, these findings are suggestive of potentially generalizable trends, but—given the small number of cases examined in this study—they would be usefully bolstered by the analysis of additional case studies in future research.

The Regulatory Environment Argument

Domestic regulation is thought to be one of the most important factors influencing the consequences of the market for force. In general, regulation is considered to temper the effects of the market. However, the case studies examined in this volume indicate that regulation is neither a necessary nor sufficient variable for the market for force to have a positive outcome on the state's monopoly on force. Furthermore, regulation is also not necessary for a market to have neutral/positive effects on the state's monopoly on force, as the market in the United Kingdom is essentially unregulated and yet has a similarly neutral effect on the state's monopoly on force. Meanwhile, the market in the Czech Republic was found to have a slightly negative impact on the state's monopoly on force, despite a regulatory framework. Only the absence of regulation was found to often be a sufficient condition (with one deviant case) for the market to decrease the state's monopoly on force in the cases examined (see Table A.4).

As the regulatory environment argument would expect, regulation appears to be an often sufficient condition for the market to have a positive/ neutral effect on the provision of security as a public good. However, regula-

Table A.4. Effects of Domestic Regulation of the Markets for Force

	Regulation Strong	Regulation Absent
Monopoly on Force		
Positive/Neutral	China, Canada, Argentina	United Kingdom
Negative	Czech Republic, United States, Guatemala[†]	Ukraine, Russia, Afghanistan[†], Ecuador[*], Peru[*]
Public Good "Security"		
Positive/Neutral	China, Czech Republic, United States, Canada, Argentina	United Kingdom, Ukraine, Russia
Negative	Guatemala[†]	Ecuador[*], Peru[*], Afghanistan[†]

Notes: United States (regulation): relatively unrestricted legal environment, though some laws were in place. Canada (regulation): Canadian Foreign Enlistment Act was inappropriate to address market, Canadian forces increased oversight. United Kingdom (regulation is absent): the partnership between the industry and the state was not regulated. Argentina, Guatemala, Peru, and Ecuador (regulation): minimal or weak oversight. Czech Republic (regulation is absent): no regulation in place. Afghanistan (regulation is absent): lack of oversight. Russia and Ukraine (regulation is absent): lack of oversight. China (regulation): market strictly controlled by Chinese police.
[*]Cases in which the market's consequences for the state's monopoly on force is negative (slightly negative cases have no [*]).
[†]Cases in which the market's consequences for the state's monopoly on force is very negative.

tion corresponds with both positive and negative market effects. Surprisingly, regulation is not necessary for the market to positively affect the provision of security as a public good.

Existing Explanations for the Markets' Variable Consequences Are Inadequate

When considering the above analyses of the alternative explanations for the variance in the consequences of the markets for force together, it becomes clear that the case studies examined herein do not provide unfaltering support for any of these explanations. As these alternative arguments do not appear to be able to explain the variation in the markets' consequences as well as one might hope, we aim below to probe the explanatory power of our own market types argument. To do so, we explore the consequences of each of the types of markets identified at the beginning of this chapter on both the state's monopoly on force and the provision of security as a public good.

The Market Types Argument

The market types argument, introduced above, argues that the consequences of a particular market for force depend on the specific logic of exchange underlying that market. The case study data examined in this volume provides relatively robust support for this argument, particularly in comparison to its support for the four alternative arguments from the existing literature that are examined above.

First, the neoliberal markets examined in this volume display an almost equal number of neutral/positive effects and negative effects on the state's monopoly on force. Hence, the neoliberal market type is not sufficient for either a positive or a negative effect. However, of the three types of markets identified here, the neoliberal market appears to be often necessary for the market to have neutral or positive effects on the monopoly on force. Hybrid markets appear to be often sufficient for negative effects, although they also display one deviant case of positive/neutral effects on the monopoly on force. Finally, racketeer markets are sufficient for the market to negatively affect the state's monopoly on force (see Table A.5).

The most remarkable contribution of the market types argument, however, pertains to its predictive capacity with regard to a market's effects. Indeed, the different market types are able to predict the *extent* of a market's negative effects on the state's monopoly on force. For instance, the neoliberal market is sufficient for *slightly* negative market effects on the monopoly on force, while the hybrid market is sufficient for negative market effects, and the racketeer market is sufficient for *very* negative effects on the monopoly on force.

The market types argument also predicts the markets' effects on the provision of security as a public good fairly well. Neoliberal markets are sufficient for a positive effect on the provision of security as a public good and are often necessary for this to occur as well (as was the case in seven out of eight instances). Meanwhile, racketeer markets are sufficient for a negative

Table A.5. Consequences of Market Types

	Neoliberal	Hybrid	Racketeer
Monopoly on Force			
Positive/Neutral	United Kingdom, Canada, Argentina	China	
Negative	United States, Czech Republic, Russia, Ukraine	Ecuador*, Peru*	Guatemala[†], Afghanistan[†]
Public Good "Security"			
Positive/Neutral	United States, United Kingdom, Russia, Ukraine, Czech Republic, Canada, Argentina	China	
Negative		Ecuador*, Peru*	Guatemala[†], Afghanistan[†]

*Cases in which the market's consequences for the state's monopoly on force is negative (slightly negative cases have no *).
[†]Cases in which the market's consequences for the state's monopoly on force is very negative.

outcome. As with the monopoly on force, the market types are also able to predict the *extent* of the markets' negative effects on the provision of security as a public good. All of the cases in which the market negatively affects the provision of security as a public good are hybrid markets, and all of those cases in which the market has a *very* negative effect on the provision of security as a public good are racketeer markets.

Notes

1. We derived the idea of relaxing the absolute categories of sufficiency and necessity directly from Charles Ragin, who argues that probabilistic criteria can be included in the assessment of sufficiency and necessity. In order to test for necessity, the researcher selects cases with the same outcome and examines to what extent they display the same cause. For the investigation of sufficiency, the researcher examines cases with the same causes, looking at the extent to which they display the same outcome. Ragin introduces different degrees of certainty about sufficiency/necessity (e.g., almost sufficient/necessary and usually sufficient/necessary). We reduce this complexity by differentiating between two degrees of necessity and sufficiency (Ragin 2000: 104–15). It is also important to note that the relaxation of the sufficient/

necessary categories on the basis of one deviant case only makes sense when there are at least three cases to base the analysis on. If there are only two cases and they display different outcomes, it is impossible to determine which one is the deviant case. In such instances, we maintain the absolute categories of sufficiency and necessity.

2. As only two nonlethal cases are included, the absolute categories of sufficiency and necessity are employed for the analysis.

3. For the purposes of this analysis, we were unable to find any cases that have *only* an export market. All countries that export security services appear to have a large domestic security market as well. Therefore, in order to differentiate the effects of export markets from those of domestically oriented markets, the cases in the preceding chapters that involve both export and domestic markets focus solely on the export of armed military services. The rationale underlying this decision is that armed military services comprise the portion of the markets in question that are primarily available for foreign, as opposed to domestic, consumption.

4. In order to have a consistent measure of state quality across the cases studied in this volume, we used the Brookings Institution's categorization of "government effectiveness" from its 2008 *Index of State Weakness in the Developing World* as a proxy for state quality (Rice and Patrick, 2008). The *Index of State Weakness in the Developing World* includes 141 developing countries and ranks them according to their relative performance in four critical spheres: economic, political, security, and social welfare. Each is measured by several indicators. We are focusing here on only one indicator in the political sphere: government effectiveness. States were categorized according to their quintile ranking in the index. Those states in the bottom three quintiles were considered to be weak, while those in the top two were considered to be strong. Some strong countries do not appear in the dataset because they are not part of the developing world. Yet, if they were to be included, it can be assumed that they would be in the highest quintile.

References

Ragin, Charles C. 1987. *The Comparative Method: Moving Beyond Qualitative and Quantitative Strategies*. Berkeley: University of California Press.

Ragin, Charles C. 2000. *Fuzzy Set Social Science*. Chicago: University of Chicago.

Rice, Susan, and Stewart Patrick. 2008. *Index of State Weakness in the Developing World*. Washington, D.C.: Brookings Institution.

CONTRIBUTORS

Olivia Allison earned her MA in international peace and security from King's College London and is currently working as a consultant in Britain on international political risk, focusing on the former Soviet Union. She is the co-author, with David Cook, of the book *Understanding and Addressing Suicide Attacks* (2007) and has published several journal articles on security and politics in post-Soviet countries.

Dr. Oldřich Bureš is the head of the Department of International Relations and European Studies and the head of the Center for Security Studies at Metropolitan University Prague. His research focuses on the areas of conflict resolution and international security, with special emphasis on privatization of security and counterterrorism. His work has been published in *Terrorism and Political Violence, Studies in Conflict and Terrorism, International Studies Review,* and several other peer-reviewed journals. His most recent book is *EU Counterterrorism Policy: A Paper Tiger?* (2011).

Jennifer Catallo received a BA in political science and an MA in international relations from York University. During her six-year tenure at the University of Toronto working as a lecturer, research associate, and teaching assistant, she focused extensively on security privatization issues. She currently works as a trainer with Desire2Learn, inspiring clients to see immense potential in information technology for education.

Dr. Molly Dunigan is a political scientist at the RAND Corporation. Prominent among her published work are her book *Victory for Hire: Private Security Companies' Impact on Military Effectiveness* (2011) and the RAND reports *Out of the Shadows: The Health and Well-being of Private Contractors Working in Conflict Environments* (2013) and *Hired Guns: Views About*

Armed Contractors in Operation Iraqi Freedom (2010). Dunigan received her PhD in government from Cornell University.

Dr. Scott Fitzsimmons is a lecturer in international relations in the University of Limerick's Department of Politics and Public Administration. He received his PhD in political science from the University of Calgary. He has published widely on mercenaries, private security contractors, and theories of military performance in such journals as *Security Studies, Defence Studies, Small Wars & Insurgencies,* and the *Journal of Military and Strategic Studies.*

Dr. Maiah Jaskoski is an assistant professor in the Department of National Security Affairs at the Naval Postgraduate School in Monterey, California. Jaskoski's first book, *Military Politics and Democracy in the Andes* (2013), analyzes military mission performance and neglect. Her research also has been published in *Studies in Comparative International Development, Latin American Research Review, Latin American Politics and Society,* and *Armed Forces and Society.* Jaskoski received her PhD in political science from the University of California, Berkeley.

Dr. Kristina Mani is associate professor of politics at Oberlin College. She received her PhD in political science from Columbia University. Dr. Mani's publications include *Democratization and Military Transformation in Argentina and Chile: Rethinking Rivalry* (2011), on the development of security cooperation and its impact on the militaries of Argentina and Chile, as well as articles on military entrepreneurship in *Armed Forces and Society,* the *Bulletin of Latin American Research,* and *Latin American Politics and Society.* She has served as a consultant to Transparency International and the United Nations Development Programme on projects related to defense industry integrity and the armed forces' role in economies undergoing political transition.

Dr. Carlos Ortiz received his PhD in international relations from the University of Sussex in the United Kingdom. His recent publications include *Private Armed Forces and Global Security* (2010), in which he casts PMCs as a necessary adjunct to state and multilateral forces in the twenty-first century. Through his management of www.PrivateMilitary.org, Dr. Ortiz's work has also been oriented toward the dissemination of scholarly resources on security privatization worldwide.

Dr. Ulrich Petersohn is an assistant professor in international politics at the University of Liverpool. He is co-author of the RAND report *Hired Guns: Views About Armed Contractors in Operation Iraqi Freedom* (2010), and his work has appeared in *European Journal of International Relations*, *International Interaction*, and *Armed Forces and Society*, among others.

Jake Sherman is the former Deputy Director for Programs (Conflict) at the Center on International Cooperation at New York University. From 2003 to 2005, he was a political affairs officer for the UN Assistance Mission in Afghanistan, and he is the lead author of *The Public Cost of Private Security in Afghanistan* (2009).

Dr. Christopher Spearin is an associate professor in the Department of Defence Studies of the Royal Military College of Canada in Toronto, Ontario. His work has been published in a variety of forums, including *Contemporary Security Policy*, *International Journal*, *International Politics*, *Journal of Conflict Studies*, *Naval War College Review*, *Parameters*, and *Small Wars & Insurgencies*, among others.

INDEX

Page numbers in italics indicate tables and figures.

Peru's military protection (continued)
  of the VRAE (Valley of the Apurímac and
  Ene Rivers), 41–42, 46. *See also* Latin
  American markets for force
Petersohn, Ulrich, 1–19, 61, 162–79,
  180–90
Petroecuador, 22, 47
Phoenix Air, 135
Price, David, 152
private-public partnerships (PPPs), 61–63,
  66. *See also* United Kingdom's market for
  force (British PMCs and public-private
  enterprise)
privatization: and Anglo-Saxon model,
  60–61, 62–63, 178n3; "privatization
  revolution," 2, 5. *See also* neoliberal
  markets for force; neoliberal reforms
provision of security as public good
  (consequences of different market types
  for), 7–8, 166–70, *167*; Afghanistan's
  private security sector and PSPs, 111–14;
  British PMCs and public-private
  enterprise, 63–66, 154, 157; Canada's
  market for force in Afghanistan, 137,
  139–41; China's quasi-managed market
  for force, 122, 126–29, 129n4; Czech
  Republic's lack of clearly defined legal
  standards, 83, 84, 85n5; defining security,
  7; and the "efficient quantity" of security
  as public good, 64; Latin American
  military protection markets and state
  capture, 24–26, 46–48; and quality of the
  state, 11; Russian/Ukrainian export
  market for privatized force (and domestic
  security overall), 99–100; and security as
  nonexcludable public good, 7–8; and tests
  of sufficiency/necessary conditions,
  168–70; U.S.-based PMCs in Iraq and
  Afghanistan, 147, 154–59
proxy partnerships: British PMCs and
  markets for force in the U.K., 53–56,
  58–61, 63–64; Cold War–era, 58–61; and
  the force continuum (lethal/nonlethal
  services), *55*, 63–64
Putin, Vladimir, 98

racketeer markets for force, 164–65, 168–76,
  169, *171*, *173*, *189*; Afghanistan, 165, 172;
  Colombia, 22; criminal force markets,
  21–22, 29–34, 165; effect of security

situation on, 172–73, *173*; Latin American, 21, 22, 29–34, 165; Mexico, 22
Ragin, Charles, 15, 180–81, 189n1
Reagan, Ronald, 61
Redut Anti-Terror, 95–96
regulations/regulatory environments,
  10–11, 16n1, 168–70, *169*, 186–87, *187*;
  Afghanistan's private security sector and
  PSPs, 108–11; ANSI/ASIS PSC.1-2012
  Standard, 16n1, 65, 153; Argentina's
  private security market, 27–28; British
  efforts to implement licensing system/
  codes of conduct, 65–66, 67; British
  PMCs and markets for force in the U.K.,
  52, 64–66, 67–68, 68n1; Canada's market
  for force, 133, 140–41; Canada's *National
  Defence Directive* on use of PMSCs,
  140–41, 141n2; China's quasi-managed
  market for force, 123–26, 127, 129n5;
  China's Security Service Management
  Regulation Act (2010), 118–19, 124–25;
  China's 2008 Ordinance on the Management of Security Services, 124–25; Czech
  Republic, 77–83, 84; Ecuador, 44–46;
  ICoC for Private Security Service
  Providers, 16n1, 65, 140, 153; Latin
  American markets for force, 21, 44–46;
  and market types, 168–70, *169*; military
  protection markets, 44–46; *Montreux
  Document*, 16n1, 65, 118, 129n1, 140, 153;
  Peru, 44–46; revolving door effects, 124;
  Russian legal debates of 2012–13 over use
  of private military companies overseas,
  98; Russian/Ukrainian export market for
  privatized force, 90, 96–99; U.K. Foreign
  and Commonwealth Office's 2002 green
  paper, 52, 64–65; U.S. Department of
  State's WPPS II, 16n1, 62–63; U.S. DoD's
  contracts for security services, 16n1; U.S.
  government support for international
  standards and regulation, 153–54;
  U.S.-based PSCs and markets for force in
  Iraq and Afghanistan, 145, 151–54, 158
Rogozin, Dmitry, 98
Rosneft, 98
Royal Air Force (U.K.), 59
RSB Group, 95–96
Russian Criminal Code, 90, 95
Russian Engineering Company, 96
Russian Military Industrial Commission, 98

ACKNOWLEDGMENTS

It was important to us that this volume not be composed of isolated chapters loosely held together by an overarching topic. Instead, we were aiming at a coherent volume held together by the same research questions. We intended each chapter to apply the same investigative approach, so that the chapters would speak to each other and would serve as comparative case studies in the broader exploration of the topic. We are hopeful that we were reasonably successful in this undertaking. Any existing shortfalls are, of course, our own—we could not have hoped for better support.

We were extremely fortunate to have excellent chapter contributors working with us in this endeavor; their diligence and expertise are the source of this volume's strength, and we are extremely indebted to them for their hard work, motivation, and patience. In addition, for their valuable advice and insights, we would like to express our gratitude to Deborah Avant, Kateri Carmola, Sabelo Gumeze, Elke Krahmann, Anna Leander, James Pattison, and Allison Stanger. Two anonymous reviewers of this manuscript also deserve special thanks for the enlightened comments they provided. We are very grateful to the International Studies Association for the research grant that began our collaborative exploration of the questions covered in this volume. Last but not least, we are greatly indebted to our editors at the University of Pennsylvania Press for their encouragement and confidence in the project.